PRACTICAL DATA M

Cambridge Technology Centre

Information Services

BCS, THE CHARTERED INSTITUTE FOR IT

Our mission as BCS, The Chartered Institute for IT, is to enable the information society. We promote wider social and economic progress through the advancement of information technology science and practice. We bring together industry, academics, practitioners and government to share knowledge, promote new thinking, inform the design of new curricula, shape public policy and inform the public.

Our vision is to be a world-class organisation for IT. Our 70,000 strong membership includes practitioners, businesses, academics and students in the UK and internationally. We deliver a range of professional development tools for practitioners and employees. A leading IT qualification body, we offer a range of widely recognised qualifications.

Further Information
BCS The Chartered Institute for IT,
First Floor, Block D,
North Star House, North Star Avenue,
Swindon, SN2 1FA, United Kingdom.
T +44 (0) 1793 417 424
F +44 (0) 1793 417 444
www.bcs.org/contact

PRACTICAL DATA MIGRATION
Second edition

Johny Morris

First published in 2006

Published by BCS Learning & Development Ltd, a wholly owned subsidiary of BCS The Chartered Institute for IT, First Floor, Block D, North Star House, North Star Avenue, Swindon, SN2 1FA, UK.
www.bcs.org

ISBN: 978-1-906124-84-7
PDF ISBN: 978-1-780170-05-3
ePUB ISBN: 978-1-780170-41-1
Kindle ISBN: 978-1-780170-32-9

British Cataloguing in Publication Data.
A CIP catalogue record for this book is available at the British Library.

Typeset by Lapiz Digital Services, Chennai, India.
Printed and bound by CPI Group (UK) Ltd, Croydon, CR0 4YY.

To Josephine, with my love, for being there.

CONTENTS

FIGURES AND TABLES

AUTHOR

Johny Morris has over 25 years' experience in IT working as a programmer, analyst, project manager and data architect. He has worked as an independent contractor for the last 20 years and in that time has worked for some of the biggest names in IT consultancy including CSC, Logica CMG and Price Waterhouse Coopers (PwC). He specialises in data migration and integration and for the last 14 years has been involved with large-scale migrations at blue chip clients like Barclays Bank, National Grid Transco and British Telecom.

ACKNOWLEDGEMENTS

I would like to thank my publisher, Matthew Flynn, who showed great patience as I struggled with the text; Jutta Mackwell for her patient chiding that finally got me over the line; and Nina Turner with whom I started this data migration journey and whose insistence on only providing the best we can is a rule I have stuck with. Dylan Jones of Data Migration Pro deserves a mention for the many conversations we have had over the years where ideas have been batted around – he has been one of the most consistent voices demanding that this under-developed corner of IT deserves better recognition. Finally, my thanks go to my wife, Jo, without whose support this book would not have been completed.

Johny Morris
July 2012

ABBREVIATIONS

API	Application program interface
COTS	Commercial off-the-shelf
CRM	Customer relationship management
DBA	Database administrator
DMZ	Demilitarised zone
DQR	Data quality rule
ERD	Entity relationship diagram
ERP	Enterprise resource planning
ETL	Extract, transform and load
GAM	Gap analysis and mapping
KDSH	Key data stakeholder
KDSM	Key data stakeholder management
LA	Landscape analysis
LD	Legacy decommissioning
LDS	Legacy data store
MDE	Migration design and execution
MDM	Master data management
MIS	Management information system
MSG	Migration strategy and governance
PDM	Practical data migration
PID	Programme initiation document
PMO	Project management office
SI	Systems integrator
SME	System matter expert
SRP	System retirement plan
UAT	User acceptance testing

GLOSSARY

Check point   A decision point at which it is agreed a new system is stable enough to go forward with or from which fallback occurs. (Also sometimes known as a 'go/no-go point'.)

Churn   The relative frequency with which records of different types are added, amended or deleted from a data store.

Conceptual entity model   A form of data model where atomic entities are grouped together to form higher level entities that are meaningful to the enterprise.

Control total   Either the sum of some meaningful value within the data being transferred or a count of the number of units of migration being transferred.

Data architect   The person responsible for the design of how the data required for an organisation, possibly held over multiple applications, is held.

Data audit   The verifiable proof that all the units of migration in the legacy data stores are accounted for in the migration.

Data freeze   The prevention of updates to records after they have been extracted for data migration and before they have loaded into the new system.

Data lineage   The history of transformation that shows how an individual data item is transformed from one system to another.

Data mapping   The rule(s) by which one or more items in the Legacy Data Store will have their values moved to one or more items in the new system.

Data migration   The selection, preparation, extraction, transformation and permanent movement of appropriate data that is of the right quality to the right place at the right time and the decommissioning of legacy data stores.

Data owners   All the people within or outside an organisation who have the legitimate power to stop a migration from happening.

Data quality rules   A set of processes and deliverables that are used to measure the quality of the data within a data migration project and to resolve or mitigate data quality issues.

Data size   The amount of data to be loaded.

Data stakeholder   Any person within or outside an organisation who has a legitimate interest in the data migration outcomes.

Data transitional rules   The temporary business operating procedures put in place to cope with the disturbance caused by data migration itself.

Demilitarised zone   The interface between the technology provider and the wider programme.

Entity type   The generic description of an entity.

Fallback   The steps that will be taken to get an enterprise back into the position it was in prior to a data migration.

Fallback window   The length of time between starting up a new system and taking the final check point that allows for the full decommissioning of legacy data stores according to the system retirement plans.

Homonym   Two words that are spelled the same way, but have different meanings.

Instance   A particular example of an entity type.

Key business data areas   The segments into which a large data migration project is broken down for management and planning purposes.

Landscape analysis   The systematic discovery, review and documenting of the legacy data stores, including their linkages, data quality and key data stakeholders.

Legacy data store   A data repository of any type that holds data of interest to the new system.

Metadata   Data about data. The data that technologists hold about the data in the business.

Migration form   The technical style of a migration.

Navigation   The links in the data that allow software to move from one data item to another. An example would be a foreign key that allows a program to get from a holding company record to all the operational company records beneath it.

'One-way street' problem   Occurs when an algorithm transforms data in such a way that the original values cannot be identified.

Policies   The explicit or tacit underlying drivers for a project and for the surrounding environment in which a project operates.

Project   A one-off enterprise event with a beginning, middle and an end.

Semantic issue A disagreement about the definition of a business term or the use of fields in corporate systems.

Sequencing The ordering of update processes into a tenable progression.

Source data store Synonym of legacy data store.

Synchronisation Enabling changes to data items in legacy data stores to be reflected in the target (forward synchronisation) or changes in the target to be reflected in the legacy data stores (reverse synchronisation) or in both directions (bidirectional synchronisation).

Synonym Two words that are spelled differently, but mean the same thing.

System retirement plan The user-side requirements of a data migration that will allow a legacy data store to be decommissioned.

Target The final destination system or systems.

Topography The map of data store linkages.

Training lag The length of time it takes to train all the staff who need to be trained in the target system.

Transitional data store A temporary database created during the process of data migration.

Unit of migration The lowest level of data granularity of meaning to the business.

USEFUL WEBSITES

www.bcs.org Publisher of this book and home of 'Johny's Data Migration Blog' – the author's regular commentary and insights into data migration.

www.dama.org Data Management International – some good data quality and modelling information, but light on data migration.

www.datamigrationmatters.org The Data Migration Matters event series with forthcoming events and past presentations.

www.datamigrationpro.com Probably the best community website devoted to data migration.

www.dataqualitypro.com Sister website to datamigrationpro with lots of product reviews, comment etc.

www.iaidq.org The International Association for Information and Data Quality – good for local events and discussions, especially via the LinkedIn® website.

www.iergo.com The author's personal website.

INTRODUCTION

WHAT IS THE PURPOSE OF THIS BOOK?

This book is aimed at practitioners, project managers and purchasers of consultant resources who have a data migration project to deal with. It is designed as a teach yourself guide to data migration. I have written it as a consultant with many years' experience in data migration to give you a series of steps developed in real-life situations that will get you from an empty new system to one that is populated, working and backed by the user population.

WHAT TYPES OF DATA MIGRATION ARE COVERED?

Data migration projects take many forms. The classic form is where a new system is to be implemented and needs to be primed with data from the legacy systems. There are also system consolidation programmes, either spawned by businesses merging or by a drive for standardisation. There are system upgrades, and these also require data migration. However, whatever the spur for data migration, the same problems will have to be faced, and this book will guide you past the pitfalls. For the sake of simplicity and consistency, unless there is a specific reason to indicate differing approaches for different types of data migration, I am going to refer to the old/existing data as the 'legacy' and the destination as the 'target'.

WHAT IS NOT COVERED IN THIS BOOK?

This book is system-neutral. It is aimed at large-scale data migration projects visible to the end-user population. It does not cover the detail of migrating, for example, from one version of Oracle® or SAP® to another. It does not cover changes to operating systems or hardware. There are courses available for changes like these, and, if there is a sufficiently large market, books will emerge. This book is aimed at the gap in the methodologies that allow you to develop the perfect system but then say nothing about how you get the best legacy data out of the flaky old systems you are trying to leave behind. This book also does not cover the regular movement of data that supports business information type applications, be they data warehouses, data marts, master data management (MDM) or management information systems (MIS). This book is aimed at a project environment where there is a clear need to move data as a 'one off' to populate a new database.

HINT

A project is a one-off enterprise event with a beginning, middle and end. A business process is continuous: individual items will move through from the start event to the final transformation, but the process itself never stops. Learn the difference. Projects require different management skills from processes, have different deliverables and different timelines, but it is surprising how easy it is to confuse them. Superficial similarities hide the essential differences. Having said that, there are techniques in this book to perform data analysis and data cleansing, and they can be used to bring the enterprise into the project, so it might still be useful reading for anyone interested in cyclic data cleansing or data quality issues.

WHO IS THIS BOOK AIMED AT?

There are two types of reader who will find this book essential reading: the executive and the practitioner. The first is the person with management responsibility for seeing the project to a successful conclusion. You might be a practising or a lapsed technologist, or you might have no technological experience at all, but you want to know how to control a data migration project. The practitioner is the technologist with a data migration project looming in front of them and who is sensibly reaching for assistance.

To the executive

You might be surprised to learn that there were no non-proprietary (i.e. not tied to one particular technology or consultancy supplier) methodologies for data migration until the first edition of this book was published in April 2006. In other words, no one had created a widely accepted series of steps that would guarantee to get the dirty old data out of old systems and transform it into clean new data to be placed into a new system in which a company has invested so much of its money. The first edition of *Practical Data Migration* quickly established itself as the primary text, with thousands of copies sold worldwide. This is the second edition of that book (*PDMv2*), updated to take account of technological changes and the maturing of the supply of services in this area.

PDMv2 will demystify the plethora of terms with which technologists love to surround their activities. It will illustrate the sort of controls you should expect to see from a well-managed data migration project, and the sorts of contracts you should write with suppliers and the amount of work you must be prepared for, even in the best managed projects. It will illustrate the steps you should expect an experienced data migration consultant to execute.

So if you are responsible for hiring consultancy resources or are overseeing an in-house project, this book will arm you with the ammunition you will need to stay on top of the project.

Section 1 is for you. It explains why data migration projects are intrinsically difficult and why there is such a high failure rate. It explains why you should insist that all parties involved in the migration work to *PDMv2* standards if you are to succeed. It gives you an overview of *PDMv2* so that you can converse with the practitioners with confidence.

The practitioner

If you are a practitioner about to embark on a data migration project for the first time (or even second or third time) you are right to feel daunted by the scale of the task. Bad start-up data is the curse of many good projects. It is not a subject that is well covered in most computing courses. It might not even seem that glamorous. Well, do not worry. Follow the methods and principles in this book and you will be guided to success. You will even make lasting allies. As explained, this book is also intended for the executive, so you might occasionally find yourself being told things that are the common currency of your daily working life. I would advise you to stick with it. Data migration uses many commonplace concepts in subtly different ways.

You should read Section 1 for an overview, then Section 2, where the *PDMv2* modules are covered in detail. If your project is in deep trouble and you are buying this book in the hope that it will get you out of it, there is also Section 3, but browse the rest of the book first because it explains key concepts.

WHAT IS NEW TO VERSION TWO OF *PRACTICAL DATA MIGRATION*?

PDMv2 builds on the success of the original. Anyone who has mastered the underlying principles of practical data migration (PDM) will find that they are unchanged here. The most significant changes reflect the introduction of new technology over the years since the first edition was published, the introduction of the demilitarised zone (DMZ) concept that reflects the maturing of the market for data migration services and the redefining of PDM in a modular fashion. This final point is in response to the many comments that asked for a more precise definition of how the products and methods of PDM interact. Modularisation also makes it easier to see how PDM can be tailored to wrap around different technologies and implementation practices. Of course there are also the many small and subtle changes that over five years of additional practice have suggested.

PARAGRAPH STYLES

I have placed the following items in boxes so that you can find them easily:

- **Anecdotes** – These record my experiences and, hopefully, amplify the point I am making in the main body of the text.

- **Hints** – These are tricks and tips that I have found to work. These should, of course, be applied with circumspection based on your knowledge of the culture and structure of the environment in which you are working.

- **Golden rules** – You will be introduced to four Golden Rules that underlie and govern the approach used. They are the most significant things to take away from this book. Learn them by heart and, whatever else you find expedient to change, stick with them and you will have increased your chances of success many times over.

- **Definitions** – As well as the Golden Rules, there are also other key ideas, unique to this approach, that need to be carefully defined.

Additionally, each chapter starts with a brief overview of what it includes, and ends with a summary of what you should take away from it.

SECTION 1:
EXECUTIVE OVERVIEW

1 DATA MIGRATION: WHAT'S ALL THE FUSS?

In this chapter I explain what an enterprise application data migration is and look at the key mistakes that lead to the high failure rate of data migrations across the board. I also explain the responsibility gap and why it is instrumental in most failing data migration projects.

WHAT IS DATA MIGRATION?

This book is about data migration, as the title suggests, but more properly it is about enterprise application migration, by which I do not mean the relocation of data centres or the regular movement of data between, say, a business system and a data warehouse. Data migration is the one-off movement of data from old systems to a new repository. It is intended to be a one-way trip with no return. More formally, I define data migration as follows:

> **DEFINITION**
>
> Data migration is the selection, preparation, extraction, transformation and permanent movement of appropriate data that is of the right quality to the right place at the right and the decommissioning of legacy data stores.

This definition is important because it highlights a key technical and project activity stage. The following breaks down the definition.

- **Selection** – In modern post-client–server environments there are often multiple potential sources of data. *PDMv2* acknowledges this and will show you how to make selections that balance technical, business and project needs.

- **Preparation, extraction, transformation** – Data quality is one of the most significant challenges to any data migration. Even where data is fine in its existing setting it might not work in the new environment. *PDMv2* will show you how transformation rules are generated that have business as well a technical relevance.

- **Permanent** – *PDMv2* is for enterprise application data migrations where the data is to be moved permanently from source to target, not for the cyclical integration that occurs between transactions and reporting systems. This is significant because there is no going back.

- **Movement** – There has been an explosion of software tools available to transport data from source to location. This book will introduce you to the various options and explain their strengths and weaknesses.

- **Right quality** – In the tight timescales of modern data migration projects you do not have time to get all of the data perfect. *PDMv2* has tools and techniques that will allow you to get your prioritisation decisions correct from both a technical and a business perspective.

- **Timing** – The business driver for data migration projects usually includes some time-based criteria. *PDMv2* will introduce you to tools and techniques that will allow you to stay in control of your project.

- **Legacy data stores** – These are usually databases or spreadsheets, but they can be reports, notebooks, rolodexes etc.

- **Decommissioning** – *PDMv2* is for enterprise application data migration. Although the legacy data stores might persist for other purposes, the data that has been extracted and the business processes it was supporting will be permanently moved to the target. Implicit in a data migration project, as opposed to a system integration process, is that the legacy data store(s) will cease. There will be a point of no return. This book will show you how to use this to your advantage in business engagement activities and to ensure the elegant close-down of legacy systems.

FIRST THE BAD NEWS

As an industry, we are appalling at data migration. The most recent figures suggest that nearly 40 per cent of data migration projects were over time, over budget or failed entirely.[1]

ANECDOTE

Outside the public sector, which has greater transparency, it often seems like everybody else is succeeding. This makes it so much harder to admit to having difficulties. The feeling I often encounter is 'If everybody else is doing it so well, why can't we?' Well, let me reassure you, nearly everybody else is doing just as badly. Those of us on the inside wince at the millions of pounds, dollars and euros we see wasted unnecessarily on failed or floundering data migrations.

So, to contextualise the above, if you are embarking on a $5 million project due to complete in 12 months, say for next March in time for the new financial year, expect it to finish in August and expect to have to go back to the board for an

---

[1] Howard, P. (2011). *Data migration*. Bloor Research.

additional $1.5 million. And that's if you are lucky. It could be longer and much more expensive.

Still feeling good about taking on this challenge? Well stick with *PDMv2* and you will have vastly increased the chance of still having a career at the end of it. Various studies have shown that using a proven methodology greatly increases your chances of on-time, on-budget, zero-defect migrations.

SO WHAT USUALLY GOES WRONG?

If the chances of getting a data migration exercise correct, on your own, using an approach developed in-house is significantly worse than using a tried and tested methodology like *PDMv2*, what are the areas that most often trip up the unwary? The following goes some way to explain.

- **Techno-centricity** – Seeing data migration as a purely technical problem. Given the choices over data selection, data preparation, data quality, decommissioning etc., the business needs to provide guidance, take ownership and provide understanding of the historic data. *PDMv2* is built around the business owning the migration process.

  The Bloor survey referenced above recorded that successful data migrations put business engagement and support of the migration so far ahead of everything else in terms of success criteria that it trumped all the other choices put together. The only one that came close was use of a migration methodology.

- **Lack of specialist skills** – Data migration analysts need to have an eclectic mix of skills. They need to have the business-facing skills of a business analyst, but also the technical understanding that allows them to interface effectively with their technical colleagues when discussing solutions and the use of migration software. They need to be able to facilitate understanding between the technical and the business players, but they also need project leadership skills to manage a virtual team of business and technical staff to deliver on time and to budget. Finally, they need an understanding of formal processes if everything they do is not to be reactive and made up on the hoof.

- **Underestimating** – Not knowing the scale of the activities that need to be undertaken leads to underestimating. This is especially true of the unforeseen amount of data preparation activity required. *PDMv2* provides a framework of activities that allows for more consistent planning and manages all data issues through a single, integrated and consistent process.

- **Uncontrolled recursion** – You will see, when I look at the responsibility gap, how easy it is to fall into the vortex of uncontrolled recursion where problems get batted back and forth across an unnecessary boundary between the project and the business.

What is rarely a problem (indeed so rare that I'm pushed to remember an example where it was the case) is the migration technology itself. This is not to say that you do not have to exercise care in specifying, writing, testing and deploying the technology, but that these are activities that over the last 30 or 40 years we, as an industry, have grown good at doing.

In addition, there is now much better software available to perform data migration functions. There are, however, a number of common confusions at the heart of data migration projects, so that when they go astray, the unwary can be led to thinking that the software is to blame when, as the people who wrote it will often declaim, it was written, tests and performs exactly to specification. To understand why the specification can be so often incomplete, you need to appreciate the responsibility gap.

THE RESPONSIBILITY GAP

To explain the responsibility gap, let me start with what I generally call the naive, or industry-standard, view of a data migration.

At one end of an imaginary pipeline there are the legacy systems. At the other end, there is the target. In between there are the data extraction routines, some transformations where data is combined, separated and modified to fit the target, and the load programs that will write the data to the target. How hard can that be?

Well, experience shows that legacy databases will have all sorts of data of questionable value.

ANECDOTE

I was consulting on a migration for a company where the industry regulator had insisted that, for competition reasons, data relating to different customer classes had to be in physically separate databases. The decision was taken to clone the main database into two, extract one set of customer records and write them to the carbon copy application. Even in these circumstances, where there was nearly zero transformation, up to 20 per cent of the records would not migrate. Changes to validation rules over time, recoveries from old system crashes and the use of fields for unofficial purposes meant that many records were rejected. And this was going from like to like. Just imagine how many more errors there might be when going from one system to a completely different system.

A large percentage of data quality issues can be fixed within the information technology function using simple programming. It is relatively easy to restructure dates to a new format, or match addresses to a known source of good addresses and correct them. However, there will always be problems that need business input. These problems are often the hardest and most intractable to fix.

ANECDOTE

A memorable event occurred on a migration in a heavily regulated industry. Having successfully completed the migration of their commercial customers they came to work on their domestic customers. On examination they found that, out of a population of several million, up to 20 per cent of their domestic customers were on commercial rates. The fix was quite easy from a technical point of view and could be completed within an afternoon. A simple table with two columns, one domestic and one commercial, was created. At migration time the load program would look up the tariff code in one column and apply the code in the other. Simple. From a business point of view it wasn't that easy: there were billing issues of over- and under-payments for people on the wrong tariffs; there were sales tax issues because the commercial customers and domestic customers had different tax rates; there were regulatory issues of not complying with running a transparent market where all domestic tariffs were openly advertised; there were public relations issues of how this would play with the media; there were commercial issues around the number of call centre staff that would be required if 20 per cent of the domestic customers suddenly found themselves on new tariffs and decided to call in. And so on and so on. It took months of inter-departmental meetings and discussion to resolve.

What also often happens is that a large number of records are cascaded back to the business as 'business problems'. Employees in middle management, who provide front-line service to paying customers, are not enthusiastic about receiving this deluge of data quality issues. After all, the project team seemed to be assuming ownership, but as those of us who have been here before know, the most difficult problems are actually the ones that the IT guys cannot fix. In the preceding anecdote it was way beyond the technical department's remit to make a call on how to handle a 'misapplication of tariff' problem.

The misapplication of tariffs was a genuine data issue caused by process failure and (probably) validation failures in the legacy system. However, there is a more common set of equally challenging problems that are often collected under the title 'semantic issues'.

DEFINITION

Semantic issues arise where there is a genuine disagreement about the definition of a business term or the use of fields in corporate systems.

A common example of a semantic issue is the definition of customer. If a business is selling to large corporations, is the customer the top legal entity? Or the department or depot that signs the purchase order? Or the subsidiary company that uses the product? Or some mixture of all of these?

Other common examples of semantic issues are product and location.

Resolving semantic issues are beyond the competency of the technologists. They can implement the definition once it is agreed, but they cannot create the definition. I often think of the example of three directors looking down on the shop floor. The human resources (HR) director sees job roles, skills and hierarchies of occupations. The finance director sees capital and operational cost centres, capital assets and consumables. The production director sees processes, equipment and labour. They are all right, but their perception is different.

Generally these semantic issues have been resolved in the legacy systems and processes, with staff routinely working around the official process so that their day jobs are possible. However, they all surface when you try to unpick the compromises and workarounds to load data.

Various locally devised uses of under-utilised fields in legacy databases also confound the technologist. They find letters in fields that are supposed to be numeric, they find strange reoccurring patterns in fields that are supposed to be unused, they find values way outside an accepted range (e.g. customers that are over 200 years old). Some of these uses are just accidents of history, program glitches and system crashes of long ago, but many are there because they facilitated a business process that was not adequately supported.

ANECDOTE

I was told an apocryphal tale when I was working with a financial services client of a table of credit card rates where one set of cards had negative interest rates. Now we all know that no credit card company is that generous. It transpired that these cards were part of a special scheme and needed processing in a different manner from the others. The negative interest rates were trapped during the payment processing batch run and the records were filtered out into an error file where they were subsequently picked up by a parallel process. This was a classic case of using a feature of the existing software to perform processing that would otherwise have been difficult and expensive to accommodate.

Finally, when it comes to automated business processes, there are all the semi-official offline processes that are performed. These range from the reworking of invoices to allow for special discount schemes that the old system could not cope with, to unofficial contact lists held by sales teams, to manual records held by warehouse staff for those limited stock items that can not be properly racked and for which the old system did not have a location.

You will come across all these issues and more, the resolution of which will involve your business colleagues. Techno-centricity, that is emphasising the technology over the human side, will inevitably lead to problems, but to see why these problems can make the difference between projects delivered on time and to budget and the 40 per cent that are late and over-budget let me look at two models of a data migration exercise: the business-class plane flight and the quest.

The business-class plane flight and the quest
As an airline passenger you sit passively in your seat and enjoy the in-flight entertainment as the clouds slip by your window. The journey is in the hands of the pilot and he or she, in turn, is depending on an unseen army of aircraft engineers, controllers, baggage handlers and ground staff to get you smoothly to your destination. If you have any contribution to make to the success of the journey it is limited to purchasing a valid ticket and turning up on time.

When things go wrong you might vent your spleen on the cabin crew and the incompetence of the airline. And quite rightly so. You were not involved with the process of getting from start to end, only with the choice of destination itself.

Now imagine a quest. It is more exciting, but fraught with the possibility of failure. There might be a leader, but each participant is expected to contribute, to a greater or lesser extent, to the success of the venture. On the classic quests of literature, each person brings a different set of skills to the task, but to be successful everyone has at some point to operate outside their comfortably familiar roles. The hero-leader might not even have direct command of his or her companions. He or she might have had to negotiate for their services and has to work hard to maintain their loyalty.

Which of these models is more appropriate to the process of a data migration exercise? Technologists normally imagine the plane flight metaphor as the better way of presenting the project. They are promising a business class service; carrying the business to its destination with little effort on their part. This keeps the business side passive and out of the way allowing the technical aspects of the task to proceed unhindered. It also allows the technologists to get out of the potentially embarrass-ing problem of having to deal with all those messy political issues. Not having to explain esoteric technical decisions to the uninitiated relieves them of an awkward anxiety.

This is compounded by an often genuine misperception on both sides that data migration is largely a technical issue. The technologists genuinely believe that they can solve the majority of the data issues, and in a sense this is true. As I said earlier, the majority of data issues are of the date reformatting type that can be fixed with appropriate technology. However, it is also unfortunately the case that the ones technologists can't fix are also the most intractable, difficult and time-consuming.

So is the plane trip an honest metaphor for a data migration? As I have shown, the experienced know that there will be problems along the way that will only be resolved with the assistance and knowledge of those people most immediately involved with the legacy systems, and that is our business colleagues. Even if everything goes smoothly you know that at the end of the process someone on the business side will be asked to sign off that the existing systems can be decommis-sioned and that the new system is fit for purpose. The plane journey metaphor breaks down before you reach the destination. You do not buy a ticket and then expect to have to sign off that the aircraft is fit for purpose before take off.

On the other hand, the quest metaphor is quite apt. There will be trials and tribulations along the way. The ultimate sanctioning authority of the success of your epic will not be the hero-leader of the quest, but either one or a collection of local panjandrums. Unexpected problems and challenges will beset you, and compromises will be needed, as well as possibly heroic efforts. Dragons will need to be slain and beautiful princesses will need to be rescued...

OK, so maybe I am exaggerating a little, but I still contend that the model of the passive plane flight is flawed from the outset. The business side is being misled (usually quite unwittingly) by its technical colleagues who often genuinely believe that it is the technology that is central to success and underestimate the scale of the tasks that they themselves do not have to perform.

At some point reality starts to dawn: usually when the number of outstanding semantic issues is beyond the project's capacity to cope with. The technologists realise that there is no way that the business can be allowed to have such a non-active role in the project. The business feels it has been misled. Someone has not been honest with it. It has been given to understand that it was going to have an easy ride and now it is being asked to make a much more significant contribution. When the plane is inexplicably diverted, or when delays occur, as a passenger you sit and curse the 'others' who you hold to blame. You might not know who they are, but you know for sure that it is not your responsibility. You do not expect to have to do anything to fix the situation. Fixing is someone else's problem. This, though, is how key enterprise contacts are treated in a typical data migration exercise. The tacit implication that their role will be limited is shattered when a huge surprise is sprung mid-way through the project.

On the quest, however, although you might know that any one problem might be someone else's fault, you are still bound into the overall success of the adventure. You see yourself as part of the solution, not as a passive observer of the problem. If you have the skills, or even if you do not, you will try to make a contribution to the success of the project.

The key difference is that in one model the business is only bound into the success at the journey's end. In the other model, it is joint owner of the process by which the journey reaches its end, as well as owning the success at the journey's end.

ANECDOTE

Allowing a business to become too dependent on the technical side in a migration exercise can have bizarre results. I worked on one migration where, in a population of 12,000 records, seven records needed special processing. Instead of going ahead with the migration and picking up the seven records later for manual action, the business side looked to the technicians to write special code to deal with them. Emails flew around, deadlines were missed, meetings were held and load windows compromised. Had the business properly owned the migration a more common sense approach would have prevailed (as indeed it did in the end, but not without an unnecessary amount of pain). As it was, the dependency culture meant that the issue was seen as a technical problem not a business problem. If the business had owned the problem, both the technical and manual solutions would have been considered and the appropriate action taken earlier and more cheaply.

The result of this misplaced expectation is known as the responsibility gap and is one of commonest features of failing migration projects. On the one side, there are frustrated technologists with questions they cannot answer, waiting for a response from their business colleagues. On the other side, there are irritated business staff drowning under a deluge of data quality requests after having been apparently promised a relatively easy ride. The principal symptom is the uncontrolled recursion that characterises a failing project where a vortex of data quality issues swirls around between a confused technical side and a disengaged business side, each side looking to the other to fix data issues in a confusion of roles.

It is into this responsibility gap that most failing data migration projects fall.

HOW TO AVOID THE RESPONSIBILITY GAP

There is an old joke about a farmer being asked directions from a lost tourist and replying: 'If you want to get there, I wouldn't start from here.' I have a similar feeling about the responsibility gap. You are far better off avoiding the responsibility gap than trying to fix it. After reading Chapter 2 on Golden Rules and Super SMART Tasks, and seeing an overview of the whole of *PDMv2*, you will see how *PDMv2* will address all the issues outlined in the previous paragraphs, thus preventing them occurring in the first place and leaving you with a controlled project where all the necessary parties are working in a collaborative way.

On the other hand, if you are reading this book late in your project's life cycle and many of these issues are being manifest, then there are suggestions in Section 3 on how to bring a runaway data migration project back under control.

CHAPTER REVIEW

In this chapter I have covered the definition of data migration, a review of the appalling industry performance in this area and looked at the various challenges you have to overcome. I have introduced you to semantic issues and why it is so hard to overcome them, and shown what I mean by the responsibility gap.

2 GOLDEN RULES AND SUPER SMART TASKS

In this chapter I introduce you to the four Golden Rules of data migration. These underlie all the other activities in this book and are the single most important set of concepts within it. Study them, learn them and live your data migration project by them. I will then introduce Super SMART Tasks and show you how important they are in delivering successful projects.

GOLDEN RULES: THE MOST IMPORTANT LESSONS

If you take nothing else from this book, then take these Golden Rules to heart and use them to inform your migration activities. If you follow all the steps laid out in this book to the letter, then you will deliver an on-time, on-budget, zero-defect migration to everyone's satisfaction. However, I am also aware that in the real world there are always local cultural, commercial and practical realities that constrain your freedom to act as you would like. Within *PDMv2* these are addressed in the policies identified in project initiation and their application to the data migration strategy, which I will look at in Chapter 4.

I therefore accept that almost any of the artefacts and processes below might be replaced by something more suited to the environment you find yourself in. I'm not saying that a substitute will work as well as the tried and tested advice I'm offering, but I acknowledge it might be expedient or even compulsory for you to follow local methodologies. However, whatever formats you operate in, abandon these Golden Rules at your peril. Each one is essential, and collectively they form the underlying philosophy of the *PDMv2* approach. Abandon these rules and you are on your own! The four basic rules will make the difference between a successful migration, with which the business will be happy, and a tortured chain of actions that lead to recriminations, dissatisfaction and even failed projects.

The rules are not always easy to abide by, however. Some are challenging, but bear them in mind as you read the book and they will make sense in the end.

GOLDEN RULE 1

GOLDEN RULE 1

Data migration is a business not a technical issue.

This is the most significant rule. It might be counterintuitive to both the technologists on one side and the business on the other. Data migration normally occurs as a result of an IT project. Those in IT are attracted to technology, so they tend to look for technical solutions. That is why there are data cleansing and loading tools in the marketplace. However, this is putting the cart before the horse. IT projects are there to answer a business need. The business understands the meaning and relative value of its data. It is this value that must be preserved and enhanced in the transformation activity that is data migration. It is from this knowledge that data cleansing, data preparation and extract, transform and load definitions can be derived. The technologists, can see the bits and bytes, but they are dangerously arrogant if they think they can see the business meaning of those bits and bytes better than the owners, creators and users of them.

ANECDOTE

I first got involved with data migration because a project I was working on had a big data 'take on' requirement. Fully half the migration budget had been expended building a migration environment. The users rejected this as unusable because, in their eyes, it was not targeted at the main data problems. So we were running late with no data and no idea where we were going to get the data from.

The technologists were backing away from the problem. After all they had built a perfectly good tool hadn't they? The design document was signed off, wasn't it?

The users were losing patience with the technologists. Why weren't they being listened to?

I was intrigued. The project had clearly gone about this the wrong way, providing a solution before it had understood the problem.

We migrated successfully in the end, but the migration tool was never used. It was the start of the process that led, after much trial and error, to the set of procedures I'm sharing with you now.

The above is not to say that there is no technical element, but, as I have shown with the responsibility gap, by emphasising technology over business knowledge, you will be committing one of the major errors that lead to project failure.

To help you understand this better, here is a typical migration story.

There is a point in the project timeline provided by a supplier of a new system that indicates when it will be ready for the first cut of a company's data. Maybe that point has slipped a little due to some unplanned changes to tailor the solution to your particular needs. The supplier's account manager and project manager do not appear that fazed by it so you assume that it is situation normal. Your project manager has assigned a lead analyst and technical resources and given them a briefing on the requirements. It is obvious where the data will come from: the system you are replacing. It is obvious where it is going. The migration team are reporting back to the steering group regularly. The load program specifications, and design, build and test stages go ahead to plan so your attention shifts to the myriad other details of a major system change.

Then you come to the first test load of real data, and it all goes wrong. Half the data is missing. Defects known to the enterprise, but not formally acknowledged, come to light, and suddenly a plethora of new data sources are revealed. You are now running late and the rework required starts to threaten your end dates.

But how could this happen? You'd only had green or amber progress reports up until now. How can computer programs that worked so well in test be so deficient when used in anger?

You might even be told by your migration guys that it is infuriatingly difficult to get the business to correct their data, even where it is faulty in the old system, never mind to make adjustments that are needed because of the enhanced processing of the new applications. Why are those business users so careless with their data and reluctant to fix it? You are asked to apply some executive pressure on these departments to provide the business resources the project needs.

You are also beginning to feel the squeeze from your software implementation suppliers. They point to the contract. Your procurement department put in some pretty stringent liquidated damages clauses to encourage them to hit target. Quite reasonably they limited their liability to those items they could control. It is your responsibility to provide them with good data. Now you have used up one of your three test loads. The second is scheduled for two weeks' time. If you miss that deadline, then the teams they had earmarked to support this activity will be standing idle, and idle time is charged on a time and materials, full-rate card basis. More than a few weeks and those charges could seriously compromise your budget.

You go back to your migration team. They give you news you do not want to hear. Yes, they could make use of the next dummy load, but only with 25 per cent of the live records. It would test the end-to-end load process and they could bolster the data run with some test data. As for the other 75 per cent of the records, well, they are still working on an answer as to when those will be right, but it is increasingly looking like you will need to switch to a phased delivery.

In the meantime your supplier sympathises with your predicament and offers the use of some additional experienced resources, on a time and materials basis, to assist your team. More expense to your already compromised budget. Can you justify it to the top-level governance board?

There are many reasons why projects go wrong like this.

Firstly, in the anarchy of the personal and mobile computer world, each IT-literate individual in each department will have their own set of spreadsheets and mini-databases, some running on corporate hardware, some on various mobile devices. Some, totally unacknowledged, will be crucial to the enterprise's processes, often filling in for the inadequacies of current systems (and if they are not inadequate, why are they being replaced?). Each will be different in format and quality, and there will be difficulties linking them together.

ANECDOTE

The largest number of individual data sources I have encountered on any one site ran to over 4,000. We narrowed it down to 3,000 potential sources and in the end used data from less than 100. And, yes, we had been told in advance that all the information we needed was in 12 corporate systems.

Secondly, there will be data issues in the legacy system. Some well known among the user community (and in part the cause of the rise in locally built solutions); others will only be discovered when the databases are examined for migration.

Of course, no one will have warned you about this. Often senior management will be unaware of, or feel uncomfortable to share, this fact. Given the silo nature of enterprise structures, the view of the user data you have been given will be that of the senior managers.

Look at it from a user perspective. Your team arrived with all their technical skills and assumed responsibility for loading the business user's data. Your business colleagues do not hear anything for a while, then suddenly a flood of data that will not load is cascaded back at them. They flounder in the deluge without tools, mechanisms or resources to cope and quite reasonably push back on you via their senior managers.

At this point something significantly bad will have happened to the project: the enterprise relationship is jeopardised. The business will have accepted the passive role offered it. The project team will have suggested that they had the technology and the tools to migrate the data from A to B. The project team will have appeared confident that their technology could cope. Suddenly the dastardly business is providing data in entirely the wrong format from bizarre locations. The elegantly written and executed software will, of course, throw up errors. The implicit contract between the business and the project has gone wrong. They have misled one another. The business side was expecting to be getting on with the day job while the technologists got on with transferring the data. Now a lot of extra work is coming their way. This wasn't what was promised! Expectations are undermined and relationships descend into a spiral of mutual recriminations.

19

A similar problem might arise with your supplier partners. From their side of the contract the software suppliers see themselves as the innocent victims of a problem with the business's data. They cannot be expected to suffer materially because of that, can they?

So why have you got to this pretty pass? The reason is, of course, that there has been a subtle (often, in politically charged environments, a not so subtle) shift of responsibility. The project has, in the eyes of the business, taken on the responsibility for getting existing data into the new system, and that includes cleansing and preparing the data. The project, however, knows that it does not have the business domain knowledge to do this. The software suppliers are also often contractually bound not to correct errors and inconsistencies in business data. The contracts between all the parties are floored by being founded on basic misunderstandings.

It might seem easy to correct this, but in my experience with modern, lean, efficient companies and departments whose key personnel might have been pulled around considerably in the development process, it can be extremely hard for a compromise to be reached. Bad feeling persists that ruins any cooperation that might have been possible. The migration team feel they have been given an impossible task with uncooperative work colleagues and unbending suppliers. The business feels abused and betrayed. You suspect that the suppliers, having been through this cycle before, should have done more to warn you. The suppliers feel they have often gone beyond the letter of the contract to assist you and are now being blamed for falling back on a contract that you largely dictated.

The answer to the project–enterprise issue is to stick closely to Golden Rule 1. From start to finish the business must own the quality of the data and the success of the migration outcome. After the programme's final day, when all of the project team pack up and head off onto new projects, it is the business that must live with the results. This does not mean that there is no room for technical competence. The project must still specify, write and test programs carefully. They still have a role to play in guaranteeing the technical appropriateness of the new data. However, long after the technologists have moved on, the business will be stuck with what they have been given. Follow the steps outlined in the rest of this book and the business will be enthusiastically tied into the successful outcome of the project, delivering the best data it can in a timely manner aligned to its budget.

The answer to the project–supplier issue lies in the careful understanding of the nature of the relationship between business and supplier as instantiated in the contract. Within *PDMv2* this is covered by the concept of a demilitarised zone (see below).

For the data source, quality, preparation and appropriateness issues, you have the *PDMv2* landscape analysis module (which is discussed in Chapter 3).

The demilitarized zone

The demilitarised zone (DMZ) is new to *PDMv2*. It reflects, to an extent, the growing sophistication of the data migration marketplace. Prior to the publication of the first edition of *Practical Data Migration*, there were quite a few well-publicised IT project failures, many of which ended up in the courts with each side trying to establish who was at fault for the failure, and with the data migration element often being central to the litigation. Of course, like many things, the visible acrimony was merely the tip of a very large iceberg of failed projects, the majority of which remain unknown to the public.

To counter this trend, procurement departments started to develop tighter contract specifications. Fixed price deals became more common with the client side demanding financial guarantees that the migration would be delivered on time. The response on the supplier side was to accept contract responsibility for a much narrower set of activities and to put clear contract blue water between what could be done within the fixed price element and what remained the responsibility of the client.

Given potential financial penalties imposed as part of the procurement, no third party could be expected to accept contractual responsibility for resolving data issues where they can have no control over the key decision makers and in-business personnel whose activity is necessary to fix semantic issues. Increasingly the contracts were drawn tighter and tighter around the 'final mile'. It is now almost always the case that it is the responsibility of the client to provide data of appropriate quality, in a format specified by the supplier, to a timetable negotiated between them, and this is often encapsulated in the contract. It is the supplier's responsibility to take that data and provide software to load it efficiently into the target.

Any slippage in providing the data is often at a cost to the client because the supplier looks for recompense for downtime. This matches the clauses in the contract imposed by the client on the supplier to provide migration software and to perform the migration physically and on time.

All of this is perfectly reasonable and to be expected, but in itself this can lead to confusion for the unwary. It might appear that the supplier is offering a full data migration service. In a sense this is true. Experienced suppliers will be offering an efficient, error-free, sophisticated data loading service that has been tried, tested and perfected on other projects. What they will not generally be offering are the services to discover, analyse, correct and prepare data from a particular business environment. After all, how can they realistically estimate the scale of that task and so put a price on it? Until you lift the manhole covers you have no idea what you will find underneath. The business might have perfect data in easy-to-access systems, with cooperative and knowledgeable staff. On the other hand, it could be closer to the norm with a mixed bag of systems, some well managed, some poorly managed, some understood and some not. The business might have some keen staff, some disinterested and some so harassed by the day job that they do not have time to look up from their desks from the moment they take their coats off in the morning to the moment they log off at night.

ANECDOTE

I have noticed yet another change recently. With the growth of profiling software (see Chapter 3) there has been the beginning of a development for suppliers to offer a pre-migration data quality appraisal. This can be done at a fixed price and provides you with a far better budget estimate of the likely scale of challenges that you will be facing when you come to set up the data migration. The use of this service is highly recommended as best practice. However, it cannot reveal how long it will take for the enterprise to agree solutions for semantic issues and therefore most fixed price data migration contracts exclude the time it takes to resolve semantic issues.

In summary, you now have the ingredients for a classic misunderstanding. The supplier trumpets their experience and skills in data migration, and they are not intentionally misleading. They might well have done the same job many times before, just not in your environment. You, inexperienced in data migration projects, assume that this means the whole journey from an unknown plethora of data sources to a single new application and fail to plan and budget for how to manage the selection, preparation, transformation and data quality issues that are going to be your responsibility.

PDMv2 prioritises the analysis of a DMZ within the set-up activities of a project in order to prevent this confusion.

Formally, within *PDMv2*, the DMZ is defined as follows:

DEFINITION

The DMZ is the interface between the technology provider and the wider programme.[2]

As I have shown, one of the main reasons for a DMZ's importance is that you cannot expect a third-party supplier to have contractual responsibility for activities outside its control. However, even where the migration is being delivered in-house using the enterprise's own technologists, there are still issues of semantic understanding and of data preparation activities that the project is dependent on the business to complete, but which the project has no direct management control over the business to make happen.

---

[2] The term DMZ as a technical description comes from its use in file transfer systems where the demilitarised zone is the area between the parties' firewalls. Data to be exchanged is placed in the DMZ by one party to be picked up by the other. In a physical sense this is still very much the practice in many data migration projects. The project extracts data from its systems and puts it into an area where it can be picked up by the supplier. The supplier processes the data and puts records that fail to migrate back into a shared area along with agreed metrics on records loaded, run times etc.

HINT

There are also, in fact, a lot of technical activities that your supplier is unlikely to complete, like the provision of network connectivity etc. So it is normal for the DMZ to bisect technical deliveries as well as form the boundary between the technical and the business sides.

As you will see when I look at setting a data migration strategy, you need to understand clearly where the DMZ boundary is on your project: what is inside, what is outside and what items will be passed back and forth across the boundary. This allows you to 'black box' the work of the supplier. If it is working to a PDM methodology, then all is well and good. If it is working to a methodology of its own devising that best fits with its experience and software, also all is well and good. You can encapsulate what they do in a standard set of processes wrapped up in a contract that safeguards both positions without having to dictate changes to preferred working practices.

I will make references to the DMZ throughout the rest of this book, and you will see the impact it has on almost every element of a data migration from initial project set up to legacy decommissioning.

How does the DMZ apply if you are using in-house resources?

Although the initial impetus for the DMZ came from a reaction to the tightening of procurement contracts, the same rules still apply to in-house run data migrations where there is no external implementation partner. As you will see when I look at the *PDMv2* model, aligned as it is to the Golden Rules, there are two clear work streams: one that is the responsibility of the technical side to complete and one that is the responsibility of the business side. You need to ensure that the exchanges between the two are clear and understood. The benefit, of course, of running the project in-house is that the whole project can be run according to *PDMv2* principles, thereby considerably reducing the amount of discussion around the items that pass back and forth between the two.

GOLDEN RULE 2

GOLDEN RULE 2

The business knows best.

As discussed in Golden Rule 1, the business players are the experts in what the enterprise does. The business has been running the legacy systems, and the legacy systems have been running the business. Within the business there is the knowledge of where all the data sources that secretly run the enterprise are located. The business has the experience and expertise to make valid judgements about the quality and appropriateness of data items.

ANECDOTE

I was consulting to a company in a heavily regulated industry on changes needed to satisfy the regulator. At a presentation to senior management, I was asked what the consequences would be if I failed to migrate successfully some of the data because of user resistance. I replied, in line with Golden Rule 2, that if the enterprise ultimately judged that they could forego the data quality the regulator demanded for sound enterprise reasons and were prepared to stand up to the regulator, then I was not in a position to disagree. It was not my data. I owned neither the process nor the result. It was a hard point to make, but after that there were no more challenges on the issue of ownership.

Once stated it seems obvious and is probably the least challenged of the Golden Rules, but it is vital, as you will see, to the rest of the *PDMv2* method that you never stray from this obvious truth. It is all too easy, in the hurly-burly and time pressures of a typical data migration exercise, to lose sight of this.

Even with the best will in the world, lots of consultation and plenty of well-written, signed-off documents, there is still a risk that the technicians will start to take responsibility for decisions. This is especially true given, as you have seen, that the majority of decisions are well within the domain of experience that technologists bring to the party. It might seem expedient, it might seem low risk, but it never helps in the long run. This is not an issue about the quality of the decision. The technical decision might be correct. This is about ownership.

However, technicians do, of course, add value to the process. They know about the technical difficulties involved with matching different data formats. They know about normalisation, common points of reference and identity. They know how to transform data and how to create transitional data stores for data cleansing. They know how to write code to extract, reformat and import data. They can perform gap analysis and facilitate the process; and facilitating the process is important.

Although the business knows best, its knowledge is usually scattered throughout the enterprise. One of the main contributions of a skilled data migration analyst is to tease out of the enterprise that knowledge that allows you to do the very best job that time and money will allow. The approach in this book has a number of techniques designed to do precisely this.

However, in everything you do, you must always acknowledge that you cannot know more about the business rules than the enterprise does itself.

GOLDEN RULE 3

GOLDEN RULE 3

No organisation needs, wants or will pay for perfect quality data.

This is the most challenging assertion in the book, but one of the most important. So many data migration projects are unsatisfactory because there was an unspoken driver at the outset to enhance the data quality of the legacy system to a level approaching perfection. So what is wrong with this as an aspiration?

Well, my personal experience tells me this will not happen. The typical project profile is one of high expectations at the outset, followed by a series of compromises en route. Budgets and schedules start to slip and then there is a mad dash for the finish. The actual data migration, often being at the end of the timeline, is the phase of the project that suffers most by this time and cash squeeze. The quality of the data becomes compromised as time gets short. It becomes a case of getting what you can, instead of what you would like.

Compound this with the change in ownership that breaking Golden Rule 1 brings or on focusing on the wrong data sources by breaking Golden Rule 2 and, on go-live, the business user is faced with a system with all the inherent problems of the legacy that they thought they were getting rid of, plus a few more. Worse still, both sides (the technical and the business) feel betrayed.

From a business perspective, the technical side will have failed to deliver on the implicit promise to produce perfect quality data and will then be perceived as arrogant and out of touch with the needs of the 'real' enterprise when the compromised data is placed before the user population.

From a technical perspective, the business will have failed to tell the technical side all the details of their legacy systems and will have thrown up a series of late challenges to the go-live date.

What normally happens then is that the project descends into mutual recriminations, and responsibility for securing data of sufficient quality to run the new system from day one is pushed back and forth across the divide between the two sides of the project: the dreaded responsibility gap. The next project down the stream will find itself mired in the backwash of this history of problems.

Data quality compromise is, from experience, the norm, so plan to accept it from the outset. The starting point is to be honest up-front. Get the message across about Golden Rules 1, 2 and 3 from the beginning of the project. This book gives practical steps that will tie in the enterprise and get the right compromise decisions made in good time by the right interested parties.

You will always find that in a modern slimmed-down enterprise, the enterprise has interests other than the project you are working on.

- Executives have many calls on their time.
- Middle managers are squeezed by the cascades of initiatives tumbling down from above and the demands of their staff bubbling up from below.
- Front-line staff are too busy with the day job to provide extensive support for non-operational work.

These are the inevitable facts of enterprise life. Add to them that the project will have a life of its own, with a fixed end date, and it is easier to persuade that compromises need to be made once the issues are fully understood. Accepting this in advance means that sensible, considered priorities can be drawn up. Leaving it until budget and time are running out leads to rushed, ill-considered decisions based on expediency and not on utility.

Be honest from the start. Lay out the issues. Accept in advance that there will be compromises. Structure the relationship so that the business decides what to prioritise and what to drop. Just as importantly, the enterprise should be able to put a brake on any developments that limit its legitimate operation.

This book shows you how to structure a data migration project so that these issues are confronted early and dealt with smoothly. A series of project deliverables will be produced that will ease the technical–business relationship from one of confrontation over an implicit contract to the cooperative partnership that will better deliver what the enterprise wants and needs.

ANECDOTE

I was working on a management information system some years ago for an emergency services organisation. I had thought, in the circumstances of a large incident, with loss of life and property and the consequent legal issues that might arise, that nothing could be lost. I was wrong. There were many details that were captured on one system or another that were not of any interest. For instance, the mobile cafeteria system recorded when particular types of rolls were sold on its point-of-sale systems. It is getting the information that matters to the enterprise that is important. Who knows what constitutes meaningful information? That's right, Golden Rule 2: the business knows best.

There is, of course, an equally misplaced assumption that you should do nothing to enhance data quality. If the data was wrong in the legacy, then it can be wrong in the target. This assumption is unfounded: even trying to move data from one repository to an exact copy is not always possible without a degree of data enhancement. Where you are moving to a completely new target with new formats etc., then some data preparation and transformation is inevitable.

GOLDEN RULE 4

GOLDEN RULE 4

If you can't count it, it doesn't count.

Almost without fail, when I join a project and ask about the data quality, I will be told, 'It's quite good in system X' or that a particular database is 'poor quality'. Similarly, when I ask what data quality threshold is required in the new system, I will be told that the enterprise expects 'excellent' or 'very good' or even 'perfect'.

However, when I ask how we are going to know if we have achieved these targets, I am met often with a blank stare. Well-managed projects have measurable deliverables and a data migration project is no exception. You need to be able to report on percentages complete. You need to be able to compare disparate potential data sources. You need to be able to perform gap analysis. To do this with accuracy you need to be able to measure your achievements and the size of gap between where you are and where you need to be. You need hard facts about the data that you can measure. Anything else is aspirational waffle.

When it comes to counting and reporting you need your reports to reflect messages that are meaningful to the enterprise. If you are reporting on readiness to migrate you need to be speaking in business terms. Once again this is an area where there can be a conflict between a technical and a business understanding of what constitutes a record.

From a technical point of view, by a record we generally mean a row from a table in a database. However, from a business perspective, a record is a whole object that has a coherent meaning, for example, like a customer. From a technical point of view a Customer might be made up of dozens if not scores of records. To prevent this confusion *PDMv2* has the concept of a unit of migration.

Unit of migration

DEFINITION

A unit of migration is the lowest level of data granularity of meaning to the business.

What I mean by this is that the unit of migration is the smallest thing the business has interest in. Examples make this easier to understand. In a billing package, the unit of migration might be a Customer. You are only interested in migrating whole Customers with all their contact information and Orders. On the other hand, you might say that, although each Order must have a Customer to attach to, you will allow Orders with data issues to be excluded, but you will not allow Orders to be part loaded. Therefore your unit of migration is Order.

The importance and implications of units of migration is expanded on in Section 2, but for now you need to understand that these are decided on by a process of negotiation between the project and the key data stakeholders in the system retirement plans (described in Chapter 3).

PDMv2 will show you how to drive out these measures and how to record them. By basing their creation on Golden Rules 1 and 2, they will be the measures that make most sense to the enterprise.

SUPER SMART TASKS AND THE MID-CHANGE CYCLE SLUMP

It is all very well agreeing to the Golden Rules, but preaching them and getting them accepted across all your project partners are not the same thing. *PDMv2* might build all its activities on them, but convincing others to work within them is not always so easy. I have corresponded with a number of colleagues who fully bought into the original PDM but still found that they were often met with fierce opposition from their business partners in that they should have any ownership of the process. Intellectual argument alone will not suffice. You have to work to develop an emotional understanding of their need to be involved. Don't forget, an experienced business employee will most likely have been on the receiving end of multiple techno-centric project initiatives (not all sympathetically managed). There is an element of unlearning to do.

The first step is to understand the psychology behind this resistance prior to learning how to overcome it. I use the concepts of the Super SMART Task and mid-change cycle slump to bolster an appreciation of why your business colleagues might be behaving in the way they do and how to overcome it.

You will be familiar with the acronym SMART when applied to tasks.[3] It is commonplace in well-structured plans. So what then are 'Super SMART Tasks' in *PDMv2*?

You often have multiple drivers on a project, but any good manager should have an eye to at least three imperatives:[4]

- **Complete the task** – This is at the centre of the Super SMART Task definition. *PDMv2* is optimised to complete the task of data migration, but that is not all that you have to do to succeed.

- **Build the individual** – This necessary aspect of people management can often mean that you might over-task an individual. You give them work beyond their current skill set and outside their comfort zone to grow the next generation of project workers. You might accept suboptimal performance in the 'complete the task' zone so that next time around you will have workers who are more highly skilled. Aside from building their skill sets you can also build the individual, and therefore make them more productive, by working on softer factors like self worth, confidence and reducing anxiety.

- **Build the team** – I imagine that you have been to team building events: some a great success, some that felt like an unwarranted distraction from your working life. However, the skilled manager will be conscious of the smaller activities that can be built into the everyday life of a project and which can help to build the team.

This has been expressed in Figure 2.1.

---

[3] SMART: Specific, Measurable, Achievable, Realistic, Timely.
[4] Based on the work of John Adair.

Figure 2.1 The three circles of activity

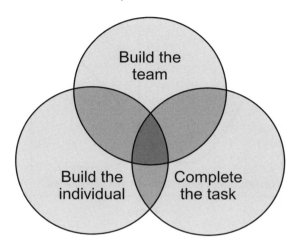

There are some tasks that sit solely in one circle, but these are fewer than you might think. Building the team is one way of ensuring that you complete the task. Building the individual is one way you have of motivating that individual to help you complete the task. However, we have all met managers who focus so much on 'complete the task' that this obsession actually gets in the way of its own success by demotivating individuals and destabilising teams.

A Super SMART Task is one that is designed to sit at the intersection of all three drivers. It builds the team, it builds individuals and it completes the task. *PDMv2* is built around Super SMART Tasks. The following example shows both how to be Super SMART and how to be less than Super SMART.

The mid-change cycle slump
So that you can fully appreciate the example you have to look first at another commonplace feature of project experience: the human reaction to change. (I think that you'll accept that most data migration projects involve some degree of change for a user population.)

Figure 2.2 shows the normal stages of an individual's reaction to change.

Figure 2.2 Standard reaction to change

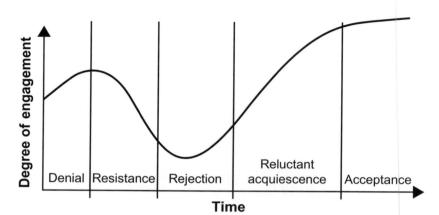

There are differing accounts of the emotional stages, which, in any case, vary according to the degree of change and the positive or negative impact of it upon the individual. However, there is general agreement that there will be a mid-cycle slump and increased resistance to change. In this model we have:

- **Denial** – This is characterised by lack of engagement and a belief that the change will never happen. This is not as crazy as it might seem. Remember that those impacted by change in a large organisation have probably been through a variety of initiatives over the years, some successful, some not, some making profound changes to working practices, but most passing almost unnoticed.

- **Resistance** – This is the guerrilla warfare phase, of politicking, of offering alternatives to the proposed change.

- **Rejection** – This phase is the bottom of the slump where, despite change now being highly likely, the individual retreats behind a set of apparently unbreachable objections to that change. What you do at this important phase can either push a user population up the slope of acceptance or deepen the slump of rejection, depression and inertia.

- **Reluctant acquiescence** – This marks the turning point where, even though the individual is unconvinced that they will in any way benefit from the change, it is now seen as inevitable. Any doubters will have been convinced of the reality of the imminent change by the arrival of the data gatherers pouring over existing systems. You can expect negotiation to begin at this point along the lines of 'I suppose I must accept the new system, but only if you can guarantee X.'

- **Acceptance** – This is where the benefits of the new application are being felt. Unfortunately this positive acceptance most often occurs post implementation when the users have got used to their new software and processes. It is the crisis in confidence that coincides with your most urgent efforts to gather appropriate data from existing legacy systems to prime your new application.

You have to understand why data matters to people to appreciate fully why people become so attached to their existing computer systems.

Why data matters to people
When in the flux of change you have to accept that data matters to people beyond its possible intrinsic value. Technologists might see it as the bits and bytes that make it up, but for an end-user it represents their business reality (often in a significantly limited manner with all its data quality challenges, but that's another story). The system might change, but the information persists, or at least it should. To aid your project you need to build the confidence of the individuals most impacted by change and you can do this by providing reassurance about the continuity of their data and significantly giving them some control over the future of that data.

Why people matter to data
On the other hand, you need the knowledge base these people have about the reality that the bits and bytes represent. Technologists can model data, pattern match and range check, but they can't know how the bits and bytes represent business reality. You've seen that, in order to resolve semantic and certain classes of data issue, you need more that just the input of your business colleagues. You are absolutely dependent on their knowledge and decisions.

Non-Super SMART Tasks
The industry standard approach to data migration is to retain as much work as possible within the confines of the project, only venturing out when the data gaps become so enormous that they cannot be filled, no matter how much ingenuity is applied internally. You team trust their software tools and databases to uncover an accurate reflection of the existing business reality. When they do venture out they find a suspicious and unhelpful user base, defensive of their data stores and gloomy about the prospects of your project bettering their lot. Your team retreats behind the barricades of project scope and are discouraged from ever encountering 'that lot' again, except as a last resort, and only then with the whip hand of superior executive sponsorship.

How to irritate and lose the trust of key business colleagues
As I have shown, you need the cooperation and knowledge of the front-line workers and managers who have been keeping the enterprise running, so why is it that our industry's standard approaches seem best designed to alienate them? Here are a few examples of techniques you might have seen that couldn't be better engineered to break down teamwork, undermine the individual and, ultimately, compromise delivery:

- **Arrogance** – Best encapsulated in 'the project knows best'. A good example of this is the rejection of local data stores in favour of the corporate data store. Imagine the scenario. Confronted with a process problem, maybe how to find the current holders of the access keys and permissions to remote sites, a worker, in their own time and on their own initiative, devises a spreadsheet of current contact details and an informal mechanism for updating with current locations. Along come the troops from the project, dismissing the spreadsheet and process at a glance because the corporate HR and asset management system holds this information. Later, when it is found that the HR system only holds the budget holding manager details, and these have not been updated when people change roles, the project goes in search of better data and finds the employee strangely uncooperative and possibly quite elusive.

- **Insult** – Often you will hear technologists being scathingly honest in their opinions of the data sources they are offered. Phrases like 'The data in this system is rubbish' or even 'This system is rubbish' are bandied about. I characterise this as the 'Your baby is ugly' approach to human interaction. It couldn't be better calculated to sour relationships.

HINT

Part of the reason for this abrasive approach is the nature of technologists. I should know, I am one. As a breed we tend to be very direct in our statements about technology. We see things in black and white and are given to pronouncing on them without consideration for the feelings of the listener. This is fine within the confines of the IT department where such exchanges are normal. We quickly learn not to tie up too much of our ego with our work, but in the real world this trait does not work to our advantage. *PDMv2* tries to discourage talk of 'data errors', replacing it with 'data gaps' or 'data readiness'.

- **Ignorance** – The project has access to all the databases and software so there is often the feeling that the project knows more than the business. We then display our domain ignorance in front of our business colleagues who have full knowledge of how it all actually works, presenting them with datasets that are less than useful. When allied to arrogance, ignorance can really alienate your most important colleagues.

ANECDOTE

A common problem I have often encountered, when working in the utilities and transport sectors, is identifying locations. It is all too common for technologists to assume that everything can be identified using a postal or zip code. Validation code is written and tested. Data is declared good or bad. Then the truth is revealed that railway sidings or industrial water meters do not have posting addresses. Even newly built domestic properties can be occupied before the relevant authority has caught up with a code. Some geographical regions do not even have postal codes outside of a few main population centres.

Super SMART Tasks

A more enlightened approach recognises the nature of the change experience and sees that you are going to need cooperation from the user base to secure decent data for your new system. You set out earlier in the project life cycle to engage with the business. You build the individual by getting the users to take on responsibility for data selection and quality. Involving them achieves a win–win situation: you secure better quality data and give them more control over their futures and more ownership of the end result. They are no longer the passive recipients of unasked-for change; they are part owners of that change. You will still experience the mid-cycle slump, but it will be you **to** whom they complain, not you **about** whom they complain.

Using rejection positively

PDMv2 encourages users to complain, to give you all the reasons why the migration is going to fail. You encourage objections and you take them seriously. You record them and reassure your business colleagues that you will address them between the project and the business. However, you are honest: you acknowledge that you will not be able to fix them all. Compromises will have to be made, as they have to be in any other area of life.

> **HINT**
>
> This technique is a variant on the old salesman's trick of asking for all the reasons why you cannot move forward to a sale. Logically, if all the objections can be answered, you must go ahead with the purchase, must you not? Except that here you have to recognise that under the surface of the objections there can be a perfectly normal but unacknowledged uncertainty in the face of change. This you assuage by increasing the involvement, and therefore control, of individuals in the change.

It might seem counterintuitive to seek objections actively. Wouldn't it be easier to ignore them? However, there is a three-fold purpose to this: it builds individuals by taking them seriously and by getting to the core of their anxiety; it builds the team by having these people look towards the migration team as fellow travellers towards an uncertain destination; and it delivers the project because in among the needless worries and preoccupations there will be real, significant issues that are unknown to the project. Finding these early is essential if you are to avoid the late challenges to migration that can sink a project.

How to engage with and gain the active support of business colleagues

Using *PDMv2* Super SMART Tasks you build one virtual team across the business that is focused on delivering the project. You do it by working at the intersection of the three circles in Figure 2.1:

- **Humility** – Relying on Golden Rule 2 ('The business knows best'), you do not assume that you know anything (or at least anything better) than your frontline business colleagues. Via the data quality rules (DQR) process (see Chapter 3) you back up every decision with a formal consultation process with the business, even the seemingly small and innocuous ones.

- **Inclusiveness** – You actively seek out and encourage the disclosure of every dataset out there. You seek out the business domain experts and encourage them to participate. You build them as individuals by listening to their expertise. You build the team by providing a forum where their contributions are taken into account.

- **Honesty** – You are seeking a peer-to-peer relationship with your colleagues and so you are honest from the outset that you will need their help at some point in the migration process. Theirs will not be a passive, business-class plane ride.

As I will explain in the following chapters, *PDMv2* is consciously built around these concepts. If you are forced by local circumstances to substitute local practice for a *PDMv2* function, make sure that your replacement operates to the same principles. In particular, I will look at activities like system retirement plans where the process of positively engaging with rejection is implemented.

CHAPTER REVIEW

In this chapter I have shown you that data migration is a risky business but, that by being aware of the major pitfalls, you can mitigate those risks.

I have introduced you to the four Golden Rules of data migration.

You have also learned about Super SMART Tasks and the mid-change cycle slump, both of which inform the structure of *PDMv2* projects.

3   *PDMv2* OVERVIEW

In this chapter I outline PDMv2 *and show how it overcomes all the issues identified in Chapter 1 by using a set of integrated modules that cover the whole scope of a data migration from project start-up to legacy decommissioning and beyond. I give a brief overview of the types of software technology available to support data migration.*

INTRODUCING *PDMv2*

PDMv2 is modularised with seven functional modules and one overarching governance and project control module. This modularisation helps, as you will see, in tailoring *PDMv2* to other project delivery methods. Figure 3.1 illustrates *PDMv2*. The arrowed lines illustrate product flows between modules. It is clear from the diagram that it anticipates a degree of recursion in a data migration. For instance, at any point a new requirement for data might emerge from the larger programme of which a data migration forms a part. You might be concentrating at this point on testing your data migration solution, but you still have to handle the requirement. This is something over which you have no control within the data migration project, but it is something you can manage.

Figure 3.1 A diagrammatic representation of *PDMv2*

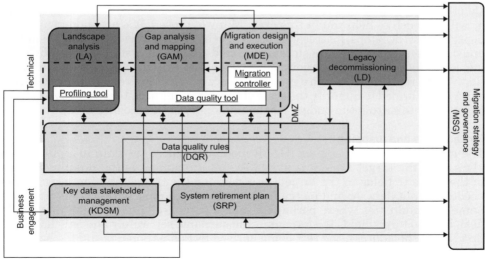

The functional modules within *PDMv2* are split over two work streams: business engagement and technical. Data quality rules (DQRs) span the two. It is important to note that even at this high level, *PDMv2* is designed from the ground up to integrate the business as well as the technical sides of the project. For *PDMv2*, business engagement is not a separate task, but is built into the way you go about your job.

Each of the modules is briefly explained below. More detailed explanations are given in Section 2, which provides sub-module, workflow-level descriptions.

Landscape analysis

The landscape analysis (LA) module uses various techniques to discover and catalogue legacy data stores (LDSs) and their relationship to one another. It is here that you look inside data stores to see how they work, what data they have and what data challenges they might contain. This is data profiling. It is performed by using both available software tools and manually. It is necessary to seek out consciously all the available LDSs, not just the official enterprise ones, welcoming all contributions. That way *PDMv2* turns a necessary technical activity into a set of Super SMART Tasks. Landscape analysis can commence prior to the design or even the selection of the target system.

HINT

If the decision on the target is still some way off, you can start on a small scale in an area that is likely to be rich in unofficial data stores. Start building the virtual team you will need to succeed. This also provides you with the opportunity to tailor the *PDMv2* deliverables to your programme management standards and to learn *PDMv2* by using it. Finally, data migration is a risky business. *PDMv2* helps de-risking by moving as much activity up the timeline as possible. Your mantra should be 'start small, start early'.

Do not expect that your selected systems integrator (SI) or software supplier can or will do much to help you in this area. Many of these LDSs are hidden away on departmental desktops, inaccessible to the reach of the SI. It is important to analyse and document how these data stores are linked (known as 'system topography') and include links across the scope boundary that receive or give data from and to stores that will be replaced. It is also a growing aspect of best practice that a fast iteration of LA is performed to quantify the scale of the data migration task you have in front of you prior to setting the budget for the remainder of the project.

Gap analysis and mapping

The gap analysis and mapping (GAM) module is where the data mapping takes place once the target system is available. Data mapping is the linking of fields in the LDSs to fields in the target, plus defining the transformation logic that is needed to split data up and merge fields. A classic example of this is reformatting name and addresses where perhaps a source database has the name in a single field, but the target holds the forename and surname separately and only holds the first line of the address, the rest being derived from a national postal file based on a postal or zip code.

HINT

It is perfectly normal for the target system to be delivered later than expected and in phases. Waiting for the target to be completely ready prior to starting data migration activities is a recipe for disaster. *PDMv2* gets around this by moving all discovery and profiling activity up the timeline to LA and the use of migration data models, which are explained in Section 2.

GAM is also where the mapping and gap analysis for legacy decommissioning design is performed so that an integrated target and archive design is developed. Again, it is absolutely standard for most SI or software suppliers not to be involved in designing a solution for those data items that the business might need (except rarely, for instance, where old transactions are preserved in case there is a tax inspection), but for which there is no place in the target. Therefore the design, build, test and execution of the archive solution is normally outside the DMZ, but driven by and dependent on the target migration design. After all, any item that is not moved to the target, but is needed by the business, has by definition to go into the archive, so these are activities that will need to be performed. *PDMv2* has them covered.

HINT

When reviewing proposals from suppliers, no matter how comprehensive they seem, comparing them against *PDMv2* will show you what is missing: in other words, what you will have to do yourself and therefore budget for. There are perfectly legitimate reasons, as you have seen from the discussion of the DMZ, for a supplier to limit their offering. Being aware of these missing elements, however, will allow you to plug the gaps.

Migration design and execution
The migration design and execution (MDE) module is where the physical design, test and execution of migration and archiving are carried out. Data migration is about more than just moving bits and bytes around. You have to be aware of business limitations, timings, audit requirements, data lineage, fallout, fallback, archiving requirements, reporting, management and control etc. MDE integrates all these elements within a single module solidly based on the business requirements expressed in the system retirement plans.

Legacy decommissioning
The legacy decommissioning (LD) module covers the physical or logical removal of legacy databases, hardware and software. It also covers the delivery of archived data storage for data items that have to be retained but which are not to be migrated to the target. There are also project close-down processes, including the handover of data quality issues (which it was not possible to fix within the project's time and budget constraints) to the in-life data quality teams (where they exist). Again it is absolutely standard for SI and software vendors to ignore the legacy decommissioning aspect of a data migration. You need to work with them through the *PDMv2* mechanisms to develop a single coherent design.

ANECDOTE

It is with some regret that I have to confess to not always finding willing recipients of those data quality issues that could not be fixed in the time and budget of a data migration project. However, at a corporate level, more organisations are making a conscious effort to manage data quality issues. As good corporate citizens we should endeavour to pass on what we can.

Data quality rules

The data quality rules (DQR) module is the centrepiece of what makes *PDMv2* unique. Sticking to the principle of Super SMART Tasks, this module manages all data quality and preparation-related activity on the programme. It integrates the legacy technical system experts, the target system experts and the business domain experts to prioritise, manage and complete all data issues, including the selection and exclusion of data sources. It is Super SMART because it builds the team by linking into the resources of the rest of the enterprise, creating a single virtual team; it builds the individual by empowering business colleagues and giving them the skills and opportunity to make a positive contribution to the project; and it completes the task by bringing much needed enterprise knowledge into a collaborative framework. DQRs are so important that Chapter 9 is dedicated to them alone.

HINT

To test how essential (and often missing) this element is in most data migration approaches, try the following. When analysing the bids of various suppliers, ask how they handle data quality issues. The common response is a long technical description of how they have sophisticated tools to trap errors. Your next question should be: 'And then what?' If you are lucky they will explain how they have an issues log that records the issues with appropriate dashboarding etc. Try another: 'And then what?' and you will be really pushing the boundaries of their method. The honest answer is: 'And then we wait while you, the project, come up with a fix.' They have no mechanism for getting that fix, only ones for uncovering errors and logging them. This illustrates the boundary of the DMZ. If you employ *PDMv2* and its DQR processes you will have one.

Key data stakeholder management

PDMv2 has its own specific role definitions for each key data stakeholder (KDSH). Key data stakeholder management (KDSM) manages the discovery, briefing and management of these individuals. *PDMv2* is very business-focused, so there are as many business as technical roles. *PDMv2* is very prescriptive when it comes to KDSHs. A full description of KDSHs is provided in Chapter 6, but from the business side the two most important stakeholders are data owners and business domain experts.

PDMv2 is quite clear about the definition of data owners.

DEFINITION

Data owners are all the people within or outside an organisation who have the legitimate power to stop a migration from happening.

This definition is not based on organisation charts of who has titular responsibility for a database. If a person can legitimately stop the migration occurring because their information is not adequately managed, then they are the data owner of that piece of information. This means that the often forgotten, but powerful, individuals like financial controllers, who can stop migrations if the results compromise their needs, are equal data owners with the people who work directly with a data store (but only for the data items that impact them). Each data owner is expected to take part in the system retirement planning process, all of which is explained in more detail in Chapter 8.

The system owners, however, are often senior executives who cannot be expected to answer every query coming out of the project personally and who, in any case, often have no direct, day-to-day, hands-on experience of using the systems in question. They will generally defer to nominated business domain experts who they empower to input to the various meetings and provide the detailed knowledge to the project.

This is all very well, you might say, but how do you get the commitment of these powerful few to your project? We all know how difficult it is to get real commitment from colleagues working in silos different from our own. In this case, you leverage the compelling event of the forthcoming system retirement to grab attention and make your needs real to people.

System retirement plans

PDMv2 does not begin its conversation with the business by asking about data mappings, data quality, data gaps, data lineage or any other esoteric technical feature. *PDMv2* begins with the ultimate goal of a data migration: turning off legacy data stores.

HINT

It might seem crudely brutal, but I have found in practice that the bold unvarnished question 'You know system X that you depend on to do your day job? Well, we are turning it off on (enter date). How will you be certain that you will be able to continue with your day job once that has happened?' works better than anything. I leave it to you to dress it up in language appropriate to your situation, but I find the unchallengeable simplicity of this statement works best.

Going back from this you uncover all the things that must be done so that data owners will be comfortable with signing off the decommissioning certificate. You seek and encourage objections to going forward. Getting these objections shows you have moved the subject over the hump of denial, down the slopes beyond rejection, to at least the negotiation of reluctant acceptance, if not to positive acceptance. Starting the conversation this way makes real the compelling event of a data migration.

You provide reassurance by explaining that you will be proceeding through a controlled sequence of iterations (the data owners will have to sign off the system retirement plan (SRP) at least three times before you get to the decommissioning certificate) that allows them to be ready and confident in the migration and that they have made you aware of all the things you must do to satisfy them.

Under the guidance of the *PDMv2* model you ask a series of structured questions that elicit the business view of the migration, looking at necessary items like business migration audit requirements, data lineage requirements, data retention requirements, migration restrictions, user acceptance testing requirements, go-live restrictions, fallback requirements, units of migration definitions, migration resource requirements and data transitional processes (all of which are explained in detail in Section 2). All responses are expressed in business terms.

The SRP is your business colleagues' main view of the migration and is a key input to migration design and execution.

Migration strategy and governance

The migration strategy and governance (MSG) module covers all the standard programme management functions that are expected on a well-managed project, plus some unique activities that are mandated by *PDMv2*. Section 2 gives a full description of MSG; however, from an overview perspective there is one task that must be completed with the involvement of the senior management of the whole programme, that is the creation of a data migration strategy and that follows in Chapter 4.

Demilitarised zone

As you have seen, the demilitarised zone (DMZ) is the interface between the work of the technology supplier and the responsibilities of its clients. The DMZ is a key component of *PDMv2* that will be, to an extent, formally defined in the contract with the supplier. However, the DMZ is wider than the contract and its formal definition will help both sides understand and manage their reciprocal dependencies. Throughout the rest of this book, I will constantly refer to the DMZ and its impact on each of the *PDMv2* modules.

INTRODUCING THE TECHNOLOGY

So far I have looked at the softer issues around a data migration because these are typically where the project is likely to go wrong. I will now introduce the standard technology that underpins data migration projects. A more detailed description can be found in appropriate places in Section 2 where the use of the technology is covered.

TECHNOLOGY OVERVIEW

There has been an explosion in the technology available to assist with data migration over the last few years and it seems that each newcomer to the market has a different take on how to perform the necessary tasks. However, broadly speaking, there are three phases of activity where specific technology support is available: data profiling; data quality; and migration control. I will also discuss generic project-supporting software (hubs and workflow tools).

Data profiling tools

Data profiling tools allow you to analyse the legacy databases and discover unforeseen features at column and row level. Some tools on the market also allow cross data source analysis. This means that you can compare, say, customer names in a sales ledger with customer names in a customer relationship management (CRM) database, even though they are from different vendors. The majority of tools work at the database level, analysing and comparing fields, but some tools will even interrogate source code to find relationships that are in the code but not in the database management system. (This only works, of course, when you have access to the source code, but is very helpful in old, locally built legacy systems where validation rules have been lost in the mists of time.)

The use of profiling tools is a vital first step in producing data of the quality that will load into your new system. As you will now be aware, you must anticipate that there will be surprises in the LDSs. It is a common misconception that the use of tools can only start once the target system has been fully defined. This is not the case. As you have seen, semantic issues, the most difficult and time-consuming to resolve, will be issues whatever the new system is. Be prepared to profile data prior to the definition of the target system.

However, data profiling tools are almost too good these days and will generate large amounts of information. You will need a process to winnow the wheat from the chaff. Fortunately *PDMv2* comes complete with just such a process: DQRs. By just using data profiling tools without the DQR process you risk drowning in a sea of possible issues. Data profiling tools are also limited in what they can access. Although some can compare spreadsheet data, most are restricted to looking at corporate standard databases and none can look easily into hard copy sources like rolodex, notebooks etc.

Similarly, data profiling tools will not uncover, on their own, the hidden data sources that are not linked by database level exchanges of data. The clerk with the data stick, moving data from one machine to another before creating figures that are re-entered manually into an old application might be essential to regulatory processes, but will be invisible to any tools. To discover these you need to rely on the more pedestrian methods within the LA module and the creation of your virtual team.

However, having dwelt on the limitations of profiling tools, best practice now recommends the use of profiling tools for projects of any size prior to setting budgets and plans for data migration. For smaller migrations there are plenty of free-to-use, studio editions of some of the leading toolsets. They tend to have enough functionality for small datasets, but are limited in their integration, and therefore application, to larger programmes. On the other hand, the studio editions are also a good way to get a feel for what is on the market even if eventually you need to scale up to enterprise level software.

Data quality tool

Once you have an idea of the target, on the one hand, and the constraints of the LDSs, on the other, data quality software allows the speedy (most are 'point and click') implementation of validation and cleaning rules. There is obviously some overlap in functionality between profiling and data quality tools. Some software can span both spheres, but most are stronger in one than the other. The difference is that profiling tools discover relationships and possible data quality issues, whereas data quality tools check for and enforce known data quality rules. It is for this reason that the leading vendors tend to have both in their software sets. Ideally the rules discovered in profiling should be passed seamlessly for implementation in the data quality software, which in turn is fully integrated with the migration controller.

Once again, there are studio editions of many of the leading software offerings. These are worth looking at to get a feel for what is on offer if you have no local expertise.

Migration controllers

Migration controllers are often known as the extract, transform and load (ETL) tools; however, they are expected to do more than merely perform these three functions. They are the essential 'on the night' software that delivers the migration. Migration controllers need to be capable of performing the following functions:

- Reading data from the LDSs (the 'extract' step).
- Validating the extracted data (preferably using the data quality software seamlessly embedded into the migration controller suite).
- Reformatting the data and blending data from multiple sources (the 'transform' step).
- Scheduling, starting and stopping the migration process.
- Writing the data to the target (the 'load' step).
- Managing fallout.
- Managing fallback.
- Reporting on execution.
- Reporting on fallout.
- Providing audits.

More sophisticated products are also capable of many other features including:

- Synchronisation (keeping the changes to source and target data in step after the data has been moved. This means that the source can continue to be used during the migration thus enabling zero downtime migrations).

- Data lineage (tracking individual units of migration to show how they were transformed, combined and written to the target. This is sometimes a necessity for regulatory reasons and is also helpful for other technical reasons covered in Section 2).

Modern, built-for-purpose migration controllers have so many complex features that it is unlikely that you would be successful in replicating them in locally produced software.

Hubs and workflow

It is commonplace these days on large projects to implement some form of hub. This is an area where documents can be shared and different software is used to facilitate collaboration. Good data migration projects are a hive of collaboration, with the disparate groups of workers sharing knowledge. Workflow engines allow the output of, say, records that have fallen out of the migration to be routed from the migration controller to the correct team for analysis. The use of these tools depends on the scale of the migration. Small, co-located teams, have less need for collaboration tools than large project teams spread over a number of time zones and continents, but the ubiquity of this software and its relative low cost compared with the benefits in productivity and knowledge sharing make it all but essential. At the time of writing there has been a surge in interest in using social networking type software for collaboration on projects. This really is an area where you need to discuss what is available for your project with your architectural resource.

THE CASE FOR SPECIALIST TECHNOLOGY

It is possible to complete a data migration using the code writing capabilities of an indigenous IT department, but there are risks. All code writing is inherently risky. Bugs work their way into the code and then need to be weeded out in testing. The more coding you do the more bugs, the more testing, the more time, the more risk. Using software designed for the job reduces the number of bugs dramatically because it is only the logic of the migration that is being tested not the logic as it was instantiated in someone's handcrafted code.

A second compelling reason is that off-the-shelf data migration software these days is incredibly sophisticated. There is no way that any company, other than a rival software vendor, could ever justify the investment to recreate even a tenth of the features available out of the box.

ANECDOTE

I do know of one large technology company that decided in a fit of hubris to build their own migration hub. I have been quietly tracking the project and after five years and considerable expense they have not succeeded in replicating even the features of one of the cheaper off-the-shelf products. I suspect that their business drivers must go beyond merely delivering a solution.

All that being said, it remains a business judgement as to just where the cost–benefit lies. Tools can be purchased separately or as part of a set. Each migration has its own set of issues. For instance, is it a true 24/7 environment (like production control systems or telephony) where you really can never shut down the systems? If so, investment in sophisticated migration controllers that allow zero downtime are called for. Or do you have a complex heterogeneous migration environment to migrate from where the use of leading edge data profiling tools capable of cross database analysis will be useful? Possibly you are in a heavily regulated environment where data lineage is vital. Maybe you have only a short window of opportunity to migrate the data, in which case tools with superior prototyping capability could be key. And so on.

Only you know your own migration challenges and drivers. On the one hand, you do not want to invest in heavyweight technology you do not need. On the other, you do not want to be hamstrung trying to manhandle a migration via an inappropriate vehicle. It really pays to take advice at this point from internal or independent experts who can refine your thinking and define your options.

PDMv2 PROVIDES ALL THE ANSWERS

A review of the issues identified in the preceding text that have historically damaged data migration projects shows that *PDMv2* provides a solution that covers all the bases but is flexible enough to be deployed in partnership with your chosen supplier's own preferred approach.

Techno-centricity
PDMv2 sees data migration as a business-led joint IT–business activity, albeit with a clear view of where technology sits and how to make informed decisions about which technology is appropriate for your project. Through the DQR and SRP processes the business provides direction over data selection, data preparation, data quality, decommissioning etc., and takes ownership not just of the end point but of the process of getting there. All this is completed within an integrated set of linked activities.

Lack of specialist skills
PDMv2 provides the tools and techniques that are all you need to perform low-risk data migrations. You can use it either as a checklist against likely internal resources or seek training in specific skills or even the whole methodology.

For those partners, like implementation service suppliers, who will perform the final 'lift and shift' and who have their own preferred approach, *PDMv2* has the DMZ concept to insulate them from having to change their approach, which might well be optimised from their knowledge of their own technology and the target systems' load requirements.

Underestimating
PDMv2 provides two ways of managing estimates. Firstly, there is the LA module that can be run separately on a fast pass through basis to generate the understanding on which estimates of scale can be arrived at prior to setting the budget for the

rest of the migration. Secondly, when the project is in-flight there is an assumption (Golden Rule 3) that more issues will be generated than can be solved, but there is the DQR process to manage the prioritisation needed to get the appropriate data of an appropriate level of quality to the right place at the right time. As I have shown, knowing there is an issue and solving an issue is not the same thing, especially if the issue is a business-side or semantic problem. Only *PDMv2* has built in the controls of these decision-making processes via DQR that reach beyond the boundaries of the project. Spotting the challenges early while working in a collegiate, virtual team, with the business taking a leading role, means that time, quality or budget can be flexed in a dynamic but controlled manner. Put together as a coherent whole you have a set of processes that allow sensible decisions to be made that will deliver the data you need at the time you want it within a budget that you can accept.

Uncontrolled recursion

Using *PDMv2* from the start of the project will build the single virtual team across business and technical stovepipes that will ensure that the responsibility gap never has a chance to develop. Via the DQR and SRP processes, you retain a tight control on your migrations using common metrics across multiple different data types, data sources, geographical locations etc.

Technology

Within *PDMv2* there is an understood place for technology and a clear decision point for deciding which technology is appropriate to your migration. However, technology is not divorced from the rest of the migration processes. Technology on its own, in any walk of life, rarely solves any problems without being wrapped in some form of meaningful best practice. Technology is embedded in the modules that make up *PDMv2* and is therefore still directed by business towards optimally aiding your data migration. If necessary, and to get the maximum benefit from your software investment, encapsulation in the DMZ means that you do not expect to have to destabilise your chosen implementation partner's favoured approach, which will optimise the use of their toolset's salient features.

To achieve all of this, however, you need to make sure that you have set up your project in the right way in the first place: in other words that you are setting off from the right starting point. For that, you need to get your data migration strategy right in the first place. This is the subject of Chapter 4.

CHAPTER REVIEW

In this chapter I have introduced you to the various modules of *PDMv2* and showed their interrelated nature. I also looked at the use of technology and you saw how it overlays the activities within the modules. Finally, you saw how the use of *PDMv2* mitigates all the risks, both technical and non-technical, that I identified in previous chapters.

4   CREATING A MIGRATION STRATEGY

In this chapter I examine the character and nature of the governance functions within a data migration project. I explain how they are a superset of the standard project governance roles, processes and artefacts. I also define the specific control flows that maximise the control of a PDMv2 data migration project within a larger programme. I show how the data migration strategy is the key early deliverable that tailors the possibilities available within PDMv2 to the environment in which you find yourself and the needs of your project.

STARTING OUT ON THE RIGHT FOOT

I have shown that there are many pitfalls to running a data migration project, but the main ones are a lot easier to avoid at the outset than fix once the project is under way. To make sure your project starts out right, you need to make sure that all the correct engagements and controls are present at the beginning and that you have the structures in place to use these controls to manage the project.

This chapter first explains what these engagements and controls are within a *PDMv2* project. It lists those that are standard to any project and those that are peculiar to data migration.

Secondly, because the start-up phase of any project is where decisions should be made about just about everything to do with scope, approach and method, reviewing these start-up decisions is a great way to reinforce your understanding of the interlinked nature of *PDMv2* and its complete coverage of the data migration space. So please read this chapter on two levels: firstly as an instruction on how to create a *PDMv2* data migration project kick-off document; and secondly as an overview of *PDMv2* itself.

PDMv2 DATA MIGRATION STRATEGY

PDMv2 insists that you should always create a data migration strategy at the outset, explicitly stating what you are doing, how you are interfacing with your numerous partners on a project like this and putting in place the controls needed to properly manage your activity. The delivery of the data migration strategy is normally led by the project manager responsible for the data migration project, but it will involve all the senior management on the programme board in decisions about scope, reporting and strategic guidance. It is both an essential document and a catalyst for getting everyone involved with the project at a senior level acquainted with the *PDMv2* approach. In that sense it is a quintessential Super SMART Task:

- It 'builds the individuals' by familiarising them with the *PDMv2* approach and terminology.
- It 'builds the team' by getting explicit agreement on scope and underlying project drivers and helping to identify the top-level KDSHs.
- It 'completes the task' by delivering the project kick-off documentation that is the cornerstone of any well-founded project.

HINT

Like many terms, 'strategy' might or might not be acceptable in this context in your environment. I have come across terms as diverse as 'proposal' or even 'project initiation document'. It is not the term that matters, but the content and purpose.

WHAT IS IN A *PDMv2* DATA MIGRATION STRATEGY DOCUMENT?

The migration strategy should be written on the assumption that the reader will not have any familiarity with *PDMv2* and only a passing understanding of formal project management techniques. It is an executive-level document, not necessarily a technical one, and should contain:

- a project overview;
- the data migration project scope;
- the data migration project budget;
- the formal project and programme organisation;
- the modules from *PDMv2* that are being deployed and local substitutes (bearing in mind the DMZ issue);
- policies;
- a project decomposition;
- the form of the migration;
- an initial migration plan;
- software selection;
- SI selection;
- the generic project office functions;
- an initial KDSHs list;
- an initial legacy data store list;
- an initial SRP;

- an initial data issues list;
- control flows and project reporting.

Each of these is considered in detail below.

Project overview

It is best practice for all documents to be stand-alone. This means that a newcomer to the project who needs an introduction to what you are doing, why you are doing it and how you are approaching the task, should be given this document and, without reference to other briefing documentation, be able to understand the project and its relationship to the bigger programme. So you need a short introduction explaining the high-level whats, whys and hows.

HINT

I normally cut and paste a good deal of the project overview from the programme's charter document or programme initiation document (PID), but it is surprising how often no one has formally articulated the whys and wherefores of the programme: which means it is down to you. This is a place for the exercise of brevity and clarity. If you can't explain the big drivers and deliverables of a project in less than three hundred words, maybe you should revisit your understanding of it.

Data migration project scope

There are two extents of scope with which you need to be concerned: the overall programme scope and the scope of the data migration project within the programme.

Programme scope often changes within the lifetime of a programme. As analysis and design proceeds, legacy data stores are added and subtracted from the scope and/or areas of functionality are added and removed. You need to be aware of these occurrences and so you need a mechanism to cope with change (outlined under the Generic project office functions heading below). However, an initial statement of scope is needed from which you can manage change and this should be in your strategy document.

There is a two-way relationship between the data migration team and the bigger programme so far as scope is concerned. Within LA you will uncover new data stores and hidden relationships between data stores that are unknown to the bigger programme. They can change the scope of the bigger programme, although it is rare.

ANECDOTE

While working on a migration for a large financial institution I came across a fully functioning data warehouse complete with a development team that was providing key regulatory data to the core business function but which was unknown to the corporate data architects.

In addition to the scope of the bigger programme and the way it cascades down through to the data migration project, you also need to define the limits of the data migration within the bigger programme. You need to manage and be aware of the detail of what is expected of you, what is expected of others and (for the good of the whole programme) if there are any gaps. By aligning your project to the *PDMv2* map you can see where the gaps might be. Who, for instance, is responsible for physical decommissioning of LDSs and software licence recovery? This is rarely the task of the data migration team as laid out in the original programme plan. More normally it is seen as the responsibility of the incumbent IT function, but it should be in someone's plan. Similarly, if you are engaged in a phased migration, you need to know who is responsible for the transitional interfaces that might need to be implemented as parts of the target application are rolled out. This is often part of the data migration team's responsibility, but not always. Use the exercise of creating a data migration strategy to ensure that you have covered all the necessary activities without overlaps or gaps. Once agreed it is less likely that this project (as opposed to programme scope) will change, but you need to ensure you can cope if it does.

Data migration project budget

Best practice recommends that a data migration project should have its own budget. It is also a guideline recommendation that it is only after LA that you can have any certainty of what that budget should be. It is not until you have completed an analysis of where you are coming from that you know how much it will cost to the lift what you need from where it is to the quality you need and prepared to the state you need. You can then move it to where you need it to go. Therefore it is normally the case that you will need to prepare an accurate budget for LA and an indicative budget for the rest of the data migration project, but this budget should be held and managed within the data migration project itself.

Formal project and programme organisation

PDMv2 does not prescribe the constitution of project or programme governance and organisation: you have to expect that they will be constituted in line with one of the industry standard patterns. You do, however, expect that such structures will be in place. If you are working to an established methodology like PRINCE, then there is a clear definition of the roles and responsibilities of the participants of a programme board. The data migration project does not usually justify its own project board, but you do expect that the data migration project manager will have access to the bigger programme's board. A lack of access to the programme board leads to problems with scope management, supplier management, planning, budgeting etc. The data migration strategy document should describe the constitution of the programme board in general and, specifically, how the data migration project will interact with it. This, of course, assumes that the programme board has already been constituted. It could be the case that the whole programme is still coalescing and that there is no prescribed programme governance formula to rely on. In this case it is perfectly acceptable to put in a place-marker that outlines the requirements above and explains how they will be safeguarded as the programme comes into being. It is important in this case to ensure the document itself is signed off by a sufficiently authoritative figure to guarantee that these governance requirements will be enacted as the situation clarifies.

HINT

I have written this chapter as if you were in the best of all possible worlds where the bigger programme is well established with clearly understood scope, governance etc. In the real world you often find otherwise. It is your judgement about whether or not you feel safe to proceed in the circumstances you find yourself.

Although you might not be able to fill in all the blanks when it comes to your relationship to programme governance, you should be able to propose how you will be managing the data migration project. A large part of this will come from the project controls described in the rest of this chapter.

Modules from *PDMv2* and local substitution

PDMv2 can be adopted wholesale and it will, of course, do the complete job for you. However, you need to be aware that this rarely happens, for two reasons.

Firstly, you need to consider the DMZ and its impact on your activities. I have already explained how you can expect each supplier to bring a set of operating practices that optimise their experience, their preferred toolset and the nature of the target. However, the DMZ is part of *PDMv2*.

Secondly, there is also the matter of local preferences. You can expect that there will be particular ways of doing things in your environment that would be adequate substitutes for *PDMv2* activities. On the other hand, part of the benefit of going through the *PDMv2* modules and their artefacts and processes is to make sure that you have everything covered.

ANECDOTE

I always use a checklist as a reminder, even though I am the author of *PDMv2*. It is just too easy, with issues such as coming to terms with new people and new ways of working in the swirl of a nascent project, to overlook or misinterpret something.

Bearing in mind that this document will be read by colleagues who have not had the benefit of reading this book, it is important to describe each module in your data migration strategy: what is does, what its principle deliverables are and so on. Any deviation from the *PDMv2* template needs to be explained. The chief reasons (other than within the DMZ) for diverging from *PDMv2* are policies, as explained below.

Policies

In any organisation there are explicit and tacit business drivers and constraints within which the project must run. Some are obvious and given to you from the start. Others are possibly not even articulated, but are nevertheless fundamental to operating successfully. *PDMv2* refers to them all as policies. Examples of the most common are given here, but be on the lookout for policies in your environment to which you have to conform.

- **Project methodology** – Is your project working within an Agile framework or do you use a more traditional waterfall methodology? Do you prescribe a specific project management framework (e.g. PRINCE or ITIL®)? These are obvious questions to ask and if you are misinformed you can be sure that, sooner rather than later, you will be brought back into line, so it is best to ask the question up front. *PDMv2* is equally at home in any modern methodological approach, but part of the job during the project start-up phase is to work out what it means to you and tailor your project accordingly.

- **Architectural** – Are you working in an environment that mandates certain software, hardware or data structures? What are your enterprise's data migration tools of choice? How far can you make independent choices? The answers to all these questions are important.

- **Risk aversion (quality versus time versus budget)** – Enterprises neither want nor need (or are willing) to pay for perfect quality data, and it is also down to the business to decide what constitutes data prepared to the right level (based on Golden Rules 1, 2 and 3). *PDMv2* has data quality rules that decide on these issues on a case-by-case basis. You are looking for guiding principles.

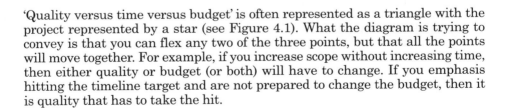

ANECDOTE

I have worked on projects (often regulatory inspired) that are best described as 'quick and dirty'. I have worked on projects that are seen as an opportunity to correct known data issues. I have worked on migrations where the time constraints are extremely tight (often these are de-mergers where the condition of sale mandates that the corporate LDSs are switched off at a defined point in the future). Most migrations sit somewhere in the middle.

'Quality versus time versus budget' is often represented as a triangle with the project represented by a star (see Figure 4.1). What the diagram is trying to convey is that you can flex any two of the three points, but that all the points will move together. For example, if you increase scope without increasing time, then either quality or budget (or both) will have to change. If you emphasis hitting the timeline target and are not prepared to change the budget, then it is quality that has to take the hit.

Figure 4.1 Quality versus time versus budget

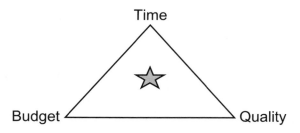

HINT

I normally find that, although I start out with quality as my main aim, once the discussion is completed I find that time and budget are increasingly significant.

You must have a conversation about this at the outset of a project with the senior sponsors and executives on the programme board. It is all about honesty and it will lead to some interesting discussions.

Be aware that not all data items will have the same quality threshold. There are always some data items that have to be absolutely accurate (like bank account details in a payments system) and others that don't (perhaps like mobile phone numbers in a CRM). You need to work through these on an issue-by-issue basis via the DQR process (more fully described in Section 2).The discussions you have at the start of the project are at a general level. It is about setting the overall policy. Later fine-tuning for individual data items will be conducted via the SRPs and the DQR processes. Setting the tone at the start is important because later conversations, within the DQR process perhaps, are better informed if you understand the top-level drivers for the project on which you are engaged.

- **Master data management** – Within any organisation there are always some data items that are more significant than others and provide the framework around which all the other data structures are built. Typically these are entities like Customers and Product. It is increasingly the case that within organisations, there is a drive to manage centrally these key entities in a master data management (MDM) system. If there is such a driver, then the chances are that it will be common knowledge. On the other hand, within a data migration project, you have a very real need to control these structurally significant data items so that you can consolidate data from disparate sources. So, if there is an MDM policy, you need to ensure that you are aligned to it.

- **Regulatory policies** – Nearly every organisation these days is subject to regulatory overview. You need to know the list of regulations that you have to adhere to, if not in detail, at least in outline, so that as you design your migration you do not fall foul of them.
- **Local policies** – This is the catch-all for all the other strategic and policy drivers within which your data migration project must work and with which it must comply.

Other common local policies might concern the employment of certain groups; the need to downsize as a consequence of the migration; the desire to up-skill certain workers in the tools you are going to use in the light of future projects etc.

Where politically appropriate, all policies that can impact your work should be noted and described in your data migration strategy.

Project decomposition

How do you manage a large project whose detail is overwhelming? Well, you break it down into manageable pieces. There is an extensive discussion on this in Section 2, but, in brief, you have a number of choices. You can follow a data-centric approach and break down your project by LDSs that deal with common data (e.g. Customer data, Product data, Sales data); you can break down your project by business function (e.g. Marketing, Sales, Manufacturing); you can break down your project by geographical area; you can break down your project by business unit; or you can mix and match all of these. Within *PDMv2* each segment in this breakdown is called a key business data area. The choice of project decomposition has a reciprocal relationship with the migration form, which I will look at next.

Migration form

> **DEFINITION**
>
> Migration form is the technical style of a migration.

There are a number of standard approaches to the way you implement data migration. Each has its strengths and weaknesses and are discussed at some length in Section 2. The following list gives the most common generic titles but, like a lot of aspects of data migration, different suppliers might use different terms. However, dig only a little way beneath the surface and you will find considerable similarity.

The commonest forms of migration are:

- **Big bang** – All the data is moved in one go and the legacy immediately decommissioned.

- **Phased** – The data is moved in separate parts, possibly geographically or by business function based over a series of migrations.

- **Parallel** – The data is moved to the target, but the legacy is allowed to run alongside it for a period to guarantee that the target is operating correctly.

- **Always up** – Migrations where the source systems cannot be taken offline (like phone systems) even for an instant. These require specialist migration tools with at least forward synchronisation and hot switching from legacy to target.

Recent developments in data migration technology mean that other migration forms are now possible.

In *PDMv2*, the initial decision of which migration form to follow is taken within the migration strategy activity because it is fundamental to many of the other decisions you have to make. It impacts choices about software selection and therefore migration partners etc. It is obviously key to migration design and execution. It might change over the lifetime of the project. You might find that you intended to go 'big bang', but that you were constrained to retreat to 'phased'. However, this change is rare. Although it is helpful to know all the migration forms in advance when considering a data migration, it is also usually pretty obvious which of the forms you are going to use. This initial decision needs to be recorded in the data migration strategy. If it really is not clear which form you will be using, then a description of the likely forms should be documented along with the steps that will be taken to come to a conclusion. There is further detailed discussion of migration forms in Chapter 11.

Initial migration plan

Your data migration strategy should be accompanied by a plan. Obviously you are in the start-up phase now, so any plan will be indicative, especially beyond LA. Therefore most plans in the data migration strategy will be fairly high level. Your plan should include the go-live date for the target system (obviously), and then you can work backwards from this.

HINT

LA, gap analysis and DQR activity will take up the biggest amount of time on a data migration project, dwarfing mapping and migration design and execution, but they are flexible in that you know you will have more issues to fix than you will have time. Therefore work your plan backwards into time boxes. This will tell you how much time you have to perform these functions and it will provide the time constraint within which you must prioritise your activity.

Use the *PDMv2* module diagram (Figure 3.1) to create your high-level project tasks, and don't forget to plan for some trial migrations.

Trial migrations

Trial migrations[5] are becoming increasingly common to the point where few major migrations go ahead without them. However, they do come with a few issues attached.

Firstly, there is the sheer scale and cost associated with them. If you are embarking on a data migration of a large enterprise application with millions of customer records derived from multiple sources, it can take some time to run and, if it is to be fully realistic, it will take a great deal of human resource effort to get all the technical and non-technical staff on site while you perform it.

Secondly, there is the question of effectiveness. Trial migrations are sometimes used in lieu of more rigorous testing. This 'throw the data at the target and see what sticks' approach to testing is the one most likely to lead to the death spiral of uncontrolled recursion that I discussed in Chapter 1 . Data issues tend to be layered and records thrown out because of one validation failure often have other failures lurking beneath the surface.

---

[5] Sometimes trial migrations are called dummy loads or dress rehearsals.

ANECDOTE

I was called into one data migration project that was on its sixth iteration of trial migration and had not managed to load a single record for real (a few had been 'massaged' through). More data issues were being revealed at each successive iteration. At the time it looked like a seventh, eighth and ninth trial migration would result in exactly the same outcome. The project was re-established based on the practices outlined in Section 3, but not without considerable pain.

Trial migrations are no substitute for thorough data quality analysis and you should be suspicious of anyone who suggests otherwise.

Finally, there is the issue of the completeness of the development. In theory, if you had enough time and resource, trial migrations would be fine. You would have a completed target system to aim at and months of iterations to get your data right. In the real word, the plan for the bigger programme will give you a fully designed, tested, configured and delivered system just a few weeks before going live. In practice, it will arrive at the last minute and fixes will be made to it right up to going live. So it is not as if the trial load will even test the target system as it will be at go-live.

For all these reasons, look at trial migrations as a fail-safe mechanism that tests a complex set of interactions, not as the bedrock of your testing strategy. I recommend you plan for them and get them put into the contract with your supplier, but aim to have zero defects on the first load.

HINT

How many trial loads to plan for is a difficult question and the answer is often down to cost and difficulty. Some modern technology, although excellent in use, is not readily amenable to quick load/unload/reload cycles. Getting the windows of opportunity where you can get a full copy of your live systems might be difficult given the number of reporting and offline jobs that are routinely run during a normal working week. Often an increasingly stale copy of the live system is repeatedly put through its paces until it is months out of date. Therefore, you need to start negotiations early with your technical system experts on both sides of the DMZ and get your intentions incorporated into the contract with suppliers, but try to get as many trial loads as you can.

Software selection

It is important to note that I am speaking here about the data migration software as described in Chapter 3, not about the target application software. The target application software is the responsibility of the bigger programme. This book gives a guide to the generic types of software that are available at the time of writing. New software is appearing all the time, so it is imperative to look at the market to see what is available and relevant to you when your project is about to start. However, software selection is still usually determined by the following constraints:

- **Scale** – Once again, size matters. Tools that are perfectly acceptable on a small, local data migration are inappropriate on a large, complex, multinational migration. The opposite is also true: expensive, powerful, feature-rich software is out of place on a smaller migration. Match the tool to the scale of the task, unless of course you have lots of experience of a particular tool, spare licences and spare people to operate a tool that might otherwise be over-specified for the task. A legitimate use of a heavyweight tool for a smaller migration might be to prototype tool and process use, with an eye to a series of migrations where the cost of learning how to use a new tool is offset by the longer term benefits.

ANECDOTE

Try to avoid the temptation of using a data migration as an opportunity to introduce a toolset that your architectural community has been looking to implement for some time. I have seen a number of projects bogged down in tool implementation issues, often around the configuration and delivery of enterprise application integration software that the architects, legitimately, want to implement as infrastructure software. They see data migration as a requirement to move data around and as the ideal springboard for their implementation. It might well be that the complete target implementation set includes a new data bus arrangement, but that should be part of the bigger programme not part of the data migration effort. Only data migration-specific software is appropriate for data migrations.

- **Budget** – The use of appropriate technology will increase the quality of the data delivered, reduce risk and increase performance, but, as I have shown above, if the risk aversion policy is low (i.e. you are going down the 'quick and dirty' route), then there simply might not be the budget to pay for expensive software tools with their associated implementation costs (including learning curves). However, if a longer timeframe is envisaged, then one project taking the hit on its budget to up-skill a department for future challenges can sometimes be justified.

HINT

Getting any new enabling technology implemented often brings with it the problem that it can never be justified on the back of any single project. However, the overall benefits, when applied across multiple projects, might justify the investment. This, of course, is because the first project must take all the implementation costs (sometimes known as 'the first passenger pays for the whole train' problem). A portfolio approach to data migration as part of a bigger data management architectural vision helps here.

Cost is always an issue, but those enterprises who want to dip their toes into the data migration toolbox (if you don't mind the mixed metaphors) can always have a look at the various open source and studio editions of software to get a feel for what it can do. It is no longer sensible to rely on 'do it yourself' approaches for larger projects, so you need to do your research and set an appropriate budget for tools.

- **Migration form** – The more sophisticated migration forms will need sophisticated migration software to support them. You will need specialist software for a genuine 'non-stop' migration. If you are going to perform parallel running, then some form of synchronisation will be needed. If you have a very large dataset and have decided on a big bang migration, then speed is of the essence, so software with a parallel processing capability might be your best option.[6] If the migration architecture is going to be more traditional (i.e. extract to staging area, consolidation of datasets, then transformation, then load), but there would be benefit in reuse, possibly of the skills and software rather than the transformations themselves, then an integrated ETL type of toolset would be most appropriate.

You will be purchasing software (certainly the profiling software) early, before your migration design is complete. This is one reason why I recommend that you have an architectural model in your data migration strategy. You will not know all the details at the outset, but unfortunately you have to make software purchasing decisions to find out those details. Some best guesses and the help of experienced data migration advice from consultants who have carried out similar migrations are essential.

- **Local software policies** – These will be captured in your architectural policies, but if you are an Oracle®-only shop for instance, then this will constrain your choice. On the other hand, you might have an existing investment in Informatica®, for instance, and it would be sensible to go along with that.

- **Local preferences** – Quite often your chosen implementation partner has a software preference and it makes sense, all other things being equal, to align with that. This way you can more easily share common understandings of data quality rules and mappings and gain benefit of code reuse.

HINT

If you are planning to maximise the benefit of code reuse across the DMZ, check out who owns the code created by partners in the contract between you. Although you will still benefit from a shared understanding that using the same software brings when exchanging mapping and data quality specifications, this will be a lot less than the benefit of full code reuse or code reuse at an additional cost. You also need to make sure that there are no version issues with the software you are using on either side of the DMZ.

---

[6] Parallel processing is a technology that allows you to run your software on multiple servers at the same time thereby vastly increasing the throughput speed.

ANECDOTE

I have worked with a number of large clients who seem to have licences for just about everything if I looked around enough. It seems like each party who needed to do a piece of work went out and bought a product that suited them. It is worth networking with the technical data stakeholders to find out what might be available to you.

However, architectural policies and preferences should not constrain your choice if there are bigger issues of performance or migration form to take into account.

- **Availability of trained resources** – This refers to both internal resources (which links back to the previous point about preferences) and external. Obviously a tool new to the market will not have the pool of talent for hire on the open market that established players will possess. Even where you are looking to up-skill internally you will get there a lot quicker if you bring in some experienced technologists to provide those hints, tips and best practices that are key to maximising the utility of any software.

HINT

When bringing in software specialists make sure that they are *PDMv2*-aware or at least *PDMv2*-agnostic. It can be destabilising to have mentors who are antagonistic to its underlying principles.

- **What is in the market?** – As I write this, I am aware that the marketplace for software tools is moving quickly. I cannot guess what will be available to you when you read this book so market research is essential. If in doubt, get advice from impartial experts who can assess your needs and point you at a selection of software tools to look at. Go to appropriate events like *Data Migration Matters* conferences. Check out relevant websites like www.datamigrationpro.com and its sister www.dataqualitypro.com. Join up with social networking groups that specialise in data quality and data management (it is still the case that a lot of the relevant software comes from the data quality vendors). Subscribe to the work of the industry analysts. Get the technical data stakeholders to download some of the free tools and experiment with them so that you have a touchstone against which to compare the various products you will be offered. Look out for aspects like the availability of the right connectors[7] and transformation widgets[8] for your environment. Some software is connector-rich. Most will have connectors for the more common targets like SAP®, but always expect that you will have to create some connectors yourself, especially for the ancient bespoke data stores you are replacing. When it comes to widgets, the more established software platforms tend to be richer. If you have a particular need, maybe for data conformance to an industry canonical model, have a look to see if there is a widget to deliver this for you.

---

[7] Connectors are the pieces of code that link your software to the source and target.
[8] Widgets are the code parcels that have been pre-written and can be included in your extraction-transformation-load flow for things like name and address de-duplication.

59

Ease of code reuse is important where a purchase will be strategic as opposed to tactical (i.e. you are looking beyond the immediate project). A software roadmap you can trust and the existence of a thriving user community are also key. The latter are becoming increasingly essential in this area of software development. Aside from the bespoke systems that are unique to your organisation, the chances are that someone else out there will have come across the same technical problems you are now trying to address. Many software vendors of data migration tools actively support their community, working to an open-source model to build up libraries of pre-built widgets at little or zero cost. Of course, how much you trust software written by a third party, which is not fully endorsed by your chosen vendor, and how you test and incorporate it into your product set is a matter between you and your architectural governance group.

System integrator selection

You will be employing some form of implementation partner on all but the smallest data migrations. This might be the software vendor or a more generic systems integrator (SI). There might be a number of third parties involved. For the purposes of this discussion I will term them all 'SI' to keep it simple. Choice of the right SI is normally dependent on the following factors:

- **Relationship to software, strategy and migration form** – There are very good reasons why SI selection and data migration software selection usually go hand in hand. As I have shown with software selection, your SI partner's migration software of choice should influence your choice of software, but that relationship is reciprocal: where you are constrained by an established policy on software, you should make it part of your discussions with prospective partners. An SI's choice of migration software is unlikely to be the most significant criteria of your decision mechanism, but taken in the round it will help clarify issues about the nature of the DMZ and how you will manage to pass design requirements back and forth.

  The migration form is also important, especially where you have a more complex type. Has this SI got demonstrable experience with this form? Do your conversations with them convince you that they understand and can provide insights into how you are going to deliver it?

- **Price** – This is always significant, but you have to look at price not just in terms of how much you are paying, but also in terms of how much you are getting in return. This means looking at where the SI draws their DMZ and how much they are doing for you (see below).

HINT

When it comes to price, check the contract to see what is quoted for variations to contract. It has been known for the less scrupulous to under-bid for the main, fixed price element, on the assumption that they can make it up on variations as the project unfolds.

- **PDM status** – If you are going to be running the data migration according to *PDMv2* principles, then check the accreditation levels of your implementation partner. *PDMv2* offers accreditation at various levels: to individuals (Certification); to implementation partners (Accredited); and to software (Compliant). Of course, not all implementers will have invested in the necessary training and implementation process reengineering necessary to qualify. There are also other methodologies that are closely coupled to the technology being implemented (for instance, ASAP® for SAP®), but, as the DMZ discussion shows, these methods generally limit themselves to the transform and load elements of the migration, and then only for the target, not for the archiving solution. They sometimes encompass the parts of LA that involve profiling and data quality analysis, but will almost never touch on legacy decommissioning, which is the end point of any data migration activity. They are also normally light on the whole business engagement swim lane.

This is not to say that a well-tried and tested approach that is closely coupled to the rest of the SI's target system design and delivery method is necessarily bad. It is often excellent at delivering a well-configured solution, having been honed through many implementations. What you need to know, from a data migration perspective, is how do you encapsulate it in a PDM wrap? To answer this you need to understand the DMZ.

HINT

You will meet many 'pig in a poke' methodologies, where a prospective supplier, in pre-sales meetings, promises you that it has a data migration methodology that 'does everything that *PDMv2* does'. 'Caveat emptor' applies here. If a supplier has something of the strength of *PDMv2*, then it will not exist without example documents, training materials, pre-sales collateral, case studies etc. Ask to see the evidence and do not be put off. Ask if it has training courses for your staff. The salesman might not be incentivised to sell training, but salesmen rarely leave money on the table if there is a sale to be made. If there is no evidence forthcoming within a week, then it probably does not exist. It is likely a case of seeding a project with people who have done it before and come with a mixed set of approaches, plus a large number of bright, intelligent, keen, but inexperienced, youngsters. If some collateral is forthcoming, then you need to match it against the *PDMv2* footprint and see where the DMZ lies.

- **Location of DMZ** – As I showed above, the DMZ is the boundary between the work the various technology partners do and the work the rest of the enterprise has to perform. It is rare that an implementation partner will offer to cover the whole data migration footprint from creating a migration strategy to legacy decommissioning. Most commonly it will concentrate on the 'final mile': the last piece of transform and load. Using the *PDMv2* checklist contained in Appendix A3, work out what it is doing and then, just as importantly, what it is not doing. This forms the edge of the DMZ.

HINT

Bear in mind that establishing the DMZ occurs at least twice. There will be discussions in the initial proposals around the support that the potential partner can give to the rest of the project, but it is in the contract that the actual details are defined.

- **Cultural affinity** – This is a hard one to gauge, especially if you are only given a glimpse of the true character of your potential partners on the referrals they should provide you with. However, all organisations sit somewhere on a spectrum from extremely hierarchical to extremely laissez-faire.[9] Additionally, some organisations are more formal than others.

  Most organisations sit somewhere in the middle of these extremes, but these days, with slimmed down management structures and an increased informality generally, the formal/informal, directed/initiative scale is sliding towards the informal/initiative end. I stress that this is not to say that you need any less formality in your structures, but it impacts on the day-to-day working of the project. *PDMv2* can, of course, cope with both ends of the spectrum. Within activities like the DQR process, honest, spontaneous, creative problem-solving is encouraged, but within the formal constraints of a set of processes and documents. Although it is rare that cultural affinity is ever consciously considered, bearing in mind that you are going to be working closely with your chosen partner in intense situations for a considerable length of time, it is worth asking the question: 'Will I and my guys be able to work with their guys?'

- **Local policies** – Quite often these days, there is a framework purchasing agreement that prescribes the partners to whom you are allowed to speak. There is nothing wrong with this. Your partner will have domain knowledge at all sorts of levels and you will have resolved the cultural affinity issues. They will also have an incentive to complete the job as rapidly and as efficiently as possible to preserve a longer term relationship. This is an incentive that a partner, whose only contact with you will be the delivery of this solution, will not necessarily have. If they have not already made the journey to using *PDMv2*, then encourage them to make the journey with you. You will then end up with a version of *PDMv2* that suits both of you in your environment.

- **Domain Knowledge** – Knowing your business area and knowing the target software are both excellent reasons for favouring one potential supplier over another, but this knowledge can be a double-edged sword. Each enterprise has its own way of doing things, its own history, its own staff. Even where you are moving to a target that is common across your industry, your heritage will be different. Be sure that you adhere to Golden Rule 2: the business knows best. Do not allow assumptions about what a field means, or how it must have been used, or where the best data is bound to come from, to compromise your decisions. Stick to the DQR and SRP processes.

---

[9] In my experience, the uniformed services are the best examples of the hierarchical structure with decisions being made at the top and cascaded downwards, as opposed to allowing more initiative at lower levels.

- **Local preferences** – Even where there is not a policy prescribing your choice, there might be a preference for a particular implementer, maybe because of previous contact or geographical considerations. This is an excellent reason to choose, but all the same caveats apply here as they do to the policy-driven partner choice.

- **References** – Of course you will seek and take up references to projects where a supplier has performed this task in similar circumstances. You will be aware that a supplier is only likely to point you at reference sites that have been cherry-picked for the smooth path they had to implementation; however, there are ways of uncovering the untold story. Ask the referee if they are aware of other sites that you could contact. Use your networking skills to tap into others' experience. Ask how flexible the proposed supplier was when it came to responding to data challenges. Did they volunteer changes that could be made to their software or was it a question of pushing at a blocked door, with every change a costly variation to contract?

ANECDOTE

I am aware of an instance where a large multinational SI was so insistent on sticking to the letter of their contract, which included not enhancing data, that they would even default a 'Y' into a field that was supposed to be 'Y' or 'N', but was sometimes blank in the legacy, without a time and materials-based chargeable variation to contract.

How good is the supplier at configuration management, especially around the format and validation of the data specification? In other words, how often did data get rejected for reasons that had not previously been communicated? How easy was it to get them to align their delivery of target and data migration software with a release strategy? How good were they at estimating build times? Did they always deliver their software on time? How good were they at estimating load times, tuning load times and suggesting alternative load strategies?

Above all, how responsive and helpful were they when things went wrong? We can all be good when things are going right. It is a matter of how good we are when things are going wrong that we should be judged by.

- **Reputation** – This is especially useful if you are in the kind of industry where information on suppliers is routinely exchanged. There is, of course, a downside to everyone climbing on board with the same supplier: their best resources start to get spread a bit thinly. Find out who else is getting their implementation performed at the same time.

- **Convincing understanding of your needs** – Here I do not mean merely a replaying of your requirements specification, but whether the supplier develops an understanding of your needs by asking intelligent questions, suggesting alternative solutions and spotting parallels with other work they have carried out. Do these questions, suggestions and parallels convince you that they have something significant to contribute to your situation?

Generic project office functions

I advise, in line with most other commentators, that data migration is accorded its own project status separate from the main and bigger programme, so it needs all the control features of any project, plus the unique aspects that mark out a data migration project. The project office is where these functions are encapsulated. You need a section in your data migration strategy on project office functions that will describe how each of the following will work in your environment. You will find, in consultation with the relevant technical experts, that you already have many of the items required and they can be slotted straight in (maybe with a little tweaking).

HINT

An experienced project manager who knows their own environment will understand how to apply this advice to their own circumstances, but if you are new to this game, then please use this chapter as a checklist of minimum requirements. Overkill at this stage is less costly than gaps that appear later and under-used features will atrophy naturally in the course of the project.

PDMv2 expects all the following standard project management functions to be present:[10]

- **Scope management, change control** – In recent years the increased adoption and sophistication of formal project planning and control methods have meant that you rarely have to create project scope structures and artefacts, but you do need to ensure that you tap into them. Although there are many ways of managing scope within projects, all have certain key features in common. Firstly, you need an agreed scope that unequivocally states what you are expected to be doing and, just as significantly, what you are therefore not expected to be doing. Then you need a mechanism where changes to this scope can be suggested. Part of the process of agreeing to the change has to be an assessment of what that change will mean in terms of cost to the project (and ultimately of course to the enterprise) and the projected benefits. Costs and benefits, where the programme is concerned, also involve effort and delivery times, as well as monetary values.

  This review is often called the impact assessment. You expect your scope management process to include a formal channel for suggesting changes, an impact assessment process and a decision process that decides whether to include the proposed change or not.

---

[10] Although it expects them to be present, it does not always find them. For instance, although it is a rare project these days that does not have formal project plans, it is still common to find that there is no formal responsibility for communications. Where an element is missing you have to ensure that the bigger programme takes on the responsibility, or that you have a workaround in place. Bringing to light these areas should be presented as adding value to the bigger programme and a demonstration of your professionalism.

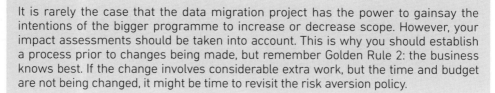

HINT

It is rarely the case that the data migration project has the power to gainsay the intentions of the bigger programme to increase or decrease scope. However, your impact assessments should be taken into account. This is why you should establish a process prior to changes being made, but remember Golden Rule 2: the business knows best. If the change involves considerable extra work, but the time and budget are not being changed, it might be time to revisit the risk aversion policy.

Within *PDMv2*, as I practise it, the conceptual entity model (see Chapter 5) is my first statement of programme scope, followed by the migration model. Bearing in mind that until the target system has been designed you do not know the detail of target specific data items, a broad brush stroke statement is good enough. If whole new areas are added or dropped from the bigger programme (like maybe sales forecasting from a CRM implementation, or supplier management from a manufacturing application), then you can add or remove the appropriate entities from your models, read through the LDS, DQR etc. lists for impacted items (which you have conveniently tagged by Entity for just such an eventuality) and react accordingly. If your project organisation (see Key Business Data Area Decomposition below) is aligned to your entities, then so much the easier to assess impact, but as you will see this is not often the case.

- **Communications strategy** – Good programmes have strong, well-understood and accessible communications strategies. Within a *PDMv2* data migration strategy you will be speaking to an awful lot of people within the business. You need to make sure that you are 'on message' with the bigger programme. It is very easy to sow seeds of confusion in the business if they hear different messages from different parties. You need to be briefed early and regularly. On the other hand, because you are also going to be mixing with a lot of people outside the inner core of those engaged in formal business engagement strategies, you can be the eyes and ears of how messages are being received (if at all) and so feed back to the communications strategy. The DQR process will also produce some good news stories: you need to make sure that these get publicised to help the bigger programme.

So much for the softer side of things. You might also have some straightforward functional requirements that need to be briefed out as formally, comprehensively and effectively as possible. These include:[11]

- o **Transitional business processes** – There are always some processes within any data migration that are needed just because of the disturbance that the migration causes. These can be to do with specific data preparation activities or special processing, like closing all outstanding orders immediately prior to migration. They are processes that only occur because you are doing a migration.

---

[11] Each of the items is defined in more detail in the Section 2.

HINT

The way I usually explain this is that if we have old business as usual before the project starts and aim to have new business as usual after the project ends, there is a bit in the middle where, because of the switch over, we will have a mash-up of old processes, new processes and some processes only there to handle the change. The processes to handle the change are the transitional business processes.

- ○ **LDS amnesty** – As I have already mentioned, in most organisations there is a plethora of spreadsheets etc. that have been secretly running the company for years. You need to have these brought out into the open so that they can be assessed for possible inclusion in the migration. In some organisations, where there is a strict policy of only using the corporate systems, you might need to declare an amnesty so that these data stores will be revealed.

- ○ **The DQR process** – There are the processes, forms and structured meeting requests that need to be briefed out.

- ○ **Migration readiness** – This is a hard percentage figure that informs the programme board sponsors etc. how many units of migration will migrate at any given time. Obviously it should increase as the data migration project nears its conclusion. It is an output from the DQR process but, within the boundaries of the communications policy itself, it needs to be communicated with the right degree of detail to the right parties in a format that they can readily digest and act upon as necessary.

- ○ **Fallback strategy** – All data migrations should have a fallback strategy in case it all goes wrong, which it can for reasons completely removed from the project itself (obviously, if you are using *PDMv2*, then the migration will not be beset by significant, show-stopping problems within itself). In the unlikely event of having to invoke it, a fallback strategy has to be briefed out quickly, accurately and completely.

ANECDOTE

I was working on a migration at a large telco when a serious outage, caused by a fire, impacted millions of customers. All non-essential activity was banned until the situation was resolved. Although it had nothing to do with the area where we were working, if the fire had happened on the weekend when we were due to migrate, then we would have been caught up in the blanket ban and would have had to invoke our fallback plan.

For these reasons always look for close cooperation with the bigger programme's formal communication process. Communications is a skill set in its own right. Try to get the best practitioner you can to help you with your messaging.

- **Planning and plan management** – Over the last 25 years that I have been involved in IT projects, project planning has come on in leaps and bounds. We are now all wedded to deliverables-based plans. We all adhere to SMART tasks. As I have shown, we expect the same from *PDMv2*. As you prepare your project office functions, you need to have space for planning, including planning cycles, plan consolidation, tracking and critical path analysis. You need to create space for formal planning that takes input from the DQR process and migration readiness, as well as from the standard analyse, build, test and go-live cycles of any IT-related project. These are related to:

  o the creation of the ETL build;

  o the creation of transitional data stores;

  o the creation of transitional interfaces;

  o the creation of our archiving solution;

  o the creation of our fallback processing.

  You will also (as I will explain below) be expecting the creation and execution of a micro-managed cutover plan. Therefore planning expertise (or at least competence) is a prerequisite of a well-run data migration project. The form it takes is usually determined by local preferences.

- **Issue and risk management** – In all well-run projects these days there will be a risks and issues register and the process for reviewing and resolving risks will be part of the general governance procedures.

However it is constituted, one key requirement of *PDMv2* is that data quality issues are not included in the programme risks and issues register. Data quality issues are a business as usual fact of data migration projects. They belong in the DQR log. If they are added to the risks and issues register they swiftly overwhelm it. Even a comparatively moderate project will have hundreds of data quality issues. If these are allowed to fall into the generic risks and issues register there is the risk of a confusion of authority with two boards considering the same question.

There is also the question of purpose. As I showed in the section on DQR, you are not only recording and tracking data quality issues within the DQR process, you are also building the virtual team that you need to solve the issues. This organic, collegiate approach to problem solving is at odds with the formal hierarchy of a risks and issues board.

Finally, you will be asking different questions of the DQR process than of an issues process. Tracking the completeness of individual issues is only part of the requirement. You need to be able to answer the question 'are we ready to migrate?' and this is not the same as 'have all known issues been resolved or ameliorated?' You need to be able to quantify a readiness to migrate in terms that the business will understand and that means talking in terms of percentages of units of migration. Given that on a large programme these units of migration can be different for different groups and that you need to summarise according to the key business data area decomposition, then you are going to be placing a series of reporting requirements on the issues register that it was not designed for.

However, there should be a known escalation path for those few DQRs that cannot be solved at the DQR board level either because of the cross-company impact (more common) or because of difficulties securing consensual agreement within the DQR process. Where a data quality issue is escalated there needs to be a cross reference linking it back to the originating DQR. Escalation within the DQR register is one of the standard resolution paths and so there will always be a cross reference to the issues register.

For all the other 'real' data migration issues and risks it is becoming common practice to use the bigger programme-level issues register for holding the data migration project's issues as opposed to holding a subordinate issues register within the data migration project. This is because today's more sophisticated issues logs allow you to partition issues by level of applicability. It also makes escalation easier. However, this is something that will be decided in the creation of your library services (see below).

HINT

If you are forced, maybe because of local policies, to add DQRs to a single issues register, then make sure there is some way to filter them out as data quality issues. You can then still have the single version of the truth about data quality and readiness to migrate that you need even if you run the risk of confused data quality management.

- **Budgeting** – You need to be able to track spend, both actual and committed, against budget. This is especially true when you have your own data migration budget, as recommended. Project budgeting is a subject that is extensively covered in many books on project management and I will not add to those here. As far as the data migration strategy is concerned, you need to understand how budgeting is going to be done on the project and make sure you have it covered. It is one of the policies covered below.

ANECDOTE

I have come across many examples of enterprises that do not account for internal spend (i.e. the cost of company resources is not tracked). This is fine, although I would track time spent by resource by task for analysis. I am still surprised at the number of projects where the control of budget has not been given enough thought. This is particularly pertinent around some of the DMZ issues that I will discuss later.

- **Library services, including configuration management** – You are going to be creating a great many products within a *PDMv2* data migration project. There are multiple DQRs with multiple versions and subtasks; there are SRPs; there is LDS documentation; there are data models, mapping descriptions, ETL rules; there are scope documents; and so on (and on). They all need to be filed somewhere so that everyone concerned with the project can be certain where the current copy is, what state it is in and who is responsible for it. You also need the history of decisions and changes. In a DQR, for instance, you need to be able to show, if challenged, how a particular solution was arrived at. Modern, enterprise programme strength repositories, like Microsoft® SharePoint®, are available to most projects these days. Make sure you set up an area in advance and create a librarian role to manage it.

HINT

Not all projects will have the benefit of a modern document repository, but do not despair, there have been many successful large-scale data migration projects that go back to the days before SharePoint® et al. It can all be done on a local file share, but it will take more effort and more policing.

PDMv2 documents are also interrelated. For example, a decision within a DQR to fix a problem during the extract phase of a migration needs to be fed into the GAM module as a requirement. Another example is when changes to scope need to be cascaded through your data models into your landscape analysis, gap analysis and mapping, and migration design and execution modules. For these reasons you need configuration management.

Configuration management and its related skill, release management, is a big topic and I will cover them in part here and in part in the section below on setting the scope and control of the DMZ. In essence, for configuration management, you need a repository that allows artefacts (configurable items) to be booked in, out and version controlled; a map of how changes to each artefact impacts on other artefacts (impact analysis); a control mechanism that regulates the changes (change management) and reduces the risks of negative impacts.

o **Configurable items** – Appendix A1 contains a list of *PDMv2* configurable items. It will make more sense once the rest of this method has been digested.

HINT

Formal management at this level would be complete overkill on a small project. As part of the data migration strategy creation process, you need to decide how much control is necessary, project by project, but it is always useful to be aware of what could be potentially impacted when you make changes.

In essence, you need to ensure that you know, for all of your significant arte-facts (software, requirements, designs etc.), which is the most current, where it is located and, if someone is working on it at the moment, who that person is.

o **Impact analysis** – To assess the impact of change, first you need to uncover the impacted items, then follow the chain of impact through related items. A *PDMv2* artefacts' impact frame is given in Appendix A2, but once again this just the starting point. Your project will be different. What triggers a change to a configurable item in the first place is described module by module in Section 2. Appendix A2 will make more sense once you are more familiar with *PDMv2*.

WARNING

Once again, this advice is not prescriptive of the controls that you must put in place. You have to judge for your project how far these relationships have to be modelled and formally controlled.

However, to reiterate, the basis of change management is:

1. to understand what the controlled items are and how they are related;
2. to ensure that when changes are first suggested you can impact assess the change by seeing how it cascades through the controlled items and estimate the scale and cost of the change;
3. to manage the change by ensuring that all impacted items are kept updated.

Some change is inevitable, especially on a data migration project where, at the outset, you do not know how many LDSs there are, what the state of the data is within them or what additional challenges the target system design and con-sequent consolidation of disparate data stores will bring. Throw into the mix that the world moves on as your project is making its way through its various stages with regulatory changes, product changes, personnel changes etc., and you just have to expect change and manage it.

- o **Release management** – Once again this is a subject sufficiently large to merit books on its own. But in a nutshell, release management is the control of all the various hardware, software, process development, data, training and testing deliverables that go to make up a single coherent release. Get any one of these misaligned and the result is, at best, a compromised delivery that is painful and beset with problems, at worst one that never gets up and running at all.

You are looking, within the context of a data migration project, at a dataset that has to be extracted, prepared and delivered to match an evolving target from an increasingly well-understood legacy. The existence of the DMZ forces its own set of internal change and configuration issues onto the migration project and I will look at these below, but any changes to the target system and the larger environment also need to be taken into account. There are two levels here: those within the control of the bigger programme and those in the wider environment. The programme should have change control in place to respond to scope changes within the programme. Well-configured impact analysis within the data migration project will feed into the decision-making process that will accept or reject changes depending on their benefit and impact.

HINT

This is all of course a 'best of all possible worlds' description. We all know that in the real world changes are quite often mandated on us by senior management and we do not have the luxury of being allowed to flex end dates. In this case you change what you can and that means looking at the risk aversion policy.

Release management comes into play by allowing you to match your total build with the release profile of the newly realigned programme, fitting the data preparation, software building and testing of your ETL releases to the new dates.

Of course you might also have to accommodate changes within the larger environment. Here an awareness of parallel projects and programmes is paramount. Where you are working in a large, complex environment, changes to systems outside the scope of your migration can still impact you, especially where you are responsible for providing temporary interfaces to a changing world. Again you must follow the steps of controlling configurable items; understanding the dependencies between them; being aware of the impending change; performing an impact assessment; planning for the change; booking out the relevant items; making matching changes; updating the versioning of the items; and aligning versions to releases to make a coherent whole.

ANECDOTE

Size really does matter here. I was working on a project for a major telco where product sets are huge, complex and constantly changing. It made the issue of release and configuration management essential. On the other hand, I have also worked on projects where, although the migration itself was complicated, it was being conducted against a background of a relatively stable environment. So although we still needed to manage carefully internal changes to our project, external change was less of an issue.

For your data migration strategy, you need to have the discussions that will allow you to design reliable configuration management, impact analysis and release management processes and describe them in the strategy document.

HINT

It is amazing how common it is for data migration projects to have apparently robust release management processes that crumble in the last two weeks before go-live when late changes stack up and there is a frenzy of additional validation and processes in response to the business seeing their data in the target system for the first time. It takes strong management (possibly enforced in the contract) to maintain control. There is no point in enhancing the target if the data does not load and it therefore does not go live.

Initial lists

There should be the following lists as part of a system retirement strategy:

- **Initial LDS list** – You will normally have been given an initial list of LDSs, but you anticipate it will hugely understate the number of data stores you will eventually uncover. It will form your starting point for LA.

- **Initial KDSH list** – You will normally have been given a list of names of those people you assume will be data owners of enterprise-level LDSs. You anticipate that you will discover other data owners and therefore business domain experts and technical system experts not only for the LDSs you have not been told about, but also for the enterprise-level LDSs, given the definition of data owners as being anybody who can legitimately stop the migration. This list will give you the initial points of contact.

- **Initial DQRs** – There is usually a list of known data quality issues with the LDSs you have been given. It might not have been published anywhere, but ask around and quite quickly you will find a few. Also it pays to be suspicious in data migration, so if you are told that your Customer file has no duplicates, then run some queries to check. Each query should have an accompanying DQR.

These initial lists, as you shall see, form the basis of your first activities as the project starts to crank into life.

HINT

These lists are provisional and will be quickly superseded, so I normally place them into an appendix to the main data migration strategy document. This way, when the data migration strategy is issued, the appendix does not form part of the signed-off document and therefore does not have to be change-controlled.

Control flows and project reporting

The establishment of streams of information that indicate to the project and programme management the health of the project and its conformance to plan is essential to a well-managed project. As I have indicated, you expect that all the standard planning, budgeting, communication, risk and issue flows will be in place, managed by the library services that you have established. You therefore expect that each deliverable will be planned, tracked and budgeted, be it code (e.g. your extraction scripts) or specification (e.g. your test specifications). However, *PDMv2* also provides additional control flows, which must be added to the project reporting function:

- **Data quality rules** – I have shown that data issues (selection issues, exclusion issues, quality issues, gap issues and preparation issues) are business as usual as far as a data migration project is concerned. Within *PDMv2* these are controlled via the DQR process. This process should be set up to report in ascending levels of granularity. At the finest granularity, you can report on the number of individual DQRs by type: how many there are in total; how many have been parked; how many have been resolved; how many you are working on etc.

  You can then move up a level and report on the number of DQRs by priority and by filtering on key business data area decomposition. You can report the number of units of migration that you know will migrate. You can report the overall measured data quality of your load set as an overall total or by key business data area. Finally, you can 'traffic light' at the top level across all the data to be migrated.

  The DQR reports also give time series data, in the sense that you can report if you are on track at an individual DQR level and all the way up the tree of granularity. This accurate, concise and highlighted reporting, with the possibility to drill down to the lowest level if required, is the kind of control that programme boards should demand of their data migration project. How this is built in is of course dependent on your library service implementation: it needs to be specified in your data migration strategy.

HINT

Knowing in advance that you will need to do this sort of consolidated reporting should lead you to build your library service in a way that makes it as easy as possible to enter data once and to have a push button reporting service. It's always easier to build this kind of reporting in advance than to retrofit it.

- **System retirement plans** – These are the key controlling documents that give you the ultimate business sign-off to go ahead with the migration. It is crucial that you track their completion and completeness. Has every data owner been identified? Has every LDS and subset of every LDS, where appropriate, been covered?

  Each SRP is signed off at least three times (once as part of the initial contact, once after the migration design has been completed and once after testing), so this becomes the key business readiness indicator and allows you to follow the progress of business readiness with all the standard slippage indicators.

HINT

Balancing the desire to keep the project moving against the desire to ensure that all the correct measures are in place before moving on is one of those tricky judgement calls. In a heavily structured environment the sign-off of the SRP would form part of the quality gate criteria. In most projects you accept a degree of lag so that the project moves on. You use the pressure of the need for decommissioning certificate sign-off to get the initial sign-offs. As a last resort you might have to go the programme board to put pressure on individuals, hence the need to ensure that the SRP is a key product in your migration strategy.

- **Migration design and execution dashboard** – Your objective with DQRs, SRPs and the LDS list is to provide the fine details from which a dashboard can be built up. You will concentrate reports on the units of migration that are defined by the business, the fulfilment of the requirements captured in the SRPs and the sign-off of SRPs themselves. These can be presented at various levels of granularity. At the very top level, a simple series of traffic lights can be the publicly available migration readiness display. The next degree of granularity is generally at the key data area decomposition level. Again, you can show units of migration impacted by migration design or DQR activity within this decomposition. After that it is pretty much down to the project to decide what subordinate levels of granularity are meaningful to report against.

- **Legacy decommissioning report** – At the end of the migration you should be reporting on the decommissioning of each LDS as it happens. This means there has to be planning and budget for the project to continue to run until the last LDS has been decommissioned (provided, of course, that physical decommissioning is within the scope of the data migration project).

DATA MIGRATION STRATEGY CHECKLIST

Appendix A3 gives a handy checklist of items that have been discussed in this chapter. Make sure each item is covered in your strategy in some form that is adequate for the task (or has been consciously excluded as overkill), and that the interfaces between each item and the other items in the list are sound.

GETTING THE DATA MIGRATION STRATEGY IMPLEMENTED

As you can see there is an awful lot to get up and running if you are going to start your migration journey off on the right foot, but it is (probably) not as bad as you fear if you have never done anything like this before. Risks and issues registers, project planning and even configuration management are all well understood aspects of any well-run IT department. Only do the things that are appropriate for the project and do not let the establishment of a perfectly functioning project office take precedence over delivery.

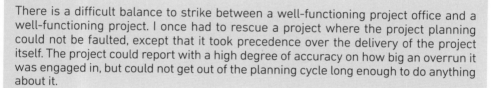

ANECDOTE

There is a difficult balance to strike between a well-functioning project office and a well-functioning project. I once had to rescue a project where the project planning could not be faulted, except that it took precedence over the delivery of the project itself. The project could report with a high degree of accuracy on how big an overrun it was engaged in, but could not get out of the planning cycle long enough to do anything about it.

It takes time for all the pieces to be in place, especially all the library services, but you might already have resources available that need to be set to work (and we all know that if we do not use the resources, then we lose them). Where do you start while you wait for the other pieces of the jigsaw to fall into place?

Quick start data migration

The place to start a data migration is with getting the DQR process up and running, linking it into LA. This will identify the KDSHs with whom you will be working to produce the SRPs. Start with business engagement first. Arrange meetings, either in groups or individually, with the data owners on the initial KDSH list, and explain their roles in the DQR and SRP processes. At the same time, if you have spare technical capacity, commence work profiling the LDSs that have been documented on the initial LDS list and use this to feed titbits of information into discussions with the data owners.

By commencing work you will be shaking out the *PDMv2* model and seeing how it fits the environment you find yourself in. Allow for a degree of organic growth. *PDMv2* is robust enough to cope with tailoring to a particular situation. It thrives on not being over-prescriptive.

CHAPTER REVIEW

In this chapter I have looked at why you need to write a data migration strategy for each data migration you are engaged in, and what goes into the strategy. I concluded by looking at what you can usefully deliverer to move the project on as the data migration strategy is being written and enacted.

SECTION 2:
TOOLS AND TECHNIQUES

In this section I will be looking in detail at the tools and techniques that are used within PDMv2. Some, that were introduced in Section 1, I will explain in more detail. Others, of a more technical nature, I will define here for the first time. This section is structured around the modules that now make up PDMv2.

5 METADATA AND KEY BUSINESS DATA AREA DECOMPOSITION

In this chapter I extend the discussion of how to break a large programme down into small sections for effective control. I introduce the concept of metadata and its use within PDMv2.

METADATA AND *PDMv2*

Data migration projects are intimately concerned with data (as the name suggests) so it is perhaps not surprising that a rigorous methodology like *PDMv2* adopts a formal approach to cataloguing its understanding of the data elements that it confronts. This approach is necessary because the process has to deal with multiple legacy data sources created by different people (some technical, some non-technical) at different times, in different places for different reasons. Some level of abstraction is needed to manage this so you can compare unlike data sources by cataloguing and analysing them, and spotting common data and gaps. Metadata modelling and cataloguing provides that level of abstraction.

DEFINITION

Metadata is data about data. In other words, it is the data the technologists hold about the data in the business.

As you will see in the following paragraphs on the use of a migration model, the complexity of comparing multiple data sources expands exponentially with the number of sources and swiftly becomes unmanageable without the use of some form of abstraction.

ANECDOTE

It seems like on every other project I work on I come across a dyed-in-the-wool hater of metadata modelling techniques. It is true these methods ended up with a bad name because, after their introduction into IT in the 1980s, they were often seen as a universal panacea of the ills of poor data management. Instead they resulted in a lot of wasted investment in corporate data models where clusters of data architects worked away for years to little apparent benefit to the enterprise. However, within *PDMv2*, the use of modelling is tactical and it only aims for 'good enough' models that are stepping stones to an eventual solution, not perfect models.

Competing techniques

There are a number of types of data model, each with its supporters. There are entity relationship models, object models, canonical models, ontology, schemas etc., and they can be embodied in XML, diagrammatic formats, complex (but precise) data definition languages and so on.

My preference is for simple entity relationship diagrams (ERDs) because, as I will show, they are easy to draw, easy to learn how to use and get you where you need to be fast. Remember these models are intermediary project artefacts not permanent deliverables. They need only be good enough for the task.

HINT

Of course you might have an architectural policy that mandates a particular modelling set or there might be a strong local preference, in which case that is the way to go. I would only caution against a representation of data that might be rigorous but really requires a two-week off-site course to master. These are, after all, models that you will be sharing with your business colleagues.

For the rest of this book I will be using my preferred ERD approach and for those who are rusty there follows a quick refresher. If you are confident in your ERD techniques, feel free to skip to the next section.

ERD refresher

I use a simple box to represent an entity (i.e. a thing in the real world, either logical or physical) and a line to represent the relationship of one entity to another. Figure 5.1 shows a simple example.

Figure 5.1 An example ERD

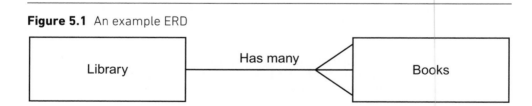

The full set of relationship symbols is shown in Figure 5.2.

Figure 5.2 ERD relationship symbols

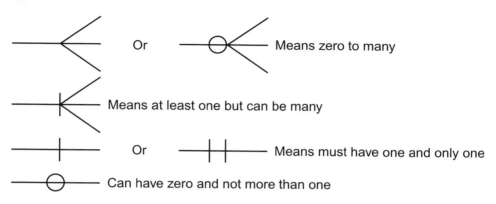

Or — Means zero to many

Means at least one but can be many

Or — Means must have one and only one

Can have zero and not more than one

The 'crow's feet', cross bar and zero symbols are drawn at the end of a relationship line closest to the entity to which they relate. By far the commonest relationship between entities in commercial IT is the 'parent–child' relationship where one higher level entity (say a customer) might have zero, but usually many, lower level entities (like invoices), and each lower level entity (invoices) only makes sense when it is part of a higher level entity (customer).

Entities can relate to themselves (the classic 'parts explosion' loved by data modellers is an example of this, where one component of a machine in made up of other components, which in turn are made up of other components). This is shown by what is known formally as an involuted data relationship or more colloquially as a 'pig's ear' (see Figure 5.3). I will be looking at some of these in worked examples because they offer interesting challenges to data migrations.

Figure 5.3 The involuted data relationship

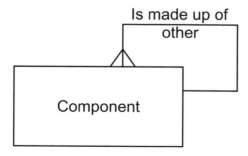

Is made up of other

Component

USES OF DATA MODELS IN *PDMv2*

PDMv2 uses data models anywhere that needs greater clarity because they offer a quick and handy way of sharing understanding that can be roughed out quickly by hand on a white board or in a notebook. They can be supported by sophisticated software, but generally they are produced swiftly using pen and paper and put into formal documentation using normal desktop drawing and word-processing tools only where necessary. However, I will discuss four examples where I will be using data models as a key component. If you choose to substitute the ERD approach with another one of your choosing, then make sure you are confident that it will suffice.

The four data models I will be using are:

- the conceptual entity model;
- the migration model;
- the target model;
- individual legacy data store models.

Each model is discussed below.

Conceptual entity model

In Chapter 4 I introduced the conceptual entity model and the role it plays in a data migration strategy where it is a key component in understanding the scope of a migration. Here is a formally definition.

DEFINITION

A conceptual entity model is a form of data model where atomic entities are grouped together to form higher level entities that are meaningful to the enterprise.

This definition, although correct from an academic viewpoint, is a little misleading. It suggests that you need to have a full entity model of the problem domain before you can create your conceptual entity model by generalising upwards. In fact, unless you have the benefit of a corporate data architect/data stakeholder, you have to make do with a working hypothesis. This might have its risks: later discoveries might invalidate or extend the relationships between entities that you initially describe. In practice, however, I have yet to get the entities themselves seriously wrong. The business knows what it does and it knows the things it needs to do what it does. It knows which aspects of what it does are covered by the systems being replaced.

HINT

The business knows what it does if you get them to examine it carefully. Often some quite essential areas (like finance) get omitted from the initial global view you are given. This is where your experience adds value.

However, agreeing the scope of the project is just the starting point for the use of conceptual entity models. You might be confronted with a few hundred (or even a few thousand) LDSs. Tagging them with the conceptual entity to which they relate will make it easier to find the LDS you need when you have to resolve a data gap. You also know that there will be data held in LDSs within different business functions with different data owners that relate to the same logical entities (how many versions of Customer do you have… and in how many different spreadsheets/databases etc?). These will have to be brought together at load time. It is easier to control this if your project documentation is data entity-based. I will cover this later in more detail when I look at the LA and GAM modules.

Similarly, when you are managing data quality issues you will find yourself under a deluge of hundreds (or thousands) of DQRs and again, as I will show in Chapter 9, linking these on conceptual entity will allow you to find matching issues and solutions and reduce redundant entries. The enterprise will have multiple data stores and the solution to one data issue might be in a data store some distance away. Documenting LDSs and DQRs using the same conceptual entities helps bring these things together.

Working down from conceptual entities also helps you to structure your activities around data-defined business domains that relate to the same things, and therefore need to be resolved by the same KDSH. I will explore this aspect in this chapter.

Migration model, target model and individual data store models
I will cover the migration, target and individual data store models in more detail in Chapter 7 (LA) and Chapter 10 (GAM), but essentially they are levels of model needed to perform comparisons of data held in differing structures, often in different technology, but which have to be combined in the migration process.

- **Migration model** – In an ideal world you would wait until the target is fully defined with a full survey of the legacy landscape and with the target model (see below) as your guide before starting the migration processes. However, in the real world, the target turns up late and is subject to modification right up to go-live. This leaves you no time to use it as the fulcrum of your analysis. You create a migration model to get around this. It is your best guess of what the target will look like. This can either be based on a view of the target (e.g. if you are working on a data migration to a well-established enterprise resource planning (ERP) package you will be given a pretty good steer towards the likely shape of items like customer address standards to work to). Where there is a single large LDS that dominates the landscape around which the local data stores cluster, then that can also be used as a migration model. Sometimes, however, you have to build the model from scratch, but if you do, always keep in mind that you only want a 'good enough' model: errors will be ironed out when (eventually) the target is available.

- **Target data model** – This is a model of the target and is the final model against which GAM will be performed.

- **Data store models** – These are the models of individual LDSs. The degree to which you can carry out modelling depends on the complexity of the LDS and of the domain in which you are working.

INSTANTIATING DATA MODELS

PDMv2 does not mandate or even recommend how to represent data models. The key to thinking about them is that they are there to serve a purpose and that purpose is to record the underlying data structures, which are common in a single representation, so that variations between data models can be revealed. Make sure they are held in the most suitable repository (and preferably one that does not blow the data migration budget). Within a single migration project there will be multiple ways of recording data models depending on their purpose. Models might be drawn freehand in workshops, then documented using basic drawing tools (such as those found in Microsoft® Office products). Models of the target can be fully documented schemas or XML documents.

ANECDOTE

I was consulting on a data migration at a large telco where there were a dozen or so databases involved in design, build, commissioning and billing of complex networks. Some were built as relational databases, some on hierarchical or even more obscure technology. By using data models that started out hand drawn, but were completed using a simple modelling tool, I was able to understand the differences between them without having to extract data. Indeed it was the model-level analysis that told me which data to extract and where the linkage gaps were.

Product or customer structures might be represented in the temporary data stores that hold the master data for migration (as I will explain in Chapter 7 on Landscape Analysis). What is important is not the detail of where the metadata is held, but the commitment to the understanding of metadata structures that can be analysed across various instantiations of the same sets of entities in different technologies. It is your job to see through the LDS representation to the essential similarities and differences of underlying data structures.

HINT

Always bear in mind that for the end-user this idea of metadata conformity is not going to be easy. Also, as I have shown in Section 1, when data is held in isolated silos there are good reasons why it might be structured differently and why these differences might not be 'wrong'. I have also shown that you need the active cooperation of your business colleagues and therefore you need to be careful in your use of words like 'right', 'wrong', 'good' and 'bad'.

This is where, as a data migration professional, you bring something to the party. Golden Rule 2 tells you that the business knows best, but it is you who understands and can compare metadata structures and who has mechanisms for getting your business colleagues to achieve the compromises needed to forge a single, composite view, out of their differences.

For now, let me concentrate on conceptual entity models and their representation as simple ERDs. The other uses of metadata will follow as I proceed through the methodology.

DEVELOPING A CONCEPTUAL ENTITY MODEL

Conceptual entities are those that correspond to a meaningful thing in the enterprise, so all the clever associative entities needed to resolve many-to-many and involuted data relationships can be discarded. Overly simple conceptual entities should also be combined. What you should have at the end of this process is a set of groups of things that make sense to the enterprise, but that completely covers, and can be traced back to, the data requirements of the new system.

Consider, as a worked example, the conceptual entities shown in Figure 5.4. The diagram already tells you something about the conceptualisation of the problem. It is saying that you accept that a Workforce (where Workforce is defined as an individual or possibly a maintenance team) is attached to a single Location. If you find teams that roam between Locations, then you need to either amend the model or create a location with which they are normally associated, or associated for management, payroll and expenses reasons. Other Locations the Workforce visits would then be expressed via Work roster and Equipment. Similarly, you can see that you are going to define a Location for each piece of equipment. Again, where the equipment is mobile (like a truck), then it would still have a primary Location for management and budgeting reasons or you will have to change the model. However, you can anticipate finding LDSs that express these as many-to-many relationships and you will have to resolve these discrepancies via your DQR process.

Figure 5.4 Example conceptual entities

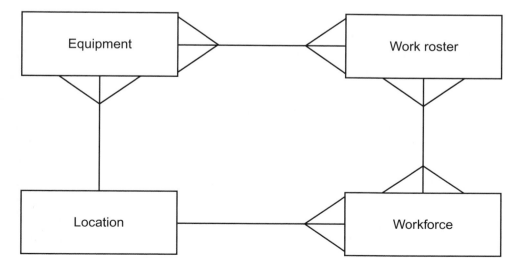

HINT

Remember all this is being done prior to the target being available, so you do not necessarily know how the target will handle these many-to-many relations. I will show you, when I get to describing the GAM module, how the use of the migration model helps to overcome these problems, but for now you note these possible challenges to the model and move on. For the purposes of cataloguing the LDSs you find, or the DQRs you perform, this is good enough: the entities matter more than the relations.

PROJECT DECOMPOSITION AND KEY BUSINESS DATA AREAS

Size matters

These days the sheer scale of projects can be daunting. You are often faced with the prospect of sifting through hundreds (if not thousands) of spreadsheets and mini-databases, not to mention massive legacy enterprise applications that have been built over decades of incremental growth. So where do you start?

HINT

There is an old schoolboy joke that I often use here:

Boy 1: 'How do you eat an elephant?'

Boy 2: 'I don't know.'

Boy 1: 'A little bit at a time.'

Large data migration projects are just the same. You need to break the big thing down into bite-sized chunks that you can digest.

In *PDMv2* the process of breaking down a big project into bite-sized chunks is known as project decomposition. The individual chunks are called key business data areas.

Key business data areas and conceptual entities

As I have said before, data migration is, by definition, all about data. From the data migration project's perspective, therefore, it would make perfect sense to base key business data areas on conceptual entities. The alternative, of decomposing by existing enterprise functional areas, risks confusing historical, enterprise functional categories (that are usually based on business process not data structure) with data structural categories. Of course the corollary of this is that you might find that your data-biased division is so at odds with the enterprise decomposition that you risk all the data migration analysts trying to arrange meetings individually with all of the KDSHs. You have to temper your academic enthusiasm with a degree of pragmatism.

There are, therefore, a number of approaches to decomposition. I prefer to use the conceptual entity model, but project decomposition based on business function might work just as well. Sometimes, where the target system is modularised, it makes sense to follow the target system's modules. That way, for each key business data area, the data migration project will be dealing with a single programme expert stakeholder.

When creating a key business data area you must also consider the migration form: big bang implementation, parallel running implementation or phased delivery. It could be that if you are adopting a phased delivery because of the geographic diversity of the enterprise, your division of activity should be along the same geographical lines.

It is also possible, on really large projects, to have a multi-level project decomposition, maybe by business function within territory.

ANECDOTE

I have worked on enterprise merger activities where the KDSHs were separated both geographically and by company. Here, it made sense to treat each source company as a separate key business data area.

Your choice is normally constrained by that of the bigger programme. Is it to be a phased migration? If so, then you might find that for pragmatic, resourcing reasons it makes sense to divide your work by phase even if that means allocating data migration analysts across what would otherwise be separate key business data areas. Phased or not, consider whether the migration is quite large or has a complexity that merits subdivision.

HINT

In most cases the decision over project decomposition is usually really obvious and will generally be driven by the needs of the bigger programme. However, it is always worthwhile reflecting on whether a particular decomposition is valid for your purposes within the data migration project. Reviewing a comparison between your conceptual entity model and the project decomposition inherited from the bigger programme might drive you to consider having 'champions' within your team for each of the conceptual entities so that a coherent view is maintained of these entities across the (usually) functional lines of the organisation of the bigger programme.

For whatever way you divide up the project (and even if you choose not to divide it at all), you should still have a conceptual entity model. You will use it to describe scope in the migration strategy; you will, as I have suggested, use it to maintain a consistency of view across the key business data areas; it will be used in LA and in the DQR process; you will need it in GAM.

This decomposition is a first-order task. You have not yet looked in detail at the LDSs, so any breakdown has to be provisional. The flip side of this, of course, is that you have to be prepared to acknowledge later on that your initial decomposition was inaccurate and be prepared to change it, with consequent extra cost. What you need is a usable set of work packages to plan and work with that make sense to the activities described later in this book, to the enterprise and to the wider programme. Best judgement is required.

CHAPTER REVIEW

In this chapter I have taken a more in-depth look at the necessity of, and how to produce, a conceptual entity model. You have seen the relationship between the conceptual entity model and project decomposition, and the tensions that have to be resolved between the, normally functional, decomposition of the bigger programme and the data-centric preferences of a data migration project.

In the rest of this section I will outline the remaining *PDMv2* modules and the impact the overlay of the DMZ has on them.

6 DEMILITARISED ZONES AND KEY DATA STAKEHOLDER MANAGEMENT

In this chapter I will look at the demilitarised zone, how to define it and its relationship to other PDMv2 tools, techniques and artefacts. I will also look in more detail at key data stakeholders: their role, how to find them, how to engage with them and how they relate to other aspects of PDMv2.

THE IMPACT OF THE DEMILITARISED ZONE

As you have seen in Section 1 a key concept in *PDMv2* is recognition of a demilitarised zone (DMZ). *PDMv2* is a pragmatic approach to data migration projects as they are actually experienced on the ground in the messy reality of real projects in real enterprises. This means that it is conscious of all the conflicts of interest inherent in the midst of large change projects.

ANECDOTE

I really enjoy giving presentations to battle-hardened data migration professionals who have 'been there, done that'. If you are reading this book as a neophyte data migration professional facing your first major migration and find some of these tales hard to countenance in your environment, believe me the response of those who have been through this before is always one of complete recognition of the issues that *PDMv2* uniquely addresses.

There are conflicts of time and expectation, conflicts between project needs and front-line staff availability, conflicts between what you need to do and what the technology allows you to do. There are conflicts between the natural interests of the supplier and those of the business, and which encompass all the other conflicts plus a few more. As I showed in Section 1, there are perverse incentives for the supplier both not to go beyond its brief in supporting the migration process and to accept less than adequate data provided it loads. This is down to modern procurement contract practices and to the different commercial imperatives the two sides are working under. This might not be what anyone wants to hear, but it is the objective reality. What you need to maximise efficiency, reduce unnecessary conflict and make sure that all parties are dealt with fairly, are clear rules of engagement that accept the reality of these conflicts. You need to put structures in place that manage areas of potential conflict and promote cooperation and compromise. The DMZ is just such a structure.

In a physical sense the DMZ is the area between two firewalls where files are placed by entity A to be picked up by entity B. In traditional data migration architectures this is still very much the case. The project will place the data to be loaded, in a format dictated by the supplier, into an agreed location where the supplier will pick it up. The supplier will put success indicators (e.g. number of records loaded) into an agreed area to be picked up by the project along with records that failed to load, error codes and reasons. The project will pick up the errors and rework them before resubmitting again via the DMZ.

In a logical sense the DMZ is also the dividing line between the responsibilities of the two parties. On the project side there is the responsibility for selecting, cleansing, enriching, preparing (including transforming), mapping, transporting and loading into the DMZ. There is also the management of business continuity activities connected with the disruption that a data migration brings and the decommissioning of LDSs. On the supplier side there is the extracting out of the DMZ, often further transformation, validation, transporting and loading to the target. However, it is also, generally, the supplier's responsibility to define the format of the file(s) that gets passed into the DMZ and the format of error records etc. The DMZ goes further than that, however. It influences all the activities within a data migration project to the extent that they are either wholly within the DMZ, and therefore the responsibility of the supplier, or wholly outside the DMZ, and therefore the responsibility of the project. There are also some shared activities, like end-to-end testing and, as you will see, DQRs, where both sides have to contribute. Within each chapter in the remainder of this section I will show how a DMZ, and where it lies in your project, influence the way that deliverables and roles are defined. To look at it another way, if you read this book in advance of solidifying your relationship within a contract, you can better negotiate a set of handoffs that suit both parties. It is at the point of handoff that protocols need to be agreed and gaps closed so that the project will run with minimum disruption due to misunderstandings.

The great thing about the DMZ concept (aside from recognising a fact of project life and giving it a name) is that once the DMZ perimeter is understood and all crossing points agreed, with supporting roles, artefacts and processes, it allows both sides to black box the other's activities. The supplier is free to deliver their side either using a *PDMv2* approach or one of their own choosing. The project is free to use *PDMv2* without it impacting on the supplier's preferred method.

ANECDOTE

'Black boxing' is very useful where the supplier is using a well-structured industry-recognised migration methodology like ASAP® for SAP® migrations. ASAP® is a classic supplier-side methodology. It is strong on final transformation, validation and mapping, and is very well integrated with the larger programme's restructuring of current business processes into ones compliant with the SAP® modules. It does not, however, address all aspects of a data migration project like legacy decommissioning, data selection or creating business engagement via the SRP process, and critically lacks a fully integrated data issue resolution process to rival DQR. I have been involved with a number of extremely successful ASAP®-based migrations where *PDMv2* has been the ideal project-side complement to this supplier-side approach.

You should always ask the questions: 'Where do the supplier's responsibilities end and is this at the boundary of a data migration?' The gap will be the project's responsibility. The DMZ lies between that gap and the supplier.

I have obviously simplified a typical data migration flow for the purpose of creating a generic structure that illustrates the point I am making about areas of responsibility, and I have not discussed things like timing, synchronisation or the differences modern ETL software can make when it reaches into LDSs and so does away with a physical DMZ and staging database. Even in these cases, there is still a division of responsibility: a logical DMZ where there is no physical one.

INTRODUCTION TO KEY DATA STAKEHOLDERS

I have shown in the previous section that for a data migration exercise to be successful it must be enterprise-led, which is an easy thing to say, but is often difficult to put into practice. Technologists would much prefer to keep their heads down and get on with the closely defined task of moving bits and bytes around rather than get involved with the messy and possibly confrontational business of gaining ownership. You must tackle this task early in a project, when motivation and enthusiasm are high, or you risk trying to find ownership later when major issues need to be resolved.

Identifying data stakeholders is not just about building alliances before things get tricky later on in the project, however. It is central to an enterprise-led approach to data migration. If saying that data migration is a business issue and not a technical issue (Golden Rule 1) is to have any meaning, then you must find those people in the enterprise who will provide direction to the project. As I will explain below, this is not about something as vague as some data champions, these are well-defined, structurally significant roles. It is also important to have allies in the enterprise that will get the tough decisions made when you need them and help you through crises. If you wait until a crisis breaks before looking for help, finding those allies will be a whole lot harder. People naturally tend to run for cover when disaster looms. What you are building here is a virtual team. You need enthusiasts and experts at many levels, and these experts are generally to be found out there in the real, everyday world of the enterprise.

Ownership
There is also the question of ownership. As soon as you create your first mapping table you will have taken ownership of the data migration project. Once you gain ownership it is difficult to move it back to the enterprise. This is especially true if you wait for issues to emerge. Remember, you must avoid the implicit promise that the enterprise is going to have a passive role in this project. The enterprise must own the ultimate delivery and the solutions to problems you will encounter along the way because the enterprise is the final arbiter of the success of the project when it comes to sign off.

The enterprise should, and almost always will, have the ultimate go/no-go sign-off responsibility. It has the power to qualify your efforts as a success or a failure. It should therefore own the problems of data migration as well as its results.

This is not to say that it has the tools and techniques to do the migration. That is why you, the technologist, have been brought in, but you are the purveyor of change. It is your business colleagues who have to live with the results.

Part of the industry-standard approach is for the technical side to propose a solution. This is formally documented and the document is signed off. You use the document as evidence in any disputes. As I showed in Section 1, disputes are almost certain to arise when the business becomes a passive party. The requirements document becomes key supporting evidence in the dispute. Such an adversarial approach is inimical to progress. Multiple meetings will be arranged and issues will be escalated to the highest authorities in the enterprise, all of which wastes time and money. Costly change control procedures will be invoked. Documents will be rewritten and reissued.

Plenty of projects founder on just these cycles of rejection and rework. It is also ultimately self-defeating because the power, in most companies, does not lie with the IT department. If what you prepare is not fit for purpose, producing documentation that shows you built to specification only serves to antagonise and alienate your colleagues. It will not make the solution any more acceptable. You will end up reworking it or both sides will have to settle for a messy compromise that satisfies neither. In my experience, if it comes down to an argument, especially on a data migration exercise, the signed-off specification will be of little use. Your work will be rejected and it will have to be redone. Only now you will have a less cooperative and more antagonistic set of users to deal with.

I am not suggesting that you do away with formal documentation. As I will show, everything you do will be formally sanctioned by the enterprise, but the documentation you produce is more flexible and does not attempt to prescribe in advance what might not be discovered until later in the timeline. However, the enterprise is intimately involved with the decision-making at each step of the way, so the cost, time and design implications of each decision will belong to the enterprise.

HINT

I always make it a mantra on a project that power should not be divorced from responsibility. The enterprise has the power to accept or reject the solution, so the enterprise must take responsibility for that solution.

Data stakeholders: finding the right fellow travellers
In Section 1 I showed that within a migration project, a quest metaphor is more apt than a business-class flight metaphor. You need to create alliances with the enterprise communities within which the knowledge lies; with those who will ultimately sign off your activities; with those who are on the other side of the DMZ. To do this you need to identify your KDSHs.

DEFINITION

A data stakeholder is any person within or outside an organisation who has a legitimate interest in the data migration outcomes.

This definition is important. Taking the definition in reverse:

- **Outcomes** – Projects are about outcomes (or 'deliverables'), that is what is provided at the end of the project and what is provided along the way to allow you to create the desired results. The physical coding process might belong to the technologists, but if, for example, a migration audit trail must be shown to satisfy a regulator, then this must become one of the outputs and must be reflected in the project processes.

- **Legitimate interest** – This is harder to define and will vary from project to project. Some projects are quite tightly targeted with a collection of KDSHs working close to the data. Other projects have a larger group of legitimate KDSHs. It is usually better to be inclusive rather than exclusive, however. If you are using *PDMv2*, then there are some mandatory data stakeholders that must be identified.

HINT

We have all worked on projects where some well-thought-of employee takes an informal interest in all projects, dipping in and out almost at whim. These people can be quite disruptive. Get them to define their legitimate interest: possibly an architectural one. Usually it is better to have them inside rather than outside, but if you want to be rid of them, remember Golden Rule 1. Once you have got buy-in from the KDSHs, get the other stakeholders to assign them a role or reject them.

- **Within or outside** – KDSHs, as I will show in some of the following examples, can be drawn from outside the organisation as well as from within. External stakeholders vary, for example, from regulators, user groups, external auditors and consultative groups to supplier partners on the other side of the DMZ and to regular business suppliers. They all need to be identified and developed into a single virtual team.

- **Person** – A KDSH, for *PDMv2* purposes, is a person not a group. That person might represent a larger group, but you need individuals you can contact, with phone numbers and email addresses, empowered to make judgements and decisions.

You will be expecting a lot from your trusted band of KDSHs and you must bind them early into the success of the project. They must know their role and accept the responsibilities that come with it. Finding all the data stakeholders and getting buy-in is one of your first and most difficult tasks. The following lists some of the common data stakeholders, starting with the two that are mandatory for every data source you find.

Data owner

Remember that in Section 1 I defined a data owner as any individual inside or outside an enterprise who has the legitimate right to prevent the migration from occurring owing to concerns over the selection, usability or correctness of the data or even the way the data is extracted, transformed or handled. You will be asking them to participate in the SRP process and ultimately to sign off a decommissioning certificate. These are the people who have the power to sanction switching off the LDSs.

However, identifying data owners can be difficult. It might seem simple, but in modern enterprises with constantly changing structures and wall-to-wall ERP systems, finding owners can be hard. Some systems seem to be used by everyone and owned by no one.

ANECDOTE

I was working on a project in a heavily regulated national company and the project required that I make changes to one of their key infrastructural systems. Although each module could be identified with an enterprise function, and therefore ultimately with a director, the system as a whole seemed to be owned by no one. In the end I settled for the senior business manager of the function in which I was working as my data owner.

Frequently the data owner is not the person in day-to-day contact with the data source. The data owner might be a senior manager who has moved into their position from elsewhere and never had hands-on contact with the system. You might find, however, that the data owner, some time and a couple of promotions ago, worked with the LDS. This can be more difficult. They might believe that they know what is going on, but beware! System use evolves with time and with personnel. You need to know how the data source is used right now, what its idiosyncrasies are, and what workarounds are in place today; not how it used to work in the past (see Business domain expert below).

One can persist up the chain of command until you reach the CEO, but you will often have to settle for group senior managers, each of whom will take responsibility for just part of the LDS. Remember the key question is: 'Who is going to sign the decommissioning certificate?' Find them and make sure they cover the whole system.

Business domain expert

You need a business domain expert who is up to speed with the way the data source is used now. This does not mean that the business domain expert and the data owner cannot be the same person (they often are on small local data sources), just be aware of the degree of up-to-date knowledge you are expecting from your expert.

Also be aware of the degree of commitment you are expecting of the business domain expert. They are supposed to be co-workers on the virtual team you are building. They must be available at the end of a phone for a quick call. They must be free to attend workshops at reasonable notice. A senior enterprise manager whose diary is booked for months in advance and who has a PA to answer email is unlikely to suit.

The business domain expert might also not work directly for the data owner. You need the best person for the job that the enterprise can spare. This is another reason for taking a top-down approach. Get data owner buy-in at the outset and resourcing issues become that bit easier to resolve.

Finally, the business domain expert should be just that: an expert. Do not be fobbed off with some junior that is the easiest person to spare. The business domain expert will be your champion in their enterprise area. Their peers should respect them and accept that they can adequately represent the business domain's interests. Their data owner must understand that you will be placing a lot of trust in their judgement on a day-to-day basis during the course of the migration.

HINT

So I've just set you an impossible task: finding perfect business domain experts. In my experience these people are usually well known in their environment, but are also often over tasked, dealing with every new initiative that comes their way. It is up to your negotiating skills and powers of persuasion to get the best you can. This is one of the reasons I recommend a top-down, enterprise-owned approach. Identify the data store owner, make the situation real to them and then get them to select a business domain expert after explaining the role. Never forget Golden Rule 1! If they do not prioritise the migration project over the others making a call on their staff then, after due warning, accept their view and get them to sign it off.

For large, complex, systems you will need more than one business domain expert, each familiar with their own aspect of the data source and its use. One representative that everyone can trust, who has the internal network of contacts to get answers to questions outside their immediate domain and can select the correct attendees at meetings is better than a plethora of experts, but you might have to make a compromise between an army of experts and a lack of knowledge.

Whoever is chosen, they need to be credible to the enterprise with recent real, hands-on, business domain experience.

Technical system experts

In anything other than a simple data source there are often aspects of the system that only the technical expert can know about. These might relate to file formats, access permissions, interfaces etc., as well as 'under the bonnet' validation that is invisible to the business domain expert. It is usually easy to identify the technical system experts. They might work for the IT department. They are often the system experts you are first pointed to when you get your initial job brief. These people are important, but not as important as the business domain experts, and definitely not as important as the data owner. Do not allow yourself to be misled into thinking that systems administrators are the same as well-informed users of the system. They are not, but many data migrations founder on the confusion of the two roles. A systems administrator is a valuable source of information on the best candidates for business domain experts. They will also be well informed on issues of data quality.

Finally, as I have stated before, it is imperative that no matter how well informed the technical side is of the enterprise issues, a data migration project must be led by, and be seen to be led by, the enterprise. If the technical side take the lead, then they will own any and all problems they find. Again, no matter how expedient it might seem to you (and to your programme manager) to use the skills of a business analyst who is the acknowledged expert in this business domain, hold out for a local business domain expert.

Technical system experts come in a variety of flavours: there are those who are expert on the LDSs you are migrating from; there are those from the infrastructure community who understand connectivity and system topography; there are those who understand the physical infrastructure and with whom you engage with to get the new system, test system and migration platforms built; there are those who understand the target system. The latter are counterparts to your in-house staff, who sit on the other side of the DMZ, but you will need access to experts who understand how the target system works from a user and technical perspective. You will need to link up with target system experts who understand how the load process to the target works, how to tune and, just as significantly de-tune, import validation routines.

Access to technical system experts on either side of the DMZ is different. On the project side you can normally negotiate for the services of your business colleagues. Of course, with the increased prevalence of outsourcing this has now become slightly less straightforward than it was. However, there are usually mechanisms for getting access to the right technologists.

Access to technical system experts on the supplier side of the DMZ is more difficult. You will see when I look at the DQR process that you will need their knowledge of what is possible when you come to resolve issues; however, there will also be a contractual line between the two parties.

ANECDOTE

In this age of increasingly tight procurement processes I have seen, many times, the weighting placed on bid price heavily skewing the selection of suppliers so that there is no incentive to provide the technical support that is needed for the migration. This needs to be addressed in the initial invitation-to-tender documents and then in the evaluation process.

Data migration analysts

Data migration analysts are the people who understand the *PDMv2* product set and the underlying approach to the extent that you can adapt your practice to the environment you find yourself in without compromising those underlying principles. You, as a data migration analyst, have certain designated roles within the *PDMv2* product set, like chairing the DQR boards (see Chapter 9), and you are responsible, often under a guiding project manager, for ensuring that the *PDMv2* product set is implemented to a quality and timeliness that will satisfy the bigger programme. You are the facilitator who creates an environment that bridges the technical, business and programme spheres of activity. The ideal data migration analyst will probably have a business analyst's skill of articulating technical issues to business people and vice versa, a facilitator's skill in creating the right environments where these conversations can take place, a data architect's skill at understanding metadata relationships, a project manager's skill at managing deliverables to time and budget, and a technologist's understanding of what the available technology can do and how to use it to best advantage.

HINT

Once again, the data migration analyst's role is not an easy one, and most candidates fall short in one area or another. The key is to understand your strengths and weaknesses and rely on the former as you build up the latter, but this is why data migration, histori-cally seen as a backwater for the less competent, is now increasingly viewed as where the best and brightest multi-taskers are to be found.

Programme experts

It is obvious that the bigger programme, of which a data migration project is a part, has a legitimate interest in the data sources. Depending on the implementa-tion methodology of the supplier, they might well start with an analysis of LDSs and processes. They will produce the target side of the data mapping require-ments. Therefore, there will be a variety of programme experts with whom you will interact in the course of a migration. Typically these will include experts from the supplier partners who are configuring the target and who will, therefore, be on the other side of the DMZ.

HINT

Here the concept of the DMZ is extremely useful. It is not uncommon for well-meaning, and often well-informed, programme experts to stray over the line into the data migration project's space and start to suggest likely data sources, sometimes even including them in signed-off documentation. Although all input is to be welcomed, it is unlikely that they are as meticulously performing LA etc. to the same degree you will be and will not ultimately be responsible for the quality and appropriateness of the data as you will be. If they are straying, then you need to examine the DMZ and move its boundaries to cover those parts of LA that they have been contracted to perform. Your role as data migration analyst will then be to ensure that the programme expert has covered the whole of the legacy landscape and not cherry-picked the data items most amenable to their preferred ETL software.

- **Programme experts versus data migration analysts** – Just as the business domain expert and the data owner are distinct roles (although they might be embodied in the same person), so the programme expert and the data migration analyst are distinct roles. Do not confuse them because confusing the legitimate interest of the programme with the legitimate interests of the project causes more problems than any other single thing. Data migration analysts are the mediators between what the programme needs and what the project and the enterprise data stakeholders need. A data migration analyst must satisfy all the data stakeholders, not just the programme.

I cannot tell you how many failing data migration exercises I have been involved with that have started from the premise of programme, not data migration project, need. It's probably just about all of them! From the outset the focus is on staffing the project with people who know the target and not the data sources. They concentrate on getting the data that the target system needs over the data that the enterprise needs. As you know, this breaks Golden Rules 1 and 2. Remember, data migration has (at least) two ends: a new system (for sure), but also an LDS end as well.

I am not recommending that you rework the analysis that has gone into the design of the target system. The bigger programme owns responsibility for that and so it has to be a given to the data migration project. Of course, as a good corporate citizen, if you spot a really bad mistake that will compromise the target, then you have to flag it up to the appropriate programme expert, but it is for them to investigate and resolve the issue. It is not your role to redesign the target. The choice of source, quality and audit trails is that of the data migration project. It is a shared responsibility with the other data stakeholders (along with data transitional rules, SRPs, and a heap of other things that I will cover later in the book).

Corporate data architect

Those organisations with a sophisticated approach to data management and administration will often have an information management function where corporate data models and data architectural models will be maintained.

Terms like 'data architect' are bandied about a lot in IT and can mean subtly different things in different departments: from an extremely technical role related to the nuts and bolts of databases and servers to a more widely encompassing one. Here is a good working definition of the data architect's role.

DEFINITION

The data architect is responsible for the design of how the data required for an organisation, possibly held over multiple applications, is held.[12]

Corporate data architects will have an overview of how the data is structured and where it is mastered in those common cases where the same data item is used in more than one place. They will also be responsible for producing, and often enforcing, institution-wide definitions of key enterprise entities.

---

[12] From BCS Careers Leaflet CWG13.

If the organisation in which you are delivering a data migration project has such a function it is extremely unlikely that you will not be made aware of it at the inception of the project. Given that these peoples' day job is reviewing data standards and maintaining data models, they make an extremely useful first port of call when you get to the process of defining the key business data areas (see Chapter 5) and producing the legacy data models. They will be well informed of the data quality issues in existing legacy data and so they make a good starting point for your first-cut DQRs that were included in the data migration strategy. They are the official corporate lead in best practice data design methods, so it makes sense to use their modelling standards, tools and methods. These preferences too should be captured in your data migration strategy document under 'polices'. Use the advice of the local experts to choose the tools that are mandated or just work best in the environment in which you find yourself. Data architects can usually identify for you the best candidates for business domain expert and the other key data stakeholders.

However, once again there is a health warning. Corporate data architects do not have day-to-day, hands-on, use of their systems. They are not a substitute for business domain experts. They are usually organisationally and culturally part of the IT function within the enterprise... and remember Golden Rule 1!

Sometimes, but rarely, they have data store owner responsibilities, but again the key question is: 'Who has the final say in decommissioning an LDS?'

The main area where there is a potential for conflict between the data migration project and the data architecture team lies in the contradiction between enforcing corporate policy with regard to private data stores and getting the best data available for the new system. Here you need to be clear about your role as the data migration expert facilitator of change, not owner of the solution. I personally always push for a full amnesty over local LDSs where these run counter to corporate policy, for the initial period of the migration exercise. However, it is often the legitimate role of the corporate data architecture team to resist this. Once again it comes down to the wider business assessing the arguments in favour of the fullest possible set of data stores against the impact on corporate discipline. The worst case is to duck the issue. It has to be faced. A decision needs to be made that all parties can agree to (and possibly entered in the risk register).

ANECDOTE

Each enterprise differs in the degree of latitude it allows its staff for local initiatives. Sometimes, even within a single organisation there might be differences. When I was working for an emergency services organisation the discipline against private data stores was absolute among the uniformed section. Among the civilian workers, however, there was a greater degree of flexibility.

Once again, though, you must stick to the rules. If there is to be a corporate data architecture stakeholder, they must be identified, with roles, responsibilities, email addresses and telephone numbers. It might be that the way the information resource function is organised means there will be separate people responsible for data modelling and physical data storage design etc. I prefer a single contact with overarching responsibility to my project, even if they pass the work around within their own department, but however it is accomplished, you should have an agreed series of deliverables and methods of communicating.

In the first phase of engagement with data stakeholders it might be that the initial deliverable will be the definition of the subsequent deliverables. However, it is essential that the full list of products is nailed down before project work commences in earnest.

Data governance and master data management experts

In most cases the enterprise group responsible for data governance (where it exists) contains the data architects or their equivalent. However, data governance is now taking on an extended role in prescribing and managing data values and data representation. Obviously the earlier you make contact with these groups the better because you will be making data management types of decision around best data sources, data structures etc. Similarly with MDM, as I will show in Chapter 7 on landscape analysis, data migration often demands the creation of MDM 'lite' where you need to consolidate reference data lists of Customer and Product etc. from disparate LDSs. If this work has been done elsewhere and you need to align to it, then the sooner you find out, the better.

HINT

Often there is a nascent data governance or MDM initiative running in parallel to your project. Just as often these initiatives stall for lack of support from front-line staff who are just too busy to engage. You, however, have the compelling event of the imminent data migration and legacy decommissioning to focus on. It is therefore possible for you to get the attention of the right people that other programmes lack. This presents you with the opportunity to give a lead into the data governance or MDM projects, thereby gaining you allies in the enterprise and kudos beyond your immediate goals. This all helps to position data migration, not as a necessary evil, but as a valuable benefit to the enterprise as a whole.

Audit and regulatory experts

Most organisations these days are subject to external and internal auditory and regulatory requirements. Data migration, both in the process itself and in its delivered data, might be subject to legitimate audit and regulatory inspection. If this is so in your case, then you will need a contact for each of these requirements. These contacts can be external to the company with which you are working, but they are more likely to be fellow employees who have the appropriate responsibility on behalf of the company. In either case, identify them if needed. It might be that the person is both the business domain expert and the audit and regulatory expert. This is not a problem. So long as you can sort out when they are speaking on behalf of the user community and when they are speaking on behalf of the regulator.

This is important; regulatory requirements usually take precedence over user ergonomics, but it is not unknown for the two to be conveniently confused for the benefit of the user population!

Data customers
Alongside the regulatory and audit functions there are often internal recipients of data. Quite often information is gathered that is needed elsewhere, outside the business domain of origin. It is sometimes necessary to identify these KDSHs. Be careful how wide you cast your net, however. Analysis of data in LDSs can often identify additional data items that need to be passed on. The choice of appropriate technical data experts should inform the project of those interfaces to secondary systems invisible to the data store owner or business domain expert. Bringing too many parties into the project risks making your work unwieldy; bringing in too few risks oversights. I'm afraid it is a matter of judgement and experience, but, hey, that's what you are being paid big bucks for, right? Only invite those who clearly have something to add.

Other key data stakeholders
It is not unusual that in the environment in which you find yourself you might need additional data stakeholders. This is fine provided you can define their role and agree it with the other stakeholders. Beware of having too many people involved, and closely define all stakeholder roles so that their influence is not allowed to extend beyond their proper competence.

Managing key data stakeholders
If you have been running the data migration project strictly according to *PDMv2*, then you will have been given an initial list of KDSHs at the outset of the project in the data migration strategy documentation. You also know that you will uncover more KDSHs during LA and possibly during GAM. You will qualify these KDSHs and have even more disclosed to you via the SRP method, so you need to take the following steps:

- **Record them** – Each LDS, no matter how big or small, will have a data owner, a business domain expert and at least one technical data expert. For a simple spreadsheet this might all be embodied in one person, but each time you encounter a new LDS capture with whom you need to speak under each of these roles (or at least with whom you need to speak to get to these people). The preference is that these names are recorded in a common programme-wide contacts database with the data migration roles they occupy (obviously a business domain expert for a corporate application can have their own spreadsheet data for which they are the data owner). You need to liaise with the bigger programme's business readiness or business communications agent, who you should have identified when you wrote the data migration strategy. There should be a single list of contacts, just make sure that you retain ownership of your definitions.

    As I indicated above, you want real people, with real contact details in your list. You need names, email addresses, phone numbers and whatever other location information is pertinent to the organisation and the migration. For instance, it might be that you are engaged in a geographical project decomposition and therefore need to have business-side KDSHs differentiated by geographical unit.

- **Brief them according to their role** – Prepare some standard briefing materials, but, in every case you can, try to brief the KDSHs personally. The roles do not require extensive training. They should come naturally, but the data owners especially need to understand the degree of commitment you are expecting of them or their delegates in DQRs and LA. Data owners need to be clear from the outset that they will be expected to sign the decommissioning certificates. Your first conversation with them will start, as I indicated in Section 1, with a clear and unequivocal statement that, in the first place, you will be decommissioning their system by a given date, and in the second, that they will be expected to sign off that this can happen. This is how you grab their attention.

You might have a challenge with data stakeholders on the other side of the DMZ. If you have been following the *PDMv2* method from the very start of the project, then the support requirements of suppliers in things like DQRs will be understood and might even be part of the contract. However, if, as often happens, the initiation of the data migration project has lagged behind the bigger programme, then there might be delicate negotiations to be had about how to access the resources you are going to need.

HINT

I have often found, especially when working on a smaller migration where access to a supplier's technical staff is unmediated, that the technologists are surprisingly lacking in enthusiasm to engage at all. They just want to 'get on with it' and not be bothered by tedious conversations with end-users. 'Just give us the data' is often their cry. Often, they are also quite stretched by supporting both the bigger programme's changing requirements and the data migration. It helps if you can demonstrate an understanding for their position on a technical level, plus use some of the examples in this book of how data migrations can struggle if the data is not appropriately selected and prepared. This will resonate with them if they have experienced data migrations in the past.

Your internal KDSHs tend to be less of a problem, but identify your requirements early, especially in large organisations, to the appropriate resourcing unit because some of the technical resources can be booked up a long way in advance. Technical resources also welcome an understanding of their role, so share as much of this book and method with them as you can. Have as much contact with business-side KDSHs as possible because you are likely to be moving them some way out of their comfort zone.

- **Use their services appropriately** – Once you have discovered, briefed and generally warmed up the KDSHs, then make sure you use them. There is nothing worse than getting a project team ready and enthusiastic then leaving things to go cold. Warming them up a second time is that much harder.

HINT

There are inevitable stops and starts on any large project, especially at the beginning when budgets and scope are being finalised, governance structures are being put in place, vendors are being chosen etc., but within *PDMv2* there are some quick wins you can use to get you going. For example, start your DQR process as soon as possible. Starting early, before there are any real show-stopping issues and prior to the time pressures at the end of the project, allows you to build the virtual team, shake out the DQR process so that it fits your environment and deliver early value by investigating known data issues that have been around for a long time. As I will show in Chapter 9 on DQRs, although in theory it might seem like you need to know the target before you can perform data quality work, in practice you know the items you just have to fix whatever the target. You will also be benefiting from your initial LA, which you can also start early (see Chapter 7).

CHAPTER REVIEW

In this chapter I have reiterated the importance of the DMZ as a concept and how you need to understand all other aspects of *PDMv2* in relationship to its existence. I then went on to explain who you need to identify in establishing your virtual team of KDSHs. Each KDSH has a clearly defined role, from data store owner to business domain expert to data migration analyst. I also gave advice on how to get the best KDSHs you can and looked at some of the confusion in roles that can lead you astray.

7 LANDSCAPE ANALYSIS

In this chapter I will look at why it is imperative that you start your data migration journey by understanding the legacy environment. I introduce the legacy data store concept and explain how to find, document and manage the large number of legacy data stores you are likely to encounter on even the most modest of data migrations. I will look at gap analysis as it relates to legacy data stores and how to steal a march on the project by performing the majority of your gap analysis before the target is defined. I will introduce you to master data management as it applies to data migration. Finally, I look at the use of software tools to perform data profiling and how this activity is integrated into PDMv2.

WHAT IS LANDSCAPE ANALYSIS AND WHY DO YOU DO IT?

A data migration is like building a bridge over a river. Both have two ends: with data migration, one end is the target and all that it promises; the other end is the legacy data. Traditionally the target has been the centre of attention. You might feel that you know about the legacy and that it is the mystery of the new that fascinates you; however, in fact, few enterprises really understand their legacy data as well as they need to if they are to be secure in their data migration exercise. It is surprising how many essential business functions are run on a platform of interlinked spreadsheets (the 'spread-net' as it is sometimes called), where users extract data from corporate systems, manipulate it externally and then re-enter it to continue the process.

> **HINT**
>
> Common examples of the 'spread-net' in operation are in sales departments where special deals for things like group or bulk purchases have been worked out that cannot be accommodated in normal processing. Also, expect to find an awful lot of spreadsheets and local databases running the company when it comes to most finance departments.

Many local data stores might only be known to a few (or even only to one individual), their significance only fully understood by those people. There are also the local uses of fields in enterprise applications that have been adopted for undocumented local use, often to allow the delivery of business processes that are not adequately supported in an old system.

ANECDOTE

Common examples of local use are the uses some notes or extended text fields are put to. I have seen a notes field hold a key holder's phone number in property inspection applications and tax code values in a surname field in human resource applications.

You need to perform landscape analysis (LA) to map this labyrinth of LDSs, their use and relationship to the known and documented business processes.

DEFINITION

Landscape analysis is the systematic discovery, review and documenting of the legacy data stores, including their linkages, data quality and key data stakeholders.

I will take this definition apart by looking at what is meant by legacy data stores, how to find them and how to document them.

LEGACY DATA STORES

DEFINITION

A legacy data store is a data repository of any type that holds data of interest to the new system.

Data migration is all about data and data is held in collections. Within the boundaries of the risk aversion policy (i.e. quality versus time versus budget) on a project, you want to get the best data you can, not necessarily the easiest to move electronically. As I will show when I come to look at the DQR module (in Chapter 9) you establish a forum for weighing up the costs and benefits of getting data from different LDSs, but for that forum to have meaning you first have to uncover all the data sources, many of which might be hidden.

ANECDOTE

I use the word 'store' as opposed to 'system', 'database' or 'file' advisedly. It is normal to get essential fragments of data from spreadsheets, card indexes and other paper files. I have even transcribed data from hand-drawn plans dating from before the First World War. Although in an academic sense these can all be characterised as 'systems', the word 'stores' conveys a more accurate description in everyday language.

Discovering legacy data stores

Identifying LDSs is both hard and easy. You will have an initial list in the data migration strategy. You will use this as your starting point, but expect there to be other LDSs out there that are possibly known only to a few people.

HINT

I start migration projects with a well-publicised amnesty on the revelation of private data stores, whatever the corporate policy on private data stores might be. I also put a strict deadline on the amnesty after which change control is rigorously enforced.

Be as inclusive as possible. It might only take a few minutes to dismiss a data store as being entirely derivative and not important, but it can cost you the price of the whole project if a key data store is overlooked. It is also discourteous to dismiss a data store out of hand. It would be arrogant to assume that you know better than an employee about how the company is run. Welcoming, not dismissing, the input of local knowledge is another way of building that wider virtual team that will deliver the project.

HINT

If it happens that you do reject a data store that you subsequently find is needed, be honest and open about your mistake. There is nothing that will build teams better than being prepared to accept an 'I told you so' lecture because your response should then be: 'Yeah, you were right. I was wrong. I apologise. Now what are we going to do about it?'

So expect additional data stores to be identified as the project proceeds. *PDMv2* accepts recursion and aspects of LA can be kept running as long as the project is in operation, but be warned, the cost of investigating late arrivals and reprogramming for them rises dramatically as the project progresses. Try to drive out as many LDSs as possible as early as possible. Use the amnesty, use the system topography, walk the shop floor looking for examples, use any technology you have available, but most of all use the virtual team you are building to volunteer hidden data stores.

ANECDOTE

Using technology can be helpful, but sometimes it can be an overkill. There is desktop search and cataloguing software that can sniff out all those spreadsheets and produce a list. However, the question is: what do you do with the list? How do you sort out the gems of isolated masters of best data from the dross of odds and ends of spreadsheets created once in a spirit of investigation, then abandoned? The answer, of course, is that you have to check with the data owners, which is what *PDMv2* is all about. On the other hand, it was by examining 'user exits' (i.e. user-created spooling off of data via an attendant reporting suite) that enabled me, on a project for a significant financial organisation, to discover an unofficial data warehouse (as discussed in an anecdote in Section 1).

Technology will also not alert you to the non-electronic LDSs that might hold crucial data for the data migration. As I will show in Chapter 10 on gap analysis and mapping, using the topography metaphor also works backwards. When you are looking for data to map you often find that there is a missing item that just has to be there to enable the business to run, but which does not appear to be in any LDS of which you are aware. There is obviously something missing from your knowledge of the LDS. Your first port of call will be the LDS list: have you overlooked the significance of a data store? (See the Hint box above on how to make this a positive thing.) If you cannot find a likely LDS in your list, then, via the DQR process, you will consult the KDSHs to find the missing item. However, as I have said above, late discovery might be better than not discovering it all, but it is not as good as getting it right first time.

LANDSCAPE ANALYSIS AS A SUPER SMART TASK

Landscape analysis is a classic Super SMART Task:

- It is a SMART task because, although you cannot know in advance how many LDSs you will uncover or how many of them will be relevant, you can 'time box' the process (again bearing in mind the risk aversion policy that prevails) and the results of your analysis will create the planning information you need to plan, budget and predict reliably the remainder of the project. Many independent industry analysts (for instance, check out the report that Bloor Research carried out in 2011[13]) assert that a thorough data profiling exercise prior to the setting of final budgets is one of the key predictors to the success of bringing in a data migration on time and to budget. As I argue below, when you come to look at the use of software tools to support LA, profiling is only part of the story. You also need business engagement and support to make sense of your findings, but the difference that diligently performing LA makes in the successful outcome of a data migration is clear.

- Landscape analysis is vital if you are to 'complete the task'. As the previous paragraph indicates, without it you are demonstrably more at risk of project overrun or failure. Knowing where you are coming from is just as vital as knowing where you are going to when you build that bridge from old to new, and this is not just about the data quality of well-known LDSs, extremely important though that is. The LDSs on the list you are given in the data migration strategy will, most likely, be the corporate systems'. You will also need the local stores either to enhance or cross check data in the corporate systems or to provide the stepping stones in your topography. You also need to know linkages between data stores that might be broken in the course of the migration so you can support the existing ecosystem as you migrate. Late challenges to go-live caused by broken data linkages that are discovered in user acceptance testing are extremely expensive to fix.

---

[13] Howard, P. (2011). *Data migration*. Bloor Research.

- Landscape analysis 'builds the individual'. Performed properly, LA rewards the data owners by recognising the contribution they have made (often in an unheralded manner) to the smooth running of the legacy business processes. It also rewards them by acknowledging their business domain expertise.

- Landscape analysis 'builds the team'. Having built up the individuals, they are far more likely to respond positively towards you and become part of your virtual team. These are the people you will be calling on from your DQR process when data gaps appear or when you have a semantic issue to resolve.

So the lesson here is: never skimp on landscape analysis. What you get wrong here can either be impossible or very difficult and expensive to fix in the migration design and execution module.

WHEN TO PERFORM LANDSCAPE ANALYSIS

Landscape analysis should be started as soon as possible after the project is initiated. As I have stated before, there is a common misunderstanding that you cannot start any data migration activity in earnest until the target is defined. This is wrong. In most cases the business is not changing what it is doing fundamentally (e.g. car manufacturers will continue to make cars, insurance companies will continue to write policies etc.). What I term the 'big ticket' items, which are things like de-duplicating your customer list, are going to be needed whatever the target. Uncovering all the LDSs that are secretly running the enterprise will take time, but will have to be done. Resolving the semantic issues I discussed in Section 1 will take time. You have the most time at the beginning of a project. It is a commodity that shrinks as you go down the timeline. In my experience the target will be delivered later than planned and be subject to many small alterations right up to go-live and beyond. Wait for that to appear on the horizon and you will be asking too much of yourself in too little time under too much pressure.

DOCUMENTING LEGACY DATA STORES

The documenting of LDSs is obviously dependent on the library services technology choices made in the data migration strategy. A fully integrated set of services is preferred where documentation on the LDSs is linked through to documentation on the KDSHs. However, I have been using these techniques to manage successfully large data migration projects using spreadsheet or local desktop database applications like Microsoft® Access. You just need to take more care to keep the various entries aligned and, on anything but the smallest project, you will require some degree of dedicated resource to manage it.

You need to create an LDS list. You need to enter on the list every LDS you encounter, but it need not take long to document data stores. Create a standard form and be pragmatic about how much detail is needed in all the columns. Larger data stores obviously require greater preparation and analysis. The LDS definition should be signed off by the data store owner and filed with the data migration project documentation. The set of LDS definitions is one of the key configurable items within the migration process. After the initial free-for-all, new LDSs that appear must be change-controlled onto the project. The later you discover these, the greater the impact in terms of time and cost they will have. It is imperative you make the programme and the user population aware of the cost of late disclosure.

HINT

I use any means possible, including posters and email shots, so that everyone is aware of the potential impact of late disclosure of LDSs. This is one of the places where you need the help of your business readiness/communications team. When latecomers come to light (as indeed they invariably do), use the programme's change control procedure to get them included in the remit of the data migration project. Be realistic in your impact assessment, these things can really trip you up!

Be warned – your LDS list will grow extra columns as the project progresses! It inevitably becomes a programme resource and additional columns will be added. The following gives some starter suggestions. These are the minimum. Your project will have its own unique requirements.

- **Identity** – Give each of the LDSs a unique project identifier: even where middle to large applications in your environment have an identifier given to them by your architect community that links back to a systems catalogue, remember that you are interested in data stores that might have been missed by the architects' audit (non-electronic data stores, small spreadsheets etc.). If you are in an environment that has a comprehensive systems catalogue, then add a cross-reference column for that code.

  Record the name by which the LDS is known. This is not as easy as it might seem. Large data stores can have different names in different parts of the organisation. Small LDSs might have no name and you might need to make one up. I tend to be descriptive, combining the name of the owner with the purpose of the data store and its technology, for example 'Johny's LDS Spreadsheet'.

  Add a short functional description. The example given above might have 'Legacy Data Store List for project X'.

- **Key data stakeholders** – As I stated when I discussed KDSHs, each LDS needs to have a data owner and a business domain expert (who can be the same person for small local data stores). You also need to record the technical system experts and other KDSHs where appropriate.

- **Data quality** – You need to record a data quality assessment for each LDS. I usually record if the assessment was impressionistic (i.e. what I have been told, but not had time to investigate) or quantitative (i.e. there has been some formal profiling that allows me to put a degree of certainty on the quality).

- **System retirement plan** – Use the LDS list to record where you are in the system retirement planning process for a particular data store. This will be clearer after you have read Chapter 8, but I record the SRP identifier and what state it is in.

- **Technical details** – Record those details here that will be useful to you when (and if) you come to get data out of a store. I usually have a column for 'data origin', that is where the data came from (i.e. is it originated and mastered in this data store or is it completely derived from other sources?). You also need to know the format: is it a spreadsheet on a PC or a DB2 database on a mainframe? You need to know the location and how to access it. Again the information held here will differ in a workstation location from the complex connection information for a corporate database.

ANECDOTE

Never underestimate the importance of knowing where a store is located and the obstacles to accessing it when you need it. I have not been caught out yet, but I have come mighty close to finding that a particular user-developed application was not available because the user in question was about to go on maternity leave and the application was on her laptop. Fortunately she had the good sense to warn me. I suppose this illustrates the importance of building the virtual team. On the other hand, it might have been better if I had asked when each member of the team expected to be on leave.

You need to know how much data is held in a data store. I normally, at least on the first pass, assess this in two dimensions: scale (being the number of bytes) and complexity (being the number of tables and columns). Both help in different ways when you come to planning the migration. Large volumes in terms of bytes require different tools for analysis (you can't eyeball two million records to spot the bad data), extraction, transport, transform and load (there are time and bandwidth considerations for large data volumes that do not apply to smaller ones). Complexity adds its own problems, typically on the coding side of things. Complex datasets tend to have complex rules for the extraction sequence. They are tricky to manipulate while maintaining their integrity and have sequencing issues when you come to load them. It is also difficult to test the migration given the complex test packs you will need to build. Finally, proving the data audit (i.e. that all the units of migration that left the legacy landed successfully in the target) can be tricky. Of course when it comes to the main, enterprise application LDS, these tend to be large in both scale and complexity.

HINT

Of course, the term 'large' differs from one environment to another. It is very much down to local experience. My rule of thumb is if the dataset is too large to inspect and manipulate manually then it is large. These days, of course, with the advent of 'big data', we are getting accustomed to massive datasets, but from a data migration project point of view, the main step change in thinking is from something you can work with manually on your desktop to something you need tools for. After that it is a question of what the appropriate tools are.

Alongside size, you also need to know the volatility of the data. How often does it change? When you get to the MDE module, I will show it might be possible to load datasets with low volatility in advance of the main migration to save time.

You also need to record information about where an LDS sits within the project decomposition and which conceptual entities are represented within it. The project decomposition is significant when you come to planning and allocating workload, but, as I have indicated, entities give you another view of the LDSs to examine, and they often prove vital in GAM.

It is advisable to tag, at the first review of a data store, what you believe its likely migration status is going to be. Is it to be fully migrated and decommissioned? Part migrated? Not migrated, but decommissioned? Neither migrated nor decommissioned? Having this conversation with the data owner, even where the LDS is not going to have any data taken out of it in the course of the migration, helps to make the fact of the migration real to the data owner and, as you have seen, this helps to build engagement.

Finally, where this is a corporate data store, there will probably be copious documentation somewhere else, and if there isn't (or even if there is) you will be adding lots of additional documentation from your profiling and DQR activity. This is where the use of more sophisticated technology than spreadsheets comes in handy. You can create dynamic links to these documentation stores, but either way you need to record where additional documentation is held.

HINT

It is often the case that in an LDS list you will have more information about some obscure spreadsheet application used by only one person in one department than you do about the largest corporate system. This is because the spreadsheet application might not be documented anywhere else, whereas your large corporate system has its own dedicated team of database administrators, system engineers, system testers, resilience managers etc., meaning that your documentation only needs a reference to their locations.

- **Topography** – Where does each LDS get its information from and where does it send it? Understanding the linkages helps you to understand if the data in a data store is entirely original (uncommon) or entirely derived (quite common where the data store is used to enhance presentation values) or somewhere in between (most common). This will help you with your data source selection. Normally, the maintenance of interfaces after the migration is not the responsibility of the data migration project, but maintenance of interfaces during the migration often is (consult the data migration strategy to find out).

HINT

Although implementing permanent links to data stores outside the scope of the bigger programme is a task for the bigger programme to complete as part of target design, when you are working on a phased migration it is often the responsibility of the data migration project to maintain temporary links between data stores that are within the scope of the programme. This should have been covered in the scope statement for the migration project that is part of the data migration strategy.

However, full discovery and cataloguing of interfaces into, out of and within the programme are also due diligence risk mitigation processes to show that the programme has captured everything. You can perform this on behalf of the bigger programme, once again demonstrating your worth.

Even where you are not responsible for interfaces within the data migration project, the source and destination information will help you form an opinion of the likelihood of this data being an appropriate source of data for the new system.

Your use of each store can be direct, in terms of data that enters the ETL flow, or indirect, where you use data from credible data stores as part of the DQR work to validate and enhance data in the main source systems.

HINT

The most accurate data in an organisation is usually that which is of most use to the person responsible for capturing and using it. For example, a salesman's mobile phone will hold better contact information than the corporate CRM for the salesman's customers. You might not be able to access easily mobile phones in salesmen's pockets, but you might consider getting them to update the CRM prior to migration.

Following the links in the system topography will also disclose other data stores that might not have otherwise come to light, which is why, when you document the LDSs, you always ask about where the data came from and where the data goes.

Once again, where this is a significant corporate application there is a very strong likelihood that all this information will be held somewhere else and you do not need to duplicate it here (although as the unofficial data warehouse example showed, you still need to perform due diligence to ensure that all the data spooled off by your ingenious users is reviewed). For the more local LDSs you need to identify the interface, either using its corporate data catalogue identifier or a series you create for the migration. You need to know the source, the destination and the transport mechanism (even if that is via a data stick and rekeying).

- **Degree of detail** – In an ideal world you would go over every LDS to the same degree of detail. In the practical world of data migration, you have to make judgements. At the very least you need to record the LDS identity information and always add the data owner, entities covered and migration status. This can all be accomplished quickly.

PROFILING, DATA GAPS AND MASTER DATA MANAGEMENT

Data quality and data gaps
Data quality challenges are 'business as usual' so far as data migration projects are concerned. Experience tells you that LDSs will have a lot of data gaps.

> **HINT**
>
> As I indicated earlier, try not to use terms like data quality 'problems' too freely. Remember that for many of the people you are talking to, the LDS you are criticising is a labour of love in which they have invested considerable effort. Remember also that the data might have been fine for the limited use for which it was designed; it just does not fit with other LDSs' view of the world. Therefore, try to use phrases like 'data gaps'.

Management of data gaps takes place in the GAM module of *PDMv2*, but obviously you will first encounter data gaps when you look at the LDSs regardless of whether or not you have a target to aim at (and if you have followed the advice above, then you will have started LA prior to the target necessarily being available).

First, though, you need to understand, from a *PDMv2* perspective, the types of gap you encounter in data migrations.

Types of data gap
If you are a devotee of data quality and engage in the various forums for data quality aficionados (as I occasionally do), then you will know that there are as many taxonomies of data error type as there are experts contributing to the debate. *PDMv2* keeps the taxonomy very simple. It has only four types of data gap and each one is structured around where you are likely to encounter that gap.

- **Reality gap** – The data in the data store does not represent reality in the real world.
- **Internal gap** – Some data in the data store does not conform to the data store rules.
- **Migration model gap** – Some data in some LDSs does not conform to the rules for legacy data even where it might conform to the rules of its own LDS.
- **Target model gap** – There are differences between the migration model and the target model.

Within LA, you are concerned with the first three types of gap.

Reality gap

You will often come across data that glaringly does not match the data in the real world. The data in the LDSs can easily fool you by being consistent with all your standard tests. It has all the right values populated consistently, it has all the appearance of something that could exist, but it just doesn't really exist. For example, you have probably experienced the phenomenon of a phantom booking that deprives you of a seat at the theatre or restaurant only to be told later that the place was a third empty. Of course there are also the examples of things of interest to the enterprise that, for some reason, never got recorded in the right place (e.g. patients who never made it onto a patient administration system or hotel rooms that never got properly entered into a booking system). You also know, especially in CRM systems, that there might be duplicate entries for the same entity. Reality gaps are fiendishly hard to find and fix. Actually, with the exception of duplicate people, where software has been developed over the last 30 years to find duplicate name and addresses, most reality gaps can only be fixed with the assistance of the business domain experts via the DQR process.

HINT

You will often hear it said that it is not the responsibility of the data migration team to fix reality gaps. If the data was bad in the LDSs, then it will be bad in the target. Firstly, you will know from the risk aversion policy where your project lies on the 'quality versus time versus budget' matrix. Secondly, for regulated data, you loose credibility if you move data that you know to be unsound. Finally, when people say this to you, check which side of the DMZ they are on and if they represent the data owner. It is far easier to be laissez-faire about things when it is not going to affect you in the future. On the other hand, if it is the data owner speaking, get them to sign off the deviation from the risk aversion policy, and, in alignment with Golden Rules 1 and 2, go with it.

Investigating and fixing reality gaps often involves either physical audits or site surveys. The discussion of how far you are going to tackle reality gaps is one for the DQR module outlined in Chapter 9.

ANECDOTE

As I indicated in an earlier anecdote, the telco migration I was involved with where I was lifting data out of an LDS to put it back into a virtual partition in the same store would not have worked without some data preparation because of corrupt data in the original. However, even if I could have shoe-horned it in somehow, restoring it this way would have created a reality gap that would have caused the system to crash. Sometimes you have to fix reality gap issues even when you do not want to.

Internal gap

Each LDS will have its own internal model of what the data should look like. In the majority of cases these models will be implicit. Even for corporate LDSs, there will be rules hidden in program code that the schema is blind to. There will also be local uses of under-used fields to cover business processes that are not adequately catered for and are also not documented anywhere. There will be historic uses of the store that were once allowed, but now are no longer allowed, that will still be represented in the data. The residue of long-forgotten system crashes and data corruptions will also be present. From a logical point of view, when you draw up a model of what the data should look like, and compare it with what the data tells you, you expect to find variances or data gaps. These are internal gaps (i.e. they are data gaps between what is in the data and what the LDS's view of the world says it should be like).

Migration model gaps

You might also find that the data structures in the silos do not match each other where the LDSs were built to support independent business silos, niche or boundary-case processing (e.g. the processing of orders for prestige or special customers). Why should they? After all they were built at different times, by different people, to support different processes, so it is no wonder that they might end up with different data structures. So how are you going to compare these structures to uncover the differences? *PDMv2* recommends that you consider a migration model.

Why use a migration model?

Let me take a step back. I have argued that in most cases performing LA before having a detailed target reduces risk and increases quality. I have also shown that, in most cases, there will be multiple LDSs for comparison. A moment's reflection assures you that where there are more than two LDSs, then each additional store potentially increases the number of comparisons exponentially. Where there is only system A and system B, you need only compare A with B: one comparison. When you introduce system C, then you need to compare A to B, B to C and C to A, so there are three comparisons. It can get very complicated when you have hundreds (or thousands) of LDSs to look through.

The answer is to create a migration model to which you compare each individual LDS (or at least the ones you have not rejected at your first pass investigation), noting their structural differences at a model-to-model level.

If you do not use a multi-level approach like this, then you risk confusing internal gaps with migration model gaps, which can have a significant impact on your approach to fixing them. Migration model gaps can rarely be fixed in the legacy because to do so would often violate the rules by which the LDS and it attendant business processes operate. The data is not 'wrong' from the point of view of that data store. You are then faced with the prospect of enhancing an LDS that you intend to decommission or fixing the gap in the data migration flow itself. These choices are considered in more detail in Chapter 9 on DQRs.

However, internal gaps can normally be fixed in the LDS because the fix does not violate any of the rules by which the data store operates. The data in question is wrong from the point of view of the LDS where it is held and can therefore be fixed where it is held.

ANECDOTE

An experience I had at a telecom client shows this distinction between internal gaps and migration model gaps in practice. It was quite clear when examining one data store that at some point in the past there had been some sort of processing glitch, either a botched data restore or a production job run twice. A whole bunch of records with the same creation dates had somehow got written to the database twice, in total violation of the data store rules. These needed to be corrected in the LDS. They were just plain wrong.

However, there were also plenty of examples of structural issues because the billing view of the circuits and the engineering views did not match up. Neither was wrong in themselves. They were built for different purposes and served different functions in different points of the sell-design-commission-operate-bill workflow. My migration model made no attempt to resolve them either. It took a largely engineering view, with a few amendments, to note the differences so I could get to work on the internal gaps that needed to be fixed. The migration model gaps were held over until GAM when the target model could be introduced and I could see how these issues had been resolved in the new system.

The final advantage of the migration model approach is that when the target model does finally arrive, you only need to look at the differences between the migration model and the target model because you have already documented the differences between the migration model and the LDSs that are to be your sources. In that final few weeks (or months) of hurly-burly activity you only have one set of differences to analyse from two well-understood models.

This is why the migration model has only to be a 'good enough' model. Obviously the closer you can get it to the eventual target the fewer differences you will find in the final mapping stages. However, you know that in most programmes the target is evolving all the way up to go-live. You are expecting differences so you are not after perfection, just something that you can use as the fulcrum of the migration effort.

When not to use migration models
Migration models are optional within *PDMv2* and do not have to be used where the target model is available. In this situation, it could be said that the target model is the migration model.

ANECDOTE

When I have worked with facilities management houses or software-as-a-service (SaaS) suppliers, they often do not need an intermediary migration model because they have a target defined and built. Similarly, on phased migrations where the migration is geographically based, the first phase might use a migration model, but after that the target is again defined.

However, I have also consulted to an enterprise that performed a facilities management function in the financial services arena. They were importing data into their system on a regular basis (two or three new clients a month). Each client had their own set of products and no two were the same. It therefore made sense for them to create a generic migration model of the target against which differences that persisted over multiple projects could be analysed: the target was configured for each new client and then the differences between generic target (i.e. migration model) and final target were analysed.

Migration models are also an overkill where there are only a few LDSs that exist in silos with limited overlap. Here, the points of contact need to be reviewed for consistency, and there is value in the direct comparison of LDS to LDS.

Modelling the migration model

Remember, migration models are 'good enough' models, but they have to be mostly complete. That is, they have to be models that you can match the candidate legacy data sources against and find the differences. There can be some specialist features that only a single legacy data source will hold that are not replicated on your model. This will be one of the documented differences between the LDS and the migration model. However, all the entities in our conceptual entity model must be represented. A common approach is to take the most dominant LDS (usually the enterprise application around which all the other LDSs cluster) and use that as a model. An alternative is to use an industry-standard canonical model as a starting point. There are models for many industries: some more useful than others. Your data architect will know if you have one or not. Some commercial off-the-shelf (COTS) packages come with a model for your industry, but be warned, these unadorned starter versions of the target, before you add all the bells and whistles, really are trimmed down and will be a long way from where you are starting from or where the configured target will end up. This will leave you with a lot of differences either side of the migration model, and your objective is to get as good a match as you can guess at in your state of incomplete knowledge. Finally, you can take your conceptual entity model and decompose that down one level, or at most two, and create a model.

ANECDOTE

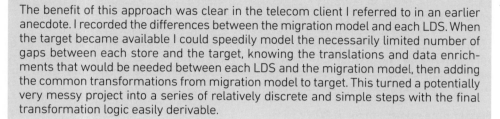

The benefit of this approach was clear in the telecom client I referred to in an earlier anecdote. I recorded the differences between the migration model and each LDS. When the target became available I could speedily model the necessarily limited number of gaps between each store and the target, knowing the translations and data enrichments that would be needed between each LDS and the migration model, then adding the common transformations from migration model to target. This turned a potentially very messy project into a series of relatively discrete and simple steps with the final transformation logic easily derivable.

Instantiating models

So what do I mean by a model? Well, let me be clear right now, this does not have to be a formal entity relationship diagram or a UML model. It could be, of course, if that is the easiest way to get quickly to an analysis of the structural differences between different LDSs or to express your understanding of how an LDS should hold its data. However, with your metadata understanding (that there is structure below the surface appearance of the data you see and which you can model and compare), you can just as readily use working models instantiated in your data quality tools. It is also possible to use a mock-up of the target as suggested earlier. There are problems with the 'throw it at the target and see what sticks' approach to data quality, however, and I discuss these in more detail in the section on testing in Chapter 11. My personal preference is to start with a rapid hand-drawn ERD, then move quickly (by quickly I mean within days) into iterations of discovery that put 'meat on the bones' of (or completely transform your) understanding. The iterations of discovery are best led using profiling tools, but can be done the old-school way of reading schemas, writing SQL scripts, talking to people and looking at screens and reports.

This is where the distinction between reality gaps and internal gaps, on the one hand, and migration model and target gaps, on the other, is important. The first two are about the detail and can be resolved locally to the problem. The second two are about structural differences, which are more general and can only be solved by looking at the bigger picture. Bigger pictures are usually easier to form using the building blocks of the individual legacy models created as level 0 or level 1 ERDs than by trying to reconcile a myriad of local data rules.

HINT

All of the above depends on the scale of the migration, but where you are faced with multiple (hundreds of) LDSs, working at too low a level will swamp you in detail. You might even consider creating migration models for each area of your project decomposition, then bubbling up differences against a project-level migration model.

So to reiterate, internal gaps and reality gaps are best discovered at an LDS model level (i.e. instantiated). Migration model gaps are structural gaps that exist between LDS models, but you simplify the process of uncovering, recording and fixing the gaps by using a migration model.

However, there is a further issue that is not strictly data rules-based, but has a relationship to the reality gap and to the structural issues that your migration model highlights. To address this you need to borrow some techniques from the master data management community.

Master data management in *PDMv2*

Master data management (MDM) has been around for sometime now. It seems that in the building of all those stovepipe solutions and even in the populating of data within the same stovepipe, we have been guilty over the last 30 or more years of failing to ensure that we have followed the classic good design best practice rule of only holding data about each instance of a business entity once and only in one place.

DEFINITION

In the discussion that follows I will be using the terms 'instance' and 'type'. A type is the generic description of an entity; an instance is a particular example of an entity type. So, for example, there is the entity type Author (which could be defined as a person who writes a book) and the entity instance of Johny Morris (who is the author writing this book).

What we have now is a situation where many enterprises find that they have multiple versions of the same entity instance held maybe in the same LDS or maybe across multiple LDSs. The common example is the Customer entity.

ANECDOTE

As an individual you are normally aware of being held more than once in the data stores of companies you do business with when you get a multiple mail shot from them, but this failure to link up the same Customer occurrence in the different data stores can be a real embarrassment when, for instance, an insurance company sends a mail shot to the address of an ex-client on whose demise they have already paid out on an insurance policy. The next of kin can be understandably distressed. It is just such issues that have led to the desire to consolidate LDSs on projects on which I have worked. This driver should be captured in the local policies and point to the need to tidy up these duplicates as part of the data migration exercise.

There are now two typical approaches to solving this problem. The first is to consolidate data stores and cleanse existing data stores where multiple instances of the same entity have been recorded. This activity has, of course, to be tied to process improvements to prevent multiple instances being recreated as soon as one's back is turned. The second approach is to employ MDM technology. MDM comes in as many flavours as there are vendors, so please excuse the simplistic view of MDM presented here, but in essence, a 'one truth' list of occurrences of the target entity is maintained and cascaded out to every data store where that entity type occurs.

ANECDOTE

A desire for a single view of the Customer entity is by far the commonest reason for using MDM technology; however, in migration projects, although consolidating customer information is still the most frequent reason, creating a single list of Products or agreed lists of Business Premises are also often required.

You will often find in data migration projects that you have a similar need to consolidate data from multiple data stores into a single view.

MDM and reality checks

Having multiple instances of the same entity in one or across multiple LDSs is a classic reality check issue. The data looks fine, but it does not coincide with reality. For example, a business might think that it has a million targets in its mailing list, but in reality it only has 750,000; the rest are duplicates. This costs the business money in terms of wasted mail shots and poorer responses to them because customer confidence is lost when a recipient receives multiple copies.

From a data migration perspective, where your initial review tells you that you have a problem, you will, via the DQR module and guided by the risk aversion policy, decide how much effort you are going to put into de-duplication.

MDM and migration model gaps

In cases where you are gathering data from multiple LDSs (and as I have shown, this is the most common scenario), each of which has been created for a different purpose, you will often find that the data has been structured differently.

ANECDOTE

I have often worked in utilities and I always say that if you get four engineers in a room you will get at least five definitions of a single piece of equipment.

The production department's view will be different from that of the financial department, and so on. However, if you are consolidating data into a single data store, then you will need a single view. An MDM approach is especially helpful where the issues are structural. This is because, as I stated earlier, migration model gaps are the least likely to be amenable to a fix in the LDSs between which the problems lie.

The stores themselves will have been created to fit their own view and it is often impossible to rejig them to fit the migration model view.

Data migration and MDM 'lite'

Having said that the MDM approach is useful, let me also say that you are probably not going to be developing a full MDM solution as a mini-project within your own data migration project. Take a look at the objective of MDM.

MDM OBJECTIVE

MDM has the objective of providing processes for collecting, aggregating, matching, consolidating, quality-assuring, persisting and distributing [non-transactional data entities] throughout an organisation to ensure consistency and control in the ongoing maintenance and application use of this information.[14]

How much of this do you need in a data migration project? Keeping in mind that everything you do in a data migration project is transitory, your objective will be limited to collecting, matching, consolidating and quality-assuring. You will only be performing limited aggregation (by which I mean taking the different attributes of entity instances that are scattered through LDSs and combining them into a single image). On a data migration project this is a task that will more likely be performed within the mappings and executed as part of migration design and execution, which is where data items from different LDSs are combined.

I would argue that you will not be distributing data throughout an organisation to ensure consistency and control in the ongoing LDS (our word for 'application') use of this information. You are, as I indicated earlier, on a mission to replace the LDSs and so it is not your job to make them more efficient except as a side product from the data quality activities you do to prepare data for migration. You do have a concern for ongoing maintenance, but only to the extent that as the project proceeds you need to have processes in place to continue the 'collecting, matching, consolidating and quality-assuring' of key entities after your first pass, because you know that during the lifetime of the project the disparate LDSs will continue to grow apart, following, as they do, their own agendas.

- **When to build a data migration MDM solution** – You need to decide if this is the best approach for the project. To some extent this is dependent on the choice of migration model. If there is one towering enterprise application LDS to which you are going to match the other LDSs (i.e. you are using the dominant LDS as a migration model) and you can consolidate the key data items within that data store, then, probably, you will not need a second MDM store. If, however, you have multiple contenders for the leading LDS and there is sufficient overlap of entity types within these stores for you to need an independent migration model, then you probably will need to build a separate MDM.

---

[14] Wikipedia (April 2012). http://en.wikipedia.org/wiki/Master_data_magagement

Each situation is different and you have to judge your requirements on its merits. It could be that there is a single dominant LDS, but it is not possible to amend data within it. It could be that although there are a number of LDSs with equal claims for leadership, there is one for this entity type that is the clear leader. It is up to you to decide.

Like the migration model, the MDM is also a 'good enough' model, especially where you are dealing with structural issues. It is the bigger programme's responsibility to give you the target data structures. It is their job to drive compromise and consolidation of views. You are interested in creating a model that will give you a clear understanding of your migration model and reality gap issues.

However, if it is the reality check that you are targeting (mostly de-duplication, but also often removal of redundant entity instances like part-created customer records that never completed a purchase), then, although the structure does not have to prejudge what the target model will look like, you have to be scrupulous about the content.

This distinction is important. Do not be forever looking over your shoulder at the target as it emerges from the mists of development, reworking your MDM as you go to match the target. Accept that it will be different and make that clear to everyone from the beginning. Resolving these differences is a job for GAM. As before, freeing yourself from dependency on the target allows you to get to work on these issues as soon as the programme is formally initiated.

- **How to build a data migration MDM solution** – *PDMv2* gives you a series of tools that allows you to construct an MDM solution whether you choose to build it around an existing LDS or to build a separate physical transitional data store. As I have shown above, it is unlikely that you will use federation or other complex techniques given the transient nature of the MDM solution you are proposing.

If you are going down the route of a physical data store that will hold the MDM structure and so that pertinent data can be collected, then you need to have it instantiated in a technical solution that is robust enough and well known enough to your technologists for them to create and support. For this reason, and because it is a throw-away application that will last only as long as the project, I usually suggest that you do not employ some new technology (like real MDM software), which involves a learning curve. A fully fledged MDM application will also have the 'persisting' and 'distributing' features that you will not have time to explore or implement. You do not want to waste effort that might be more gainfully directed at finding gaps and supporting the DQR process in resolving them.

Matching entity instances is very much what you are interested in on two levels. On the first level you need to retain the unique identifiers that will allow you to perform an aggregation function during the migration execution. On the second level you need to understand the different semantics by which different LDSs hold matching entity instances and have documented the transformations that are needed between them. This again shows how the MDM and migration model approach have to work hand in hand. It is where the use of formal LDS models help you by abstracting that which looks different into a common language, where real differences can be separated from the apparent differences (which are only present because of different technology).

De-duplication is usually one of your main drivers, and, as in any consolidation exercise, making decisions about which of two or more competing data values to accept is a problem that the DQR process (described in Chapter 9) is designed to resolve. You can also rely heavily on the use of third-party tools to resolve them. The increased sophistication of data quality software designed for discovering and managing data quality issues has greatly aided the DQR process.

You will probably be unable to justify the cost and risk of implementing the 'persistence' and 'distribution' features of fully functional MDM software, so you will have to rely on transitional business processes, backed up by checks on data consistency using data quality software to maintain MDM in line with ongoing data updates in the LDSs. Transitional business processes (see Section 1) are those business processes that are only in place because you are performing a data migration. Now, you will need to construct some and get them briefed out to support your ongoing commitment to keeping the MDM platform up to date.

HINT

Of course, if you are competent in MDM and have spare MDM software licences, then implementing your requirements in an MDM application provides numerous benefits. Just keep at the forefront of your mind that you are only after a 'good enough' solution, not a perfect MDM solution. Do not allow the creation of an MDM platform compromise your delivery dates.

Therefore, by using data quality rules, transitional business processes, gap analysis, technology with which you are familiar, and software designed to be used in integration environments (principally data profiling and data quality), you can collect, aggregate, match, consolidate and quality-assure the key entities you need for the project. In other words, you will be performing only part of the MDM function (by leaving out 'persistence' and 'distribution').

ANECDOTE

I have found that although you are performing all the steps that would be normal in establishing an MDM, you are often forbidden from using that name because somewhere in the organisation a 'real' MDM project is under way. I was working with one client that had a huge number of products that needed cataloguing and aligning across multiple LDSs and I had a functioning MDM solution in place. The team in the organisation that had been charged with implementing its own MDM heard about this and I was very nearly forced to shut down my MDM (which would have been catastrophic for the programme). I just got away with it by renaming my collection as 'reference data'. Once I had finished, the official MDM team were happy to accept what I developed as 'seed corn' for their project.

I suppose the moral of this tale is to be flexible with names and show value by handing back to your colleagues the knowledge you have won.

SOFTWARE TOOLS TO SUPPORT LANDSCAPE ANALYSIS

Software tools that support LA have come on in leaps and bounds over the last few years, and developments are progressing at an equally rapid rate. There is a risk, therefore, that anything I write will be out of date before this book hits the bookshops. I will therefore try to be as generic as possible to give a feel for what software there is and what it can do.

HINT

Software is changing all the time. For the latest data migration software tools and the best ways to use them, visit the website www.datamigrationpro.com and its sister www.dataqualitypro.com. Both are edited by my colleague Dylan Jones (who suggested the term 'landscape analysis' to me for the work I need to do that is wider than, but includes, profiling). Both websites are not aligned to any vendor, but offer sound insights into data quality, profiling and ETL tools in a collegiate, social network setting. Also, have a look at the work of groups like DAMA and IAIDQ that are dedicated to spreading data quality best practice by the collaboration of professionals working in this area.

The key applications for LA are profiling and data quality tools. The difference being that profiling tools are designed to uncover rules in LDSs, whereas data quality tools are designed to check data for compliance with rules they have been given. In LA, you use profiling tools to analyse the LDSs you encounter to help populate the LDS list, build up your metadata understanding of the legacy environment and to generate potential anomalies that will be investigated via the DQR process. You use data quality tools to support MDM activities and this is often the way you instantiate out a migration model that you can then use against individual LDSs to find migration model gaps, which once again will be investigated and controlled via the DQR process.

IMPACT OF THE DMZ

Landscape analysis is predominantly the preserve of the client because of the way modern procurement contracts are drawn up. Even if they are not prejudiced by penalties in the delivery of a data migration, they normally lack the knowledge of the client's LDSs. There are exceptions, however. Increasingly, the more experienced and sophisticated suppliers will offer data profiling services, including de-duplication. However, as I have shown, these are targeted at the corporate LDSs where the tool-based approach can offer substantial benefits. They do not look at the local LDSs, and certainly not at any non-electronic stores. They will not be able to look at reality check issues. Often, they do not offer the same service for looking at the legacy topography. There is always the risk that you get blinded by the reports, from the shiny new tools to the things they can't reach. On the other hand, employing professionals skilled in the use of profiling tools, who analyse the majority of data as it is stored in enterprise applications, generates rules that can be reused in the data quality tools, and gives you DQRs to start work on. Obtaining some far more accurate information for estimating the remainder of the project is something I would strenuously recommend for any but the very smallest of projects. It is something you can do quickly (in a couple of weeks) with the correct tools, and it gives you a kick-start to a project.

CHAPTER REVIEW

In this chapter I have looked at the role of the landscape analysis module within *PDMv2*. I covered legacy data store discovery, documenting and analysis, and the definition and roles of key data stakeholders. I covered the use and instantiation of data models and their role in gap analysis. Finally, I looked at the growing use of master data management techniques in *PDMv2*.

8   SYSTEM RETIREMENT PLAN

In this chapter I introduce you to system retirement plans and demonstrate how they are one of the essential Super SMART Tasks within PDMv2, performing a fundamental role in business engagement as well as providing the user requirements for the migration.

WHY HAVE A SYSTEM RETIREMENT PLAN?

I showed in Section 1 that data migration projects are frequently a psychological challenge to the very people you need to engage with in a migration project. You might need the expertise of the user population to ensure that you do not create the technically perfect data migration that kills the enterprise. On the other hand, the very act of engagement makes the imminent demise of their trusted LDSs apparent, which could alienate them from the project.

You use system retirement plans (SRPs) to force the issue, to make the change real. You encourage rejection so that you speed up the process towards negotiation. You also provide the reasons why you cannot migrate as the starter of a data migration requirements list. Performed correctly, SRPs are a great example of a Super SMART Task in that they build the individual by helping them get a measure of control and influence over the process of change. They also visibly show that you are listening to concerns. SRPs build the team by bringing into your team the data owners, business domain experts and other KDSHs. They crucially help you complete the task by making the project aware of all the local knowledge that you need and do not possess, which covers those areas of which you can have very little knowledge.

SRPs are Super SMART Tasks because they are individual, discrete (simple) tasks with concrete (measurable) deliverables that can be delivered (achievable) by normal project workers (realistic) in a planned way (timely).

WHAT ARE SYSTEM RETIREMENT PLANS?

DEFINITION

A system retirement plan documents the user-side requirements of a data migration that will allow a legacy data store to be decommissioned.

This definition, although correct, needs to be thought through from a user's perspective. Firstly, SRPs have to be tangible in a way that that data owners and business domain experts can access. I will include some suggestions regarding this later on, but it is a topic that needs to be resolved in advance when you devise the library services and in conjunction with the business engagement lead. Secondly, you need to document all the things you need to have in place before you can decommission an LDS that is essential to a crucial business process. Obviously, as I showed in Chapter 7 on landscape analysis, not all LDSs are equal. You will dismiss some (the majority, in most cases) at first appraisal as derivative and not to be migrated. Others might contribute by confirming data that will be migrated from elsewhere, used to enrich data or fill in data gaps during migration. Normally, only a crucial few will be the basis of the migration and demand the full treatment.

HINT

As a technologist and project person, you can probably think of more categories to include in the SRP than your business counterparts. Use the following suggested headings as a starter and be ready to accept others. It builds trust if you can suggest things that the business has not thought of. It shows that you are genuinely committed to making the transition as smooth as possible.

You are after an organised list of requirements that you must fulfil before you can migrate the data and turn off the LDSs. The following checklist is a minimum requirement. Be open to negotiation because it is all part of the Super SMART Task. Start with the reasons why you cannot migrate and turn these into requirement statements. Never accept a partial list, which gives the data owner the right to come back later with more reasons for not migrating. Try to get your business colleagues to come up with at least one requirement for each heading. Do not worry about getting some trivial requirements that do not make it beyond a first consideration, often these are the indicators of your business partner's naturally negative response to change. Bringing them out and writing them down is often all that is needed to consider them before dismissing them.

HOW AND WHEN TO IMPLEMENT SRPS

The data owners should be the first people you speak to once the project is mobilised, and SRPs should be the first thing you discuss with them. However, as I have said before, you must expect that you will come across some LDSs after you have already commenced your formal engagement activities (perhaps even run a few DQR cycles etc.). In principal, however, the first engagement you have with a data owner should concern system retirement, not data quality (or mapping).

HINT

I find in practice that this is less of an issue in reality than it might appear. Those people already engaged with the migration will be expecting to create SRPs when they disclose their LDSs. Those who are not will more than likely have heard of them and will, in any case, be confronted with an SRP meeting as their first point of engagement. Use your relationships with the business readiness team you identified when you were creating the data migration strategy to get the message out that system retirement planning is on its way as part of the project.

Three visits

You will visit the data owners at least three times when you come to create and sign off SRPs.

HINT

Arrange a face-to-face meeting if you can, especially for the first meeting. SRPs are as much about building a relationship as they are about gathering requirements. Expect to have to cajole and encourage full disclosure from reluctant data owners who might just be wishing you would go away. This is where you might need some executive sponsors to lean on a few people. Make sure they are briefed and understand why you need SRPs completed now.

Always insist that an SRP is signed off, by whatever means that is accomplished in your project environment. This is the data owners' commitment that they have asked for everything they need you to do to enable them to sign eventually the final decommissioning certificate.

You will meet the data owners again at the end of GAM to check that what has been designed meets their requirements (there are some variations in precisely when each of the headings can be signed off, see below). Again you will expect a signature. This is the point where the reality of what can be delivered for the budget, technology and time available, will come up against the desires expressed in the first pass SRPs.

HINT

I find it useful to say in the first SRP meeting that I will, of course, endeavour to deliver everything on the list, but that I have to be realistic in terms of what is possible and that compromises might be called for. This is being honest. Most people appreciate that. However, I make it clear that where one of the requirements is challenged then I will be back to them to discuss the possible impact of competing requirements.

Finally, you will see the data owners at least one more time: once the target has been built and testing is complete (including migration testing). This third sign-off is the decommissioning statement that gives you the go-ahead to complete the migration and shut down their LDSs.

HINT

Where there is user acceptance testing (UAT) after the physical migration, there might be an additional sign-off, after the testing, but before migration takes place, to confirm that it is OK to initiate the data migration. The decommissioning sign-off then occurs (possibly) after some parallel running, indicating that the LDSs can now be turned off. This is all dependent on the form of migration and how cleanly you can roll back if post-migration UAT fails.

I will now discuss the minimum headings that go into an SRP.

SRP MINIMUM REQUIREMENTS

Training
Although training on the target is the responsibility of the bigger programme, it is worth checking that the business is getting the levels of training it thinks it needs. Often, there are activity silos being consolidated and there is a requirement for awareness training (as opposed to full-on training) in different areas that might not have been picked up. There is also a recognition by data owners that their team might not need training in a particular area, but that they would like to be informed that a department or function on which they depend is satisfied with the training it has received. All of this is easily accomplished, because you will, of course, have the SRPs for the other areas as well.

The most significant issue you need to resolve is the length of the training lag and whether it will have an impact on your chosen migration form.

DEFINITION

The training lag is the length of time it takes to train all the staff who need to be trained in the target system.

The training lag impacts you when it takes months to complete the training for a large number of groups. The risk is that the first group will have forgotten what they have been told, or you migrate before the last group have been trained. The length of the training lag might force you to consider a phased migration, when a big-bang migration would have been your preferred choice.

Testing

Testing is covered in a sub-module of the MDE module. UAT is specific to the SRP. Remember you are asking the question: 'How do I know that when I decommission this application that you will still be able to carry on with your business function?' Part of that answer, of course, is that the target has been tested. Here, however, you have to be careful. The responsibility for the target solution is with the bigger programme. You are testing that the data has arrived complete and usable in the right place. So, in that sense, you are looking only at a subset of UAT.

On the other hand, as I will show when I look at data retention, it is likely that the data migration team will be responsible for the archiving solution, and this needs to be tested just as thoroughly as the target. You need to establish a close relationship with the programme testing team. This is something you should have covered in the data migration strategy. You need to have access to the test plans and test areas so that you can assure the business, before the migration, that the data will indeed migrate to where it wants it, in a format that remains useful to it. You need to align your acceptance testing with their tests. This is where you really benefit from a dress rehearsal or dummy load of live data into a test instance of the target. It gives the business domain experts the chance to see the data as it will look in the target and to interact with it.

Firstly, an SRP needs to specify that the business wants to perform its own tests to confirm it is satisfied with the migration. Secondly, you devise your tests (including those for archiving, data audit and data lineage) as you gain a greater understanding of the nature of the new system. The most common form of testing that a business domain expert will want to perform for reassurance is also the least scientific, but often the most effective. It is the 'look and feel' test. Selected users are allowed access to the new system after data load, but before the rest of the user community is allowed on, to run their eyes over the screens, and report any anomalies they can find. You can be sure that the business domain experts will do this anyway, whether you formally sanction it or not, so make a UAT test part of the SRPs. Doing this further reinforces the data owners' sense of being part of the team.

Finally, you need to have the tests signed off before you can proceed to decommission the LDSs to which they relate.

HINT

Make your data migration project as good an experience as possible for all the participants (I have stated this elsewhere in this book, but it bears repeating). Involving the business domain experts at go-live is a good way of building the team on which your success depends. You might not experience any benefit from it directly if, like me, you move on immediately to other projects, but it helps the next guy down the pike.

Data retention

Some data your business needs at hand all the time; some data they need to call for if it is required; some data they need only if a regulator asks for it; some data they no longer have any need for at all. The question when it comes to your data migration is: how do you categorise your data? The technologists and the business will have different views and you need to get agreement.

From a project perspective, the less data you need to migrate the better. Less data means less data cleansing, faster transfer times and a less cluttered system. The older the data that you try to migrate, the more likely you will encounter data issues associated with changes to validation.

The business is likely to want to carry over everything 'just in case', but there might also be edge cases where old data needs to be looked at (for instance, if there is a regulatory inquiry over a complaint). The business will also be required, for regulatory reasons, to retain some records for a long time after their business usage date (e.g. detailed tax records that need to be kept for seven years).

What is needed is an understanding of how data items are accessed and with what urgency over time. In other words, the data that needs to be online, the data that needs to be near online and the data that can be offline are determined by the frequency the data is accessed and the acceptable length of time (whether or not this is captured in a key performance indicator) you are allowed in order to retrieve it. These conditions change with the age of the data item, for example an order that is being delivered and billed now needs to be online with immediate access; an order that has been delivered and billed two months ago might need to be stored in a reporting database so that it can be retrieved in case there is a warranty enquiry; the billing details of an order that is out of warranty might need to be kept in offline storage for a further period in case there is a tax enquiry (such enquiries are rare and you will get plenty of notice and time to prepare accounts).

Armed with this kind of understanding, and tackling the problem when there is plenty of time for discussion, means that you will make sensible decisions. It is all too common for the data migration analyst to arrive on a troubled project and find the technical side and the business side almost at war over the amount of data to migrate. This is due to a misunderstanding on the part of the data migration project. Your task is to decommission the LDSs. All the data that is in those data stores will either by migrated or lost. Data that it is necessary for the business to retain must be migrated somewhere, but it does not have to be to the target system. Once you have resolved the data retention requirements for different classes of data you can feed that into your decommissioning design sub-module (which is part of the MDE module).

ANECDOTE

Archive design, build and test are often an afterthought in many system implementations that have their emphasis on the delivery of the new system. This is so much so that I have often been called on to migrate a system where the previous generation of system is still there in the background, still running and being paid for because the previous migration ran out of money before they could build an archive solution. There are even apocryphal tales of three generations of systems still taking up server room space and valuable operating budgets.

Data audit and data lineage

Data audit and data lineage are related, but they are not quite the same.

DEFINITION

Data audit is the verifiable proof that all the units of migration in the legacy data stores are accounted for in the migration.

In other words, you can show that all the Customers in an old CRM package migrated to the new CRM, or have been removed as duplicates, or are old Customers that you are no longer interested in or are Customers records with too many data irregularities to migrate. Data audit is often done using control totals.

DEFINITION

A control total is either the sum of some meaningful value within the data being transferred or a count of the number of units of migration being transferred.

For data migration, control totals are normally restricted to a count of records rather than adding up the values in a particular field. The count will be performed once in the LDS, then again in the new system. The two values should be the same (less, of course, the records not migrated for the reasons identified above).

HINT

This is not always so straightforward. As I will show when I look at data mapping in the GAM module, one record in an LDS might become many in the new system or vice versa. The calculation then becomes trickier. You need to work with the data store owner and business domain expert to devise a set of control totals that make sense both from a technical as well as an enterprise viewpoint.

An example of the above is where you are migrating an accountancy application. Here it is rare that the same chart of accounts will be replicated in the target as it was in the legacy. It is more usual to use account balances to so show that nothing has been lost, added or changed during the migration.

Data lineage is the more detailed tracking of what has happened to each individual unit of migration as it passed through the various stages of the migration, from being extracted from the source, to being loaded into the target. Sometimes this is necessary because the transformations and enrichments that go on during the journey from source to target are so complex that you need to retain intermediary values to enable you to fall back if you need to (I will deal with fallback below). However, for the purposes of the SRP you need to find out if there are any regulatory or other reasons why more information about the journey is needed than a simpler control total count.

ANECDOTE

Electronic, contractual relations that have to be retained for legal purposes are the commonest reason I have come across for the need to implement data lineage controls.

Go-live restrictions (windows of opportunity)

Most business processes go in cycles. There might be a statutory reporting cycle, with a big hiatus at financial year-end when after a mad rush to process as many orders as possible the world stops while the business waits for the year-end processes to run. However, there are other cycles as well. Spaces of time exist within those cycles when you can get access to the strategic LDSs from which you will be getting large amounts of data. It is quite often this window that determines the timeframe within which you operate.

ANECDOTE

It is not just the business cycle that can determine the end date of a project. Long bank holiday weekends are another favourite time for migration exercises. I'm sorry to say that the quiet days between Christmas and New Year are often my busiest period, when most staff are off and there is plenty of spare capacity on machines. Like great chefs, data migration experts often work hardest when their clients are enjoying themselves!

Being tied to a window of opportunity is one of the many reasons why data migration projects are so often time-based. You cannot afford to overrun when it might be 12 months before the ideal time comes around again. You must be ready on the night.

ANECDOTE

I have found the summer months are generally a bad time to plan large-scale business engagement activities in Northern European countries. Every other person is away on holiday. Some clients even have a moratorium on implementations in August.

In addition to windows of opportunity that are well known within a whole business, there are also times that are no-go for local reasons (e.g. there might be conferences that drag all the client-side KDSHs away; there might be reporting cycles that detract from availability). Find out what the worst times are for the data owners.

Remember, at least at first, that you are happy to be given all the reasons why the migration cannot go ahead.

Windows of opportunity are usually revealed on the first pass, although one-off events might appear at any time in the life of the project to prevent you from acting when you would like.

Customer experience

You include 'customer experience' in an SRP for several reasons.

Firstly, because you want to be pro-business and it is the customers who ultimately pay all of our wages. It is also a less arrogant approach.

Secondly, meetings between the technical side and the business side are often couched in technical terms and neither side thinks to ask about the impact on customers unless there is a prompt. You need to know if there are any customers who need special attention (e.g. the biggest customers or the ones who can cause the most trouble if you get it wrong). You need to know if there are customer groups that you can network with to increase the power of the virtual team. Most of all, you need to be aware of what the impact of your activities are going to be on the customers.

ANECDOTE

I have plenty of tales about how changes that were genuinely well intentioned have backfired. From the consolidation of billing dates that nearly brought down a helpline, to the redesigning of bills that led to thousands of billing complaints being automatically generated by a customer's electronic billing reader that had not been reprogrammed. One obscure example I remember well regarded the payment dates for landlords and the impact this had on windows of opportunity in a social-care migration. Nobody thought of them as customers of the system because they were not the *raison d'être* for the group I was migrating.

Inclusion of the customer is another example of a Super SMART Task. It gives you knowledge of any constraints that you could not be aware of any other way; it helps build the individual by reassuring the business-side KDSHs; and it builds the team by bringing into the team the views of one of the most important groups in any business.

Taking on board the customer will save you considerable embarrassment later, I assure you. It is also an area where no amount of technology can help.

Fallback

You should not consider going ahead with a data migration project without a fallback plan. Although you will have prepared for all eventualities there is always the unexpected that can stop the migration in its tracks. It might be an environmental event (like flooding), a technical problem (like a key supplier going out of business and so failing to provide you with support in time), or logistical (like transport strikes preventing KDSHs being available at the right place at the right time). This is in addition to the small possibility that something you do on the project might go wrong.

ANECDOTE

I have never had to invoke a fallback plan on any migration on which I have been involved, but I would not like to go into a migration without one.

What you want in the first-cut SRP is a statement of the boundaries of fallback. Which parts of the systems are essential from the moment the target is switched on for the first time? What are the most essential parts of the processing that must be supported? Which parts can be delayed in the absolutely worst case? Who will need to be part of the discussions? Who will need to be informed? If you have to fall back how can you be certain that the data has not been changed in the process?

This information is fed into migration design, out of which will come a fully configured technical fallback plan that is based on the requirements.

ANECDOTE

On more than one occasion I have had to prepare a 'fall forward' plan. Once, where the migration was being implemented for a regulatory compliance reason and more than once where I was involved in de-mergers. In the first case, my client had to be compliant by a particular date or faced severe penalties, possibly the loss of their licence to trade if the new system was not in place. In the second, there is often a date written into de-merger contracts of when you have to have exited the previous partner's systems. If you haven't they will simply cancel your access and wipe the data. In both cases I created 'fall forward' plans that meant that the business processes might have been ugly and inefficient, but they would have been tenable and the business could have continued with its data secure to try again with on another day.

Resources

You need to understand what personnel and physical resources are going to be needed from the business side so that you can plan for them and make sure that they are available. You know that you will need to get sign-offs at various points. Who are the people who will do this? Who are the people who will be supporting the DQR process? Whose opinion will the data owner rely on to confirm that they can sign the decommissioning certificate?

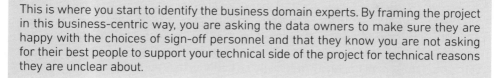

HINT

This is where you start to identify the business domain experts. By framing the project in this business-centric way, you are asking the data owners to make sure they are happy with the choices of sign-off personnel and that they know you are not asking for their best people to support your technical side of the project for technical reasons they are unclear about.

In your first pass discussions around the SRP, you will be given a list of business domain experts and business-side technical data experts that will almost always be incomplete. As your work progresses, you will inevitably find that you need to reach out to other business domain experts to fill in detail, especially in the DQRs process. The list of business domain experts, therefore, grows with the project.

You then have to make sure that you are aware of any constraints on the availability of these resources and plan accordingly, especially in your cutover planning.

You also need to know about physical resources. Will you need access to local PCs and, if so, do you have the passwords? Will you need access to certain buildings and, if so, do you have the relevant keys and alarm codes?

Unit of migration

You must agree the units of migration with the business so that you can express yourselves in their terms. Remember, units of migration are the lowest level of granularity from the business perspective that it makes sense to report on. It might be that you will be migrating at Customer level, so if a single order fails the whole Customer is rolled back. It might be that you roll back at Order level, so as long as each Customer has at least one order, they can be migrated. Units of migration can be compounded so that it is possible to report at Order and Customer level. Whatever you choose, you need to confirm that it is meaningful to the business.

You need to get a first-cut view of units of migration at your earliest interviews. They do not often change from a reporting perspective as the project progresses, but compromises are often accepted in what you will be allowed to count as a complete migration of a unit of migration. To stick with my example of Customers and Orders, if Customer is your top-level unit of migration, you will often find that, as you get into the detail and find those Orders that have complex issues, you will be allowed to migrate Customers even if all the Orders beneath them can not be migrated, provided, of course, that you have a plan for how to manage the orders that are not migrated.

Another challenge you will face is that different data owners will prioritise units of migration differently.

HINT

An example of this might be where you have a dispersed geographical network with customers who can have dealings with more than one geographical area. From a CRM perspective it might be advisable to migrate customer by customer, thereby keeping each customer in only one system, but from a practical perspective, especially where you have a phased migration form, it might be better to migrate whole customer within geographical area.

Transitional business processes

Transitional business process are, as I mentioned earlier, those business activities that only occur because a data migration is occurring. They might be to do with how you deal with 'in-flight' transactions that start in LDSs, but have to complete in the target. They might be to do with how you manage fallout and fallback. I usually include them in the SRP because that is the key business-facing document. These days, with document management systems, which allow more loosely coupled documentation than the old monolithic tomes once produced, it is possible to link to them from within the SRP as opposed to having them physically present. (This is something to resolve when you plan your library services.) Even so, it is still worth bringing them up in the first SRP meeting so that the data owners start to visualise and plan for how they are going to manage the migration in terms of organisation and personnel.

Decommissioning certificate

From everything I have said so far, it should be clear that the decommissioning certificate needs to be front and foremost in everybody's mind. Whether you have a physical certificate or just make it plain that the last sign-off is the point of no return is down to your sense of drama and to the imaginative powers of the data owners.

SRPS AND SUPER SMART TASKS

A combination of KDSH management and SRPs prevents a data migration from spiralling out of control due to a series of late challenges to the migration. SRPs are essential to the completion of the mapping and to the migration design and execution.

SRPs build the individual by helping your business colleagues to support the project by getting all their fears, well founded or not, off their chests. You are doing more that just listening to them: you are suggesting all sorts of headings they have not even thought about, reassuring them that you know what you are doing and that their precious data is safe.

SRPs get you your business domain experts. Having made the migration real to the data owners, when you get to the subject of UAT and sign-off you will get the level of business domain expertise that the data owners deem necessary.

SRPs are also SMART. They can be planned for once you have uncovered all the LDSs. They have concrete deliverables that can be tracked. They are eminently sensible because they bring into the project knowledge you could not obtain any other way and that is essential to delivering your objective.

IMPACT OF THE DMZ ON SRPs

The client is always responsible for delivering SRPs. This is not to say that you cannot outsource the legwork of going around the data owners to carry out the interviews. Indeed trained, bought-in, resource can be ideal for this. However, in the classic client–supplier relationship, this activity is so dependent on the engagement of the data owners that, although you can outsource the activity, you cannot outsource the responsibility.

CHAPTER REVIEW

In this chapter I have looked at system retirement plans in some detail: at what they contain; why you need them; when and how you develop them; and how you document them.

9   DATA QUALITY RULES

In this chapter I introduce you to a key tool: data quality rules. I will show you:

- *how to construct them;*
- *how to use them;*
- *where to use them;*
- *what a well-constructed data quality rule looks like.*

INTRODUCING DATA QUALITY RULES

Data quality rules (DQRs) are central to *PDMv2*.

- They keep ownership firmly in the hands of the business (Golden Rule 1).
- They expose to the project the knowledge hidden in the business (Golden Rule 2).
- The process of deriving them ensures that the business addresses time and resource limitations (Golden Rule 3).
- They form a contract between the business and the technicians about what constitutes quality data and how to go about securing it (Golden Rule 4).

On a well-run data migration project, you will spend far more time, effort and resource on DQRs than on any other activity. So what are they?

DEFINITION

Data quality rules are a set of processes and deliverables that are used to measure the quality of the data within a data migration project and to resolve or mitigate data quality issues.

I have intentionally overloaded the definition of a DQR to include the process, the steps within the process and the deliverables, both individually and collectively. This overloading is not a problem in practice. Bearing in mind that a business population is in a state of flux, adding more terminology to distinguish between a

DQR as a business rule and a DQR as a project template, only serves to confuse. Your aim is to make 'DQR' part of the vocabulary of a data migration project. A single definition means that you will not be faced with data stakeholders presenting you with 'data problems' that you need to solve. They will be requesting additional DQRs, but, as I will show when I look at the DQR process, they will have accepted the necessity of business involvement in the resolution. They will have become part of the solution: the one virtual team that delivers the data migration.

HOW DO YOU GENERATE DQRS?

DQR are principally created in the LA, the GAM and the MDE modules of *PDMv2*, but in reality this means just about anywhere: at the water cooler; during a conversation about target system design; in SRP interviews etc. This is one of the main reasons that you need to have a single, clear, unequivocal route to inform the project about data quality issues. You want to prevent the project being riddled with multiple locations of data quality information that makes it impossible to form a single picture of what the data readiness is and when you will reach the threshold of acceptability in time to migrate as planned. Every gap that gets revealed needs to go straight into the DQR process, even if the solution is self-evident. DQR is a set of forms, a DQR board and a process (as shown in Figure 9.1). Following the process flow will allow me to show you each of these in turn.

Figure 9.1 The DQR process

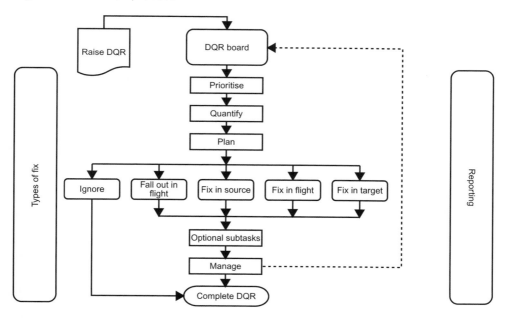

THE DQR PROCESS

Raise DQR
Every data quality, selection or preparation issue should have a DQR. I cannot over-stress the importance of this. There should be no other repositories on the project: not in requirements documents, not in functional specifications and certainly not in code. I have given some suggestions below on how to manage this.

DQR board
I have outlined below the composition of the DQR board, but it will have equally weighted input from the business side, from the project team, from the legacy technical data experts and the target technical data experts. It will be chaired by a data migration analyst and its role is to arbitrate between the differing perspectives of the relative importance of, and the most appropriate solution to, data-related issues.

Prioritise, quantify, plan and manage
The DQR board has four tasks to accomplish: prioritising, quantifying, planning and managing. They are shown as sequential tasks in Figure 9.1, but in reality they are interrelated and might be concurrent.

- **Prioritise** – You know that on all but the simplest data migration project you will have to prioritise activities because you will uncover more issues than you can hope to accomplish to the tight deadlines that are demanded by the business. This prioritisation must balance the demands of the target with the requirements of the business.

ANECDOTE

It is usually the case in traditional techno-centric migrations that the concerns of the project and the target take precedence over the concerns of the business, but with often disastrous consequences. I have seen, from the inside, a company that underwent a data migration that was 'successful' from a technical perspective, but then saw its market share fall from number one nationally to number two as the business operatives struggled with misapplied data that caused a haemorrhage of customers to its chief rival.

- **Quantify** – Each DQR needs to be quantifiable so you can comply with Golden Rule 4. You need hard figures to work with to see how you are progressing towards your goal. You need hard figures that you can bubble up through the layers of granularity to your top-level dashboard of data readiness. The DQR board decides what the appropriate metrics for each DQR should be.

- **Plan** – The hard figures you have allow you to plan the steps you will take to deal with any issues raised. You should view each DQR as a mini-project in its own right. By running all the DQRs in the same format, controlled from the same place, you can start to answer the question of just how ready you are to migrate and when you will have crossed the threshold of acceptability that allows you to proceed.

- **Manage** – You have a plan and measurable deliverables, so as a control you can feed back the degree of success you are experiencing. The DQR board will monitor the delivery of a previous DQR as part of the prioritising and planning activities of new DQRs. Quite often a DQR that seemed significant at the start of the process will be downgraded in favour of activity on one discovered later.

Methods

There are five generic reactions to any DQR:

- **Ignore** – It is likely that you will ignore the majority of data quality issues that you encounter. These are generally the low-level reality issues (e.g. missing or clearly wrong telephone numbers). They were a problem that the business never found irksome enough to fix in the LDSs and they will persist into the target because you have bigger issues to resolve.

- **Fix in flight** – This is probably the second most common solution. Here, you might plan to enrich the data with data from a third party or other LDS. You might be going to perform some form of transformation that will correct the data (like defaulting a 'Y' into a Yes/No field where it is blank). Maybe you are going to do something more sophisticated like parsing or consolidating data items. Obviously changes like this must be recorded in your DQR, but you must also pass them on to the team responsible for the design and build of the transformation element of the design. This means that your DQR process has to take into account the DMZ and pass such requirements into the MDE module.

- **Fix in source** – This is the most popular first suggestion of how to fix an issue, but, as I have shown elsewhere in this book, it is not always possible.

- **Fix in target** – You can do two kinds of fixes in the target. Firstly, you can degrade validation in the target, either temporarily or permanently, so that the legacy data can get through. Secondly, you can move the data over, knowing it to be wrong, but with a plan to fix it after the migration. It goes without saying that this fix is a risky option. You need to make sure that you have robust data transitional rules in place to ensure that the data is corrected. This fix means that the data migration project can run on for some time after the physical migration has occurred.

ANECDOTE

I worked on one project (an order processing application) where, because the target software was layered, with an application layer and a database layer (very common these days), I could bypass the application layer and move data straight into the database layer where the validation was less severe. However, when a dubious order entered this way was subsequently retrieved and viewed on screen, it had to be corrected before it could be rewritten to the database. I really had to trust my business colleagues that this would be acceptable to their peers. It is not an approach I would recommend, but two years later, when I spoke to them again, this process of natural quality enhancement had cleansed their data.

- **Fallout in flight** – This might seem an odd fix method, and it is usually reserved as a last resort, but there are occasions when writing and testing code to manipulate the really obscure edge cases is really more costly, and risky, than allowing them to fall out in the migration and then dealing with them manually.

If you consider this fix method, you should determine in advance how many cases you are dealing with (which is another reason why you need quantitative analysis).

ANECDOTE

I first came across the 'fallout in flight' fix on a migration in an engineering environment when a certain type of switch gear had been designed as a series of custom builds. The whole data structure was fiendishly complicated and was represented completely differently in the target. There were less than five types built to this design in a population of hundreds. It was easier, cheaper and less risky to let it 'error out' in migration than to re-input it manually.

HINT

I often say that you can perform zero-defect migrations with *PDMv2* (which is true because I routinely do them). By this, I mean there is no unexpected fallout. Using the fallout mechanism as part of a DQR strategy is 'planned' and is not therefore a defect.

Optional subtasks

The DQR process, as I have outlined it here, is at a high level. It gives an overview of how you are going to deal with a particular issue. Often that is enough (especially if you are using the 'ignore' option), but frequently you need to specify a series of tasks (e.g. the LDS technical data expert will create an extract, then the target technical data expert will provide some enrichment, then the business domain expert will update records in the LDS etc.). In this case, you need to create a series of subtasks: each in the form of a SMART Task with a deliverable, a resource and a delivery date. You can then track them at an individual task level.

Complete DQR

Finally, after possibly going through some iterations at the 'manage' task stage to reprioritise activities, you will complete the DQR. At the end of the project, you will have 'completed' all the DQRs, even those you failed to deliver on, ready to be handed to the in-life data management team (if there is one).

Types of fix

The types of fix available to you adds another dimension to the ways you can (or cannot) correct data quality issues. Each type can be applied to each of the methods listed above.

- **Manual fix** – Altering records in the LDSs, through the front-end screens, is still an excellent way of correcting reality, internal and migration model gaps, providing that the number of records to be corrected are relatively few and the corrections do not require changes to the LDS's application logic. Later I will discuss the software tools that can help you.

As with the fixing methods, often the most economical approach to correcting gaps is to allow records to pass through the migration uncorrected and fix them manually on the target. It is sometimes necessary, in order to fix the gap, to perform a physical audit of the business objects being migrated. You might have to get your business colleagues to go into the warehouse and count shelves or into the server room to list racks. There might be no other way of getting data to the correct degree of accuracy. The audit data might be entered directly into existing LDSs, but you can also find yourself creating transitional data stores to hold the data for the duration of the migration, especially where there is a target model gap of a data element or relationship that you have not needed to collect information on before. Be warned, though, manual activity takes time and effort, usually by front-line staff that are hard-pressed already with their day job.

ANECDOTE

In my experience, for every business colleague you meet who will shirk activity they could easily accomplish, there will be another three who will overestimate the amount of work they can do on top of their own work. Be prepared to allow more time than is requested by them, but never discourage them. This is a good reason for starting as early as possible so that everyone gets a feeling for what can be accomplished in the environment in which you all work.

- **Automated fix** – You can automate gap fixes in the LDSs, often more easily than you can in the target. This is, of course, fraught with risk and will often need its own test cycle (although I have worked in many environments where 'clean up' jobs are routinely run by internal IT). Once again, this is most often used for reality, internal and migration model gaps.

The whole ETL journey gives you plenty of opportunities to automate data transformation:

  o You can implement exclusion rules on extract for data items that you have decided you will not be picking up for migration. This is one way of physically implementing 'ignore' or 'fix in target' methods.

  o You can create transformation rules that allow you to manipulate data and so fix data gaps. This is the commonest way of correcting target model gaps.

  o You can create validation rules that will exclude data (there should, of course, be nothing you have not planned for).

  o You can also create load rules that allow you to deal differently with 'ignore' and 'fix in target' methods or with target gaps in general.

145

I showed in Chapter 7 on LA that you can consider the use of MDM techniques when analysing and fixing structural and data value issues within legacy data. These are clearly a form of technology and can be used during the ETL journey to validate or to correct data in the transformation stage.

Similarly, you might use third-party data. Often this comprises postal address files for name and address fixing, but it might also be industry-sanctioned lists for confirmation with industry canonical models. (Third-party lists can be used both in an automated or manual fashion.)

You should consider all the options available to you for a DQR, whether automated or manual (or a combination of the two) and for whatever method, when using MDM or other transitional data stores. You need as broad an input into the decision-making process as possible, both from the technical side and from the business side. This has an impact both on the position of the DMZ and on the composition of the DQR board.

Reporting

One of *PDMv2*'s strengths is that you can provide project reports with all the levels of detail required for a major project or for a smaller local project. As I have already mentioned, starting at the lowest level of granularity, an individual DQR is a SMART Task (or collections of SMART Tasks) in its own right. A DQR is tracked through the DQR board, with late-running tasks highlighted for investigation, reprioritised against a new DQR and so on. You need a clear escalation path to the main programme's risks and issues register for cases where the issues cannot be resolved within the DQR board.

HINT

As I indicated earlier, DQRs are kept in their own repository, not held in the bigger programme's risks and issues register. You should only flag up the exceptional one or two DQRs that are either going to have a huge impact on the programme or where the board cannot reach agreement, not the hundreds of activities that will be progressed as data migration 'business as usual' tasks.

You should be reporting to the programme board the percentage of units of migration that you predict will migrate successfully today, next week and by the date of the planned migration. To do this you need to be able to group DQRs such that the metrics can be accumulated by unit of migration. You need to plan additional activities into the data analysis that generates a quantitative statement. This allows you to report on the individual unit of migration identifiers, so that you can accumulate the numbers of units of migration that will not migrate. This is because DQRs are often layered (e.g. a single customer might have a bad address and an invalid credit rating, but these might be the subject of different DQRs). The alternative is to put all the DQRs into a data quality engine that will validate all the rules against all the source data. This is one of the benefits of using a data quality tool. If you do not take these steps there is the danger of overstating the number of units of migration at risk of not migrating by taking the count from each individual DQR. There is also the risk of underestimating the scale of data quality challenges if units of migration are put into a validation-type engine where records are rejected at the first validation failure. This is the reason why using a mock load approach to data quality (or as I less charitably refer to it 'throw the data at the database and see what sticks' approach) is highly risky. One data quality challenge can hide a second and a third and so on. I will return to this theme when I look at testing strategies in the MDE module.

From a DQR (or even from individual DQR tasks at the lowest level), you can build up a picture by key business data area, by business function, by unit of migration type, and by any combination of these. As part of the creation of the data migration strategy, you need to have considered the reporting aspects that the programme is going to need. It is easier to plan this in advance than retrofit it, but following the DQR process will give you the lowest level information that will allow you to build the rest.

Reporting warning

The full picture of where you are and how much activity there is to do to get your data to the right level in time for migration will only appear toward the end of LA. Up to this point you are in discovery mode and will not have a concrete figure. The problem is that with each successive discovery your data readiness appears to be getting worse. You might need to prepare the senior management for this, or even not publish a data readiness projection until the figure stabilises. Getting to the desired migration readiness threshold in the time available can also be helped by revisiting the risk aversion (or 'quality versus time versus budget') policy to see which of those parameters you can flex. You can always exercise the 'ignore' method more often than you planned. At least you will be in a position to start the conversation early, armed with facts to argue your case.

ANECDOTE

In my experience it is nearly always the case that once you get your business colleagues engaged in a proper peer-to-peer conversation, with everybody working as a single virtual team towards the same objective of a workable target system, that the 'ignore' option gets exercised far more frequently than in the early stages of the engagement.

HOW A DQR BOARD WORKS

Solving data challenges on a data migration project is all about teamwork.[15] You need the data analysts' expertise to uncover most of the internal, migration model and target model gaps. You need your business colleagues to tell you about all the reality gaps and some of the internal and migration model gaps. You need the target technical data experts to explain and document the target model (they might also

---

[15] Teamwork is needed on any data quality initiative, but with migration you have the compelling event of imminent system demise to help you with buy-in.

help with target model gaps, see the paragraphs on the DMZ that follow). If you are looking at manual methods of fixing, then you will certainly need the business domain experts, often supported by internal technical data experts who will build transitional data stores and run reports to help. You will need technical data experts on both sides of the DMZ to explain what is possible and what it will cost in budget and effort to perform the automated methods of resolving DQR. You will need the input of target technical data experts when you come to reducing temporarily the validation thresholds for aged data. You need everyone's input into prioritising which DQR to pursue and which to leave on the DQR register as unresolved.

No one voice should take priority. It is often the case that the voices of the technical data experts become loudest: the results are the kinds of data migrations that hit the news headlines for all the wrong reasons. Using DQRs and the DQR board properly will prevent this from happening.

Constitution of a DQR board

The DQR board is made up of business representatives in the form of business domain experts, technical system experts for both the LDSs and the target, and, optionally, other KDSHs (covered below). The board will be chaired by a data migration analyst. I will cover each of these roles below. Remember, you are trying to build a team and build individuals, as well as complete the task. At the end of the day, though, you will get who you are given and have to do the best you can with them. You can push and try to persuade, but adhering to Golden Rules 1 and 2 means that if you have had the SRP discussion with the data owners and they are still willing to give you only a business analyst as a business domain expert, then that is what you must use.

- **Business domain experts** – As I outlined in Chapter 6, business domain experts and the data owners who sit above them are the key groups with whom you have to engage if you are to have a smooth data migration. The business domain experts must have delegated authority to suggest possible fixes and to agree priorities for the DQRs and at least to commit some resource (probably their own) into manual fixes. Their key attributes are an up-to-date knowledge of how the business works today with the LDSs you are discussing. They will know all the workarounds, hidden LDSs and the undisclosed data issues of which the technical data stakeholders might be unaware. They also need to make a commitment to turn up for the meetings, but, as I will show, gaining this can be easier than you might think. Of course, in a large and complex enterprise, no one can be an expert in all parts of a business process. The best business domain experts can tap into that unofficial network of personal connections that run most enterprises to find the right person for you.

- **Technical data experts** – These take a number of forms.

  - **LDS technical data expert** – You obviously need to know about what goes on under the bonnet of an LDS and for that you need access to LDS technical data experts. They are not the same as business domain experts. Although a business analyst who has spent most of their working life building systems in a particular department might be extremely well informed, unless they are on the staff budget of that department, they will not be seen by their business peers to be one of the staff. Ideally, you want front-line workers.

- Target technical data expert – This is one group that you rarely have a problem identifying. From the very outset of the bigger programme, through the appointment of suppliers and letting of contracts, there will have been a focus on getting expertise on this new technology into the programme. However, it is often the case that the workload, on the supplier side of the DMZ, is split into a number of parts. There are the technical data experts who understand how the target works, and there are technical data experts who understand the ETL software. You need access to both groups. This has implications for the DMZ and how this is represented in the contract (see below).

- Other technical data experts – There are a mass of technical data experts who are outside the programme proper, but whose skills you need to call on from time to time, such as network engineers, platform providers, direct memory access experts etc. You will need to add these people to the KDSH list, but they will not take part in the regular DQR meetings, and will be invited only where a DQR task requires their input.

- **Other experts** – There are other peripheral groups, like audit and regulatory experts and data architects, who you might want to include on an irregular basis. It might seem like data architects should always be involved, but, if you do, you will be spending most of your time discussing low-level details that are below their level of interest. However, you know your migration, so you will be able to ascertain what degree of involvement they should have.

- **Data migration analyst** – The board is chaired by a data migration analyst. This 'Jack of all trades' has to have sufficient technical understanding to be able to engage with the technologists, but enough business-facing skill to communicate technical issues to business folk. The chair of a DQR board has to be independent. Obviously in the hurly-burly of a highly creative meeting, they are allowed to throw in their suggestions, but the key to success is to be the facilitator not the leader. This is challenging because, at first, the business side will typically look to the data migration analyst to take the lead. It might be surprising, but for many on the business side this might be their first experience of being listened to. They need permission and encouragement to speak.

The data migration analyst is also responsible for the organisational details: calling meetings, taking and publishing minutes, publishing agenda, updating management reports, updating the DQR forms etc.

HINT

These days few organisations insist on formal minutes. Once running properly the DQR board is self-reporting. The updated list of DQRs are a record of what was decided and you will have a standing agenda, similar to the one below, that will only need minor adjustments. I tend to send out a quick bulletin of the key decision points as well, as a sign of commitment.

Size of a DQR board

There is a limit to the number of people who can usefully contribute to any discussion. This is something to bear in mind when you are considering the key business data areas as part of the data migration strategy proposal. Attendance will start to drop off if a board is too big and most of the discussions are around issues that relate to only one part of the business. Therefore you often have to create a number of DQR boards across a project. A 'board of boards', meeting less frequently (perhaps monthly), can resolve resource conflicts and get confirmation from the business that the balance of DQR activity reflects the whole business. You are also more likely to get input from busy, senior data owners to this more executive-style overview meeting. This group will not want, or have time, to go through the DQR list; that is a job for the lower level boards. Instead, there should be a briefing at the entity or unit of migration level, describing pinch points, data readiness and general direction.

Running a DQR board

As I have shown, the DQR board essentially prioritises high-level plans and manages DQRs. It is not about solving issues (tempting as that might be) unless the solution is 'ignore'. The agenda should be:

- Evaluate new DQR.
- Progress report on existing DQR.
- Reprioritise or redirect resources as necessary.
- Agree plan for next cycle.

Keep meetings short, but hold them regularly.

HINT

I like to keep my DQR meetings to one hour, no more. Once everyone gets used to being brief and focused, the meetings become highly productive.

It is extremely important that you schedule the meetings regularly and that you stick to the schedule. The DQR board meeting is the most important event that will keep a data migration project on track. Make this plain to the project sponsor, programme manager, line manager and anyone else who might want to pull you into another meeting that clashes with the DQR. Ask yourself, if you show a lack of commitment to the DQR process, then how do you expect your business or technical colleagues to show commitment?

ANECDOTE

When I consult to projects on a mentoring and best-practice advice basis, I always ask to sit in on the DQR meetings as an observer. It is the one place where you can take the pulse of the project. Is the business engaged? Are the technologists responding to issues in time? Is the DMZ managed properly? Answers to questions such as these come out of the DQR board.

HINT

It does not matter what an issue is about, bring it into the DQR process for resolution. You have all the necessary resources to hand, plus a great understanding gained by working with one another.

HINT

Where there are real risks that as the data migration analyst you are going to be constantly pulled into other meetings, then appoint a deputy chair to do the job in your place. Do this as a last resort, however, because as I've said above, the DQR board is the place where you can get a feel for all the soft measures that the bare statistics on progress do not tell you.

Initiating the DQR process

Start the DQR process as early as possible. You can start LA as soon as the project has been initiated. You can generate DQRs as soon as LA is under way. In fact, as I have shown, you will have collected a list of 'starter' DQRs as part of the data migration strategy. Convene the first DQR board and get going. Like any other method with which you are unfamiliar, the first few cycles will be clumsy, but as you gain confidence and as the team starts to gel, the process will start to work organically. Every team is different because it is composed of different people at different points in their careers, with different educational and experience levels and different sets of interpersonal relationships.

HINT

As I often say, do not wait for the perfect moment. Just do it, and do it now.

Do not start, however, with a technical data stakeholder-only team. As soon as you appear to accept responsibility for data quality, you will find it difficult to move that responsibility back to the business. Use the SRPs and the LDS analysis to identify potential DQRs and the local business domain experts to join the DQR board. Convene the first meeting and make a start.

On a large project, which might be years in duration, introduce the DQR process slowly. Get the meetings scheduled perhaps monthly (never schedule less frequently than once a month). As the pace of the project builds, increase the frequency to fortnightly, then weekly.

Pick some easy, early wins and don't worry that the target is a long way off. It will always be obvious which items need to be fixed, wherever you are migrating to.

ANECDOTE

In 30 years of IT project experience in scores of organisations, I have only ever once worked in an environment where the whole basis of the business was changing. That was in the UK when the local government tax system switched over from a property-based tax to a personal tax. Everywhere else, if, for example, the organisation was a car maker before the new system, it was a car maker afterwards. If it was a utility before, so it was afterwards. In a practical sense, it is always obvious which reality checks and internal gaps need to be fixed before you can contemplate migrating.

The first DQRs you look at are likely to be investigative. In other words, you will be asking questions about the data that will get you from the qualitative to the quantitative (e.g. you are told that there are duplicate names held over two or more systems, so you run a DQR to quantify that, plus to pick up any other issues that come up).

HINT

It is my preference, as a project manager, to have more short tasks that complete quickly rather than fewer but longer running tasks. I therefore prefer to have an initial DQR that investigates and quantifies, and then spawns a number of other DQR, rather than a single DQR that runs for a long time. However, I am aware that this is merely a preference of mine.

As you get further into the DQR process and the LA starts to mature, the balance of investigating DQRs and fixing DQRs starts to shift towards the latter.

Obey Golden Rule 4
Never trust qualitative statements that are not backed up by hard evidence.

To old hands at any data-centric activity, the preceding sentence might appear a little like teaching your grandmother how to suck eggs, but all the same it is worth saying. The statement is especially true of assertions that some data is perfect. This is often the case with referential integrity constraints. Always run a quick DQR to check. It is better to have run a hundred quick checks than get caught out with one major issue at load time.

ANECDOTE

On the telecom migration that I referred to earlier, I encountered a set of tables where it was 'impossible' that any of the items in table A could possibly have duplicate parents in table B. I ran a DQR and found that a single batch was indeed duplicated. I could not tell how it had happened but surmised, because of matching date-time fields, that at some point in the past, either because of a system crash or faulty processing, one batch of updates had been run twice. If I had tried to load, the whole load program would have crashed at a point where full rollback would have been the only option.

Broadcast success

It is often the case that these early successes start to get to grips with issues that have been plaguing the business for ages. Work with the communications or business engagement team you identified in the data migration strategy to tell everyone in the business about your successes. Too often we do not advertise enough our successes, but rather concentrate on problems. Success attracts people. It shows that you are not just a cost to the business, but are delivering value even before you introduce the new system.

Creating DQR

This should be as easy to do as possible from a business user perspective. A single mailbox to which emails can be sent is good (but see the notes on technology below). A DQR form should be raised subsequently. Generally this will be done by the data migration team. On larger projects, where a project management office (PMO) for the data migration project is justified, then there will be some PMO support for the paperwork. Where there is not such support, then it generally falls to the data migration analyst to keep the paperwork in order.[16]

DQR document

A specimen DQR form is available in Appendix A4. I have used this form on real (and successful) data migrations in a number of companies; however, I am also used to tailoring it to the needs of different projects. Use it as a starting point.

The document is split into four sections:

- an identity section;
- a data quality assessment section;

---

[16] From when I first defined this process back in the late 1990s to now, the choices of format that a collaborative document like a DQR can take has changed dramatically. Back then it was easy to envisage an email exchange and eventually a Word document being created. Now, as I will show in the technology section below, we have more (and better) choices. Even as I write these words I am aware that we have gone from wikis, through in-house collaborative tools like Microsoft® SharePoint®, to a dawning age of social network-type products that exist in public and private clouds. The pace of change is quickening. These choices should be considered in the library services section of your data migration strategy; however, I shall write the rest of this chapter as if you were working in an old-school file-sharing and Word document world, which is a common basis we can all understand. The principles are the same, but the technology available now is a whole lot better.

- a method and optional tasks section;

- a metrics section.

Looking at these one at a time:

Identity section

This area provides ways of identifying and cross-referencing the DQR. It has the following subsections:

- **Short name** – This is a one- to three-word descriptive name for the DQR. It helps you to find quickly a DQR by eye from lists etc. and gives a handle to use when you refer to it in conversation.

- **Cross reference** – DQRs can be raised (or 'spawned') by other DQRs or by fault logs etc. It is useful to retain the audit trail. This is where the unique reference for the prior artefact would reside.

- **Raised by** – This should be the person who initially raised the DQR, not the person entering it into the log. You might need to go back to them for clarity at some point.

- **LDS/entity** – A DQR can relate to one LDS. Enter the LDS's unique ID here. DQRs also often relate to entities from the conceptual entity model, especially where you are trying to understand how a particular entity should be represented in a migration model. Recording the entity name and LDS unique ID from the LDS list makes it possible to report on percentages complete against LDS and entity.

- **Date raised** – Tracking by date allows you to see, when the DQRs start to pour into the data migration PMO, if you are keeping ahead of the flood or falling behind. This helps you manage the process.

- **DQR ID** – Each DQR should have a unique ID for filing and identification purposes. I normally number mine DQR*nnnn*, where *nnnn* is a sequential number starting at 0001. The prefix helps to ensure that when they are discussed or passed around the programme, the DQRs are easily distinguished from fault logs, risks and issues logs etc.

- **Priority** – I have seen people getting quite inventive when assigning priorities, but I tend to stick with three: 'must be fixed or the project will fail'; 'extremely useful to be fixed'; 'cosmetic'.

- **Status** – Status entries can be quite varied depending on the workflow you devise for DQRs in your circumstances, but I tend to keep it simple with four: 'new'; 'open'; 'cancelled'; 'completed'.

Data quality assessment section

This section is where you get to grips with the detail. You start with an extended description of the problem. Next, when DQRs are raised, you usually only have a qualitative assessment. You tend to be told, for instance, that the data on switches in the equipment table is 'quite good' or maybe 'poor', but you need hard figures so that you can comply with Golden Rule 4. You need to move rapidly to quantitative assessment. For each issue identified in the qualitative assessment, either a quantitative statement is required or, where there is no way of realistically measuring the true value of the qualitative statement, a mitigation can be added.

ANECDOTE

I was working on a project for a large utility company and there was doubt about the adequacy of some of the very old (Victorian) underground asset records. Clearly it was not tenable to dig up the assets to look at them. I had to accept that these records were as good as I was going to get and estimate the data quality based on the limited sample of assets that had been exhumed over the previous two years. Remember Golden Rules 1 and 2: be led by the business on what is adequate and realistic.

By and large, you are trying to follow Golden Rule 4. To retain control, the project needs to know what set of steps you are going to carry out and how you are to measure your success. The quantitative statement should record the number of key data items impacted out of the total population (e.g. 200 out of 2,532 sites, or 400 out of 3,000 suppliers).

Each quantitative statement must be accompanied by a testable verification rule (e.g. run a query to check that each supplier code on the purchasing system matches an account code in goods receivable).

Remember that you will be recording both known errors and known strengths. Check both.

Method section

A method statement is required whenever a DQR is suggested. It gives a brief explanation of what you are going to do (including 'do nothing') and explains what mitigation, if any, is going to take place to accommodate less than perfect data. As I indicated earlier, the method statement is often sufficient, but where more detail is required, you will add DQR tasks that have the following format:

- **Task ID** – Giving each task a unique ID helps if you are linking tasks into other project software. It is often not necessary. If you use the format of DQR*nnnn.nnn*, then there is an overhead if you decide to insert an additional step.

- **Description** – This describes what the task is and what it will deliver.

- **Who** – This identifies the person responsible to the DQR board for making sure the task is delivered.

- **When** – This gives the delivery date.

Obviously the sum of the DQR tasks should complete the method statement. Breaking down data cleansing, the principal activity, into methods and tasks allows different levels of control by the programme office. I do not normally recommend that the low level of detail in the tasks is copied onto the larger programme plan. Method statements are usually sufficient to form the larger programme level activities.

The duration, resource and effort values for the tasks can be rolled up to calculate the duration, resource and effort value for the method.

The tasks are monitored within the data migration subproject and the larger programme office can be confident that reported completion percentages are accurate reflections of deliverables from lower level tasks.

Metrics section

Use this to document how you will measure DQR progress. For instance, it might be agreed that you will be satisfied (bearing in mind Golden Rule 3) that the DQR will be considered complete when you can get the quantitative assessment up to 95 per cent. So you can have a difference between a 100 per cent complete DQR and the percentage accuracy of the data for that DQR. The percentage accuracy is needed for an overall data readiness assessment, the metric for project control within the DQR process.

SOFTWARE SUPPORT

Back in the beginning, when I first got involved with data migration, there was really very little support for DQRs. You would hold face-to-face meetings to go through a list prepared on spreadsheets that related to Word-based DQRs held in shared network folders. Now the choices are far more extensive, but in an enterprise you are normally limited to working with whatever is available. You rarely have the privilege of a separate budget for DQRs (unlike for data quality or profiling software).

The following outlines what the set of requirements might be in areas where you need support, then you will have to use your design skills to build a working solution with the tools you have available.

- **Recording DQRs** – You need some way of raising DQRs and capturing the data outlined above. Word documents have worked fine for years, but there are more efficient methods. You need to summarise all the DQRs for the DQR board. In the past this has meant cutting and pasting statements from DQR forms to a spreadsheet (with all the time overhead and possible transcription errors that entails). You also need to link out from the DQR forms to the plethora of underlying reports, screenshots, data correction sheets etc. that support the DQR tasks. You need to record 'percentage complete' statements and so on. Many people are now using project reporting (adapted risks and issues registers) for DQR management. Others have utilised fault logging, or first- and second-line support software to record DQRs and manage their execution.

ANECDOTE

In my experience there is always a trade-off between capturing all the fields you want on a DQR in a helpdesk system, and the advantages of industrial-strength software. Often, though, the available software wins out on balance, especially where you are performing a once in a business lifetime activity, and so availability is a premium over a perfect fit.

At the time of writing there are also some very interesting developments in CRM solutions, especially web-based ones, where the collaborative elements of social networking websites are being integrated with an enterprise-wide impromptu, small project team approach.

Local wikis and collaborative hubs where documents can be shared are also available, so there is plenty of choice. Have a look at what is available around you.

Finally, there are telephone conferencing and video/web conferencing solutions. Given that you are trying to have a regular meeting, of short duration, involving people from all over the business and some outside the business, phone conferencing is an ideal fit.[17]

ANECDOTE

Phone conferencing, like email or mobile phones, is one of those technologies that once you have used it, you cannot imagine doing a data migration without it. I find myself confused and a bit confounded now when I work with clients who do not have phone conferencing. If you have to get a bunch of people to co-locate so that they can have a meeting, and those people are geographically dispersed, there is a real challenge to the ideal of a one-hour meeting. It is difficult to justify people travelling for most of the day to attend a one-hour meeting. If you are faced with this, then you have to reconsider your key business data area decomposition.

ROLE OF THE DMZ

The DMZ passes through the DQR process in the standard *PDMv2* model. Although it is nearly always the case that initial data preparation, data readiness and resolving DQRs are the responsibility of the client, the process needs the support of the target system technical data experts to understand the complete range of possible technical fixes that can be applied. Their input is needed to consider 'in-flight' or 'on-the-target' fixes, although the majority of DQR activity will be on the client side of the DMZ. You need to ensure that this is catered for when contracts are negotiated.

CHAPTER REVIEW

In this chapter I introduced data quality rules. I looked at the structure and use of DQRs, how they are created and managed, and how to get a DQR process up and running.

I stressed that DQR is where you can monitor the heartbeat of a data migration project and that it is critical to the success of a data migration project.

---

[17] I'm not so sure about web conferencing. There is a temptation to go for interesting presentation formats rather than getting through a shared list very quickly.

10 GAP ANALYSIS AND MAPPING

In this chapter I will look at how the artefacts from the previous chapters help you overcome the challenges of data mapping and data gap fixing. I will also cover the 'one-way street' problem and the impact that it has on data lineage.

GAP ANALYSIS

The gap analysis and mapping (GAM) module is where the technical tools and techniques *PDMv2* makes available to you to discover, analyse and quantify data gaps are documented. This is because, whether the data gaps appear in LA, GAM itself, the DQR process or even MDE, those tools and techniques should be consistent. From a practical perspective, when it comes to planning and staffing, the skills needed are best defined in one place. In this sense the gap analysis part of GAM could be thought of as a service sub-module to the DQR process through which all data preparation and quality issues must pass. This will become clearer if I quickly review the types of data gap covered so far.

Types of data gap
The data gaps I have introduced to you so far are:

- **Reality checks** – These are where data in LDSs does not match business reality. They are found primarily in LA, but can also appear in the DQR process and, where you least want them, in UAT.

- **Internal gaps** – These are where the data in an LDS does not match the rules for that LDS. These are found in LA and in the DQR process, but can appear in testing.

- **Migration model gaps** – These are where there are differences in data and data structures between LDSs. They are found in GAM as a service to LA.

There are also data gaps that can only come to light once the target is introduced and a comparison of the legacy model and target model is made for mapping purposes:

- **Target model gaps** – These occur where there are differences between the data you have in the LDSs and in the target systems' data requirements. They will not become visible until the target model is introduced in the mapping sub-module of GAM.

- **Topographical gaps** – These are gaps that come to light when you try to navigate from data item to data item and find that an essential linking data item is missing. Generally they suggest that there is a missing LDS, although sometimes the target system has a requirement for a link that was not necessary in the legacy. You sometimes also uncover them when you try to build a legacy data model and cannot see how a required navigation was performed.

DEFINITION

In this context, a 'navigation' is the links in the data that allow software to move from one data item to another. An example would be a foreign key that allows a program to get from a holding company record to all the operational company records beneath it.

Types of fixes

I have also shown that there are a number of types of fixes:

- **Manual audit** – This is where you have to survey your business environment to collect data that was either not collected at all beforehand or collected to an inadequate level of quality.

- **Manual fix** – This is where you fix data by hand, normally in an LDS, but also sometimes in the target.

- **Use of third-party data** – This is where you perform data enrichment to add data items that were not previously present or not present to the necessary level of quality. The source of data for data enrichment can be from third-party sources (like a postal service address file to validate and correct addresses) or from your own manual audits.

- **Automated fix** – This where data gaps are fixed using computer programs either in the source, in the target or in flight.

- **Discovery of missing LDS** – As I have shown above, this is a common solution to topographical gaps, but it is also applicable to target model gaps. Both only really appear during the mapping element of GAM.

GAP ANALYSIS AS A SERVICE

When it comes to discovering data gaps, you would expect to have the skills, tools and resources to be able to support the discovery of internal, legacy model, target model and topographical gaps. There is, these days, software available to support gap analysis, but frequently, because of budgetary constraints or simple expediency, it is often necessary to resort to more manual methods.

- **Reality checks** – Unless there is a trusted third-party source of confirmation, then there is no substitute for reality checks but to use the business domain experts' knowledge of the domain in question or to perform an audit/survey. Usually you do a combination of the two. The technical support for this within GAM is limited to providing cuts of data in repositories suitable for the auditors to use and a transitional data store to hold their updates in cases where they are not going to update the LDS directly. These transitional data stores can be anything from pre-printed forms to databases, but spreadsheets are the commonest form of assistance. Having them built by technical people within the project means that you can guarantee some degree of consistency, robustness, error checking etc., plus it helps reinforce the team ethos that you are all helping each other.

- **Internal gaps** – I explained in Chapter 7 on LA that the use of profiling tools will assist in the discovery of internal gaps. You can also instantiate an LDS model in a data quality tool and run that against the data in the LDS. I will look at data quality tools in the software support section of this chapter.

- **Migration model gaps** – The migration model, either in diagrammatic form, instantiated in data quality tools or as a built database, can be used to model the gaps between the logical structures of the LDSs and a single common point of reference. This will leave you, as I have shown, with a set of known differences that you can choose, via the DQR process, to act on immediately or note and defer until the target model is stable enough to allow you to know for sure if these differences are significant enough to require action.

HINT

Once again I have to stress that it might seem that you cannot make a judgement about what is a significant structural difference and what is not before you have the target model, but in practice you can with a high degree of accuracy.

- **Target model gaps** – Obviously, you cannot uncover target model gaps until you have a target, which, as you know, is usually late in the programme. Even when it is delivered to plan, that plan date is a long way down the project timeline, too close to go-live to allow you much leeway to fix any tricky semantic issues. The target is also, typically, under constant change as a consequence of user testing and late fixes. However, if you have followed the 'reality check → internal gap → migration model gap' process, then, by the time the target stabilises you will have the overwhelming majority of data gaps under the control of the DQR process. The target model is often instantiated as a real, physical, repository into which you can test load your data. The use of dummy loads as a testing approach is covered in the testing section in Chapter 11 on migration design and execution, but remember, gap analysis is not the same as testing.

HINT

One of the things I say on projects is that you test **out** defects, but you build **in** quality. Testing should be the last defence against poorly executed code and to confirm assumptions about run times, cutover organisational issues etc. Gap analysis is about discovering requirements for data preparation (i.e. part of the requirements gathering of a data migration project).

Often you are not given a fully configured test instance into which to load data, but rather a set of data templates possibly in the form of an XML schema or even a collection of spreadsheet documents. I will explain later that when you consider the DMZ in the context of GAM, configuration management and version control are absolutely vital, but first I'll explain each of the instantiation options in turn so that you can decide which is the most appropriate for your migration.

Data model instantiation options

There are a number of instantiation options for you to consider. Once again I am going to deal with them generically in the full knowledge that there are all kinds of subtle and not so subtle variations. What you need from a model instantiation is the ability to find all the data gaps so that they can be catalogued and dealt with via the DQR process. The technical lead on a data migration has the responsibility to recommend the most suitable for the project. However, there is no single best approach, so on most projects you use different types of model at different times.

- **Logical model** – I recommend that you commence a data migration journey with a conceptual entity model. You use this firstly to define scope in the data migration strategy, and then again for cataloguing DQR and LDSs. If the conceptual entity model is a level 0 model, then there is often value in creating level 1 and 2 models (i.e. decomposing the top-level model down a couple of layers). You can then swiftly compare the structural differences of LDSs built in entirely different technologies. The advantages of logical models are that they are quick and cheap to produce and review: they can be hand drawn, then reproduced in any desktop drawing tool. Their disadvantages are that you need to have the skills to create and interpret them (and that is a book in itself). I would also not recommend going down any further than a level 2 model (i.e. a model with discrete entities, but without all the attributes completed). What you are looking for are structural gaps (which will show up at this level). Formal data models are useful for finding migration model and target model gaps at the data structure level provided you have the skills.

  Although I do not recommend including the entity details in the diagrammatic model, it is possible to accompany the structural model with a data dictionary that goes down to attribute level.[18] Whereas it is easier to see the structural gaps at an entity level, field level issues (data type, field length, patterns, parsing rules etc.) can only be determined at field level. This is what you need to define a migration model if you are not creating a physical database. Again, you are interested in the differences between your migration model and the individual LDS models, so your data dictionary needs to be designed to hold details of the differences (i.e. these reference to the appropriate DQR where these gaps are recorded). Data dictionaries support migration model and target model gaps and the mapping specifications.

- **Data quality tool model** – Whenever you write code to interrogate an LDS you are doing so against a data model implicit in the code. If you are using LA tools or if you are relying on a database schema and ad hoc queries, you are qualifying and defining a logical data structure. When you are implementing

---

[18] A data dictionary is the list of all existing fields and the rules for their usage.

LA, you are looking initially for internal gaps. If you are using a profiling tool, then it will show you the potential anomalies in the dataset. You need to investigate the anomalies to understand what the LDS's own data model should look like and what the internal gaps are (i.e. in a sense you are discovering what is right and what is not from the perspective of that LDS). If you are using the schema plus some reverse engineering from analysis of what the business domain experts tell you (not all the business data rules will be in the schema), then you will get the same result. The profiling tools will get you there more quickly and more thoroughly at one level, but you should do the front-end reverse engineering if you want to understand fully the subtleties of the legacy dataset.

When it comes to the second phase of LA (building a migration model), then you can also accommodate this (backed up, as I indicate above, by logical models) in a set of queries as opposed to a fully built physical model.

The benefit of this approach is that you are not attempting to perform two physical migrations: one from the LDS into the migration model and one from the migration model to the target. Of course, if the migration architecture relies on the use of a staging database, then there is no advantage, but on the other hand, if you are planning to migrate fully live, without a staging database, then this approach reduces the build requirement and, if you maximise code reuse, it provides the basis for the transformation logic in the final ETL sequence. The downside of relying on queries is that in most supporting software there is no in-built control of the queries being produced, so there is nothing to prevent contradictory rules being checked for (e.g. one query checks that a field is only filled with numeric values while another checks that its values match a list that includes non-numeric values). Data quality software tools that enforce a consistent view of the data model, do so with their own in-built data dictionary.

- **Physical migration model** – Here you build a repository and put data into it from the LDSs. Obviously, if you are basing a migration model on the most dominant LDS in your environment, then it is unlikely that you will be able to import into it the data it usually receives. You will need to manage the migration using one (or a combination) of the methods described above. It is an option that is particularly attractive if your migration architecture calls for a staging database or if your software supplier has a version of software that is quickly and easily available (albeit with necessary customisation to accommodate the requirements of the client). I stress again though, what you are not necessarily doing is trying to perform a full dummy load into the intermediary data store. Unless you have very small data volumes and the data structures are relatively simple, there is a real risk that you will get drawn into a painful and time-consuming iteration of failed loads. It is better to use the physical data store as the source for a data dictionary from which you derive a battery of queries that will test all the conditions for all the units of migration. Each failure then becomes a DQR and, as you have seen from the DQR process, the team decides if and how to fix it. You will get a better overall picture more quickly.

DATA QUALITY MONITORING AS A SERVICE

The technical support for data analysis sits in the GAM module, so this is also where you locate the support that the DQR process needs to monitor DQRs. There are two levels to this. The DQR process expects regular feedback on the progress of DQRs and, because DQRs are written with verifiable, quantitative statements, this is what you measure to monitor that a DQR is on track.

As well as supporting in-flight DQRs, GAM also supports the monitoring of the state of data fixed by a completed DQR. This is especially the case where you used the fix-in legacy option. Data that is fixed in the legacy can decay over the remainder of the migration and so a monitoring DQR needs to be put in place to check that things are not getting any worse.

This means there has to be a clear workflow from DQR to GAM, and that the technical team from GAM needs to be involved with the DQR process.

MAPPING

Many people, thinking about data migration for the first time, see data mapping as being what it is all about. This was certainly true for me. However, I hope that you are realising that data migration is a lot more.

Mapping sits in the *PDMv2* GAM module. It brings together:

- the requirements from the SRPs for business-side mandatory data and the history that needs to be captured in the target;
- the history that will be transferred to the archive solution;
- the 'fix in flight', 'fail in flight' and 'do not migrate' requests from the DQRs;
- the understanding that the target model gap analysis provides you with of the relationship between target and legacy;
- the understanding that the migration model gap analysis provides you with of the relationship between LDSs;
- enhanced LDS knowledge from LA;
- MDM models of reference data;
- third-party data identified during DQR activity;
- transitional data stores holding data collected by survey or audit as a result of DQRs.

Mapping faults from testing are also fed back via the DQR process, as is any unpredicted fallout from migration (although such fallout is evidence of a failure to perform properly the pre-emptive data preparation and data quality activity).

All of the above is structured by a common conceptual entity and key business data area breakdown. It leverages the expertise of the virtual team of KDSHs, who by now are tightly bound into the success of the project.

Using *PDMv2*, you expect to produce an archive design alongside the target migration design. The scope statements in the data migration strategy will tell you who is performing the design and build of the archiving solution, but it is normal for the extract aspects of the archiving to be performed by the same team as that performing the extract aspects of the target solution migration design.

Where to start mapping
Data mapping might appear daunting at first. The new system has hundreds (or even tens of thousands) of fields that need to be filled with data from hundreds of potential LDS sources. There are gigabytes (terabytes?) of archive data. However, in practice, although it can be a sizable work package, if you have prepared properly, then you will find that it is simply a matter of ploughing through the task. The overwhelming majority of data items present no challenge and can be mapped rapidly. It is only where there are gaps, choices or special processing that difficulties emerge.

Start at the top
Top-down design is always best. As a starting point, align work packages with the key business data area decomposition. Break down the mappings into conceptual entity bundles (if they are not aligned to the key business data areas) and go to the LDS catalogue.

> **HINT**
>
> It is at this point that you will realise the benefit of having the library services sorted out at the very beginning of the project. All *PDMv2* artefacts (DQRs, LDS catalogues, SRPs etc.) will be searchable on key business data areas and conceptual entities. Make sure this is true for your understanding of the target as well.

The target gap analysis will have identified the points of similarity as well as the points of difference between the target and the migration model. The migration model gap analysis will have done the same for the points of similarity and difference between each LDS and the migration model. The internal gap and reality check analysis will have done a similar job for the lowest level data items. All the issues will be recorded in DQRs, which are cross-referenced to LDSs, key business data areas and conceptual entities.

You will have recorded end-user business requirements in the SRPs, and reviewed them against the design at the end of the migration design phase for a business sign-off confirming that all the requirements were met in the migration design. This ensures that business data requirements are included in the design and so they should be referenced both in the *PDMv2* mapping and the design sub-modules. In the mapping phase, you are mostly interested in the data retention and (possibly) customer experience aspects of the SRPs.

> **HINT**
>
> All this seems very mechanistic, but continuity of engagement is the best guarantee of a deep understanding for a data migration analyst. It means that where there is project staff turnover, and where you increase the numbers of staff to cope with the peak in work caused by data mapping, incoming staff have a wealth of detailed analysis to work from.

Move down the hierarchy

Having partitioned the mapping activities by key business data areas and conceptual entities, and having assembled the work packs of LDS catalogues with an associated data dictionary, DQRs and SRPs, it is time to move down to a deeper level of granularity and start linking entity to entity, then field to field. This is where a formal data modelling approach pays off. If you have decomposed the migration model diagrams down to a set of level 2 diagrams, and you have cross-referenced these entity descriptions to entries in the LDS catalogues and data dictionary, then it is relatively easy (although necessarily long-winded given the number of connections you have to make) to link source to target.

It gets difficult at this point to describe the process in more detail because there is such a variety of software available, each with its strengths and weaknesses, to the extent that there is little generic detail I can add. I will try to address some of the more common software variants below, but first let me define some common terminology that will help.

Common vocabulary

Sometimes different terms mean different things to different people, so, to help you, the following gives a few terms with their definitions as I will be using them in the rest of the book.

> **HINT**
>
> There are synonyms for most terms in IT. Almost every definition I use in this book (especially the ones I coined myself) will be challenged by someone who has a penchant for using a different vocabulary. If you encounter a variant, do not be afraid to ask for an explanation and try, as I try, not to be too dogmatic about one label or another. It is more important that the project as a whole uses the same terminology than to embark on a spurious search for the 'correct' set.

- **Extraction rules** – You rarely need to migrate all the data from the LDSs to the target. The target data dictionary is the starting point, but there will also be guidance on what is needed for the target, what is needed for archiving and what will be left behind, in the SRPs and the scope statement of the data migration strategy. Extraction rules tell you what is to be included in the extract defined by data item (e.g. for the target, all Customers who have placed an order in the last two years).

- **Exclusion rules** – By definition anything that is not included is excluded; however, even within the extraction rules, there are exceptions. These are normally related to 'do not migrate' fixes from the DQR process, but they can also come from SRPs. Again, exclusion rules are defined by data items (e.g. exclude Customers for whom you do not have a UK billing address). The benefit of distinguishing them like this comes when you get to instantiating them in code (i.e. in MDE). Depending on your architecture and the complexity of the rule, you might implement them in the extract or in the transformation steps.

- **Navigation rules** – In anything other than a simple data migration, you often have to link data items from more than one table or even more than one LDS. You have to enrich data from external sources and use values you have stored in MDM repositories. You need rules to 'navigate' from table to table; from one LDS to another; from LDS to external data source or MDM platform. This is an area where the technical side often feels the most comfortable, but beware, it is the data that the KDSH consensus suggests is the most important, not the data that the technical data experts are satisfied with. These are sometimes not the same. You have to balance the advice of the technical data experts against that of the business domain experts.

HINT

Remember you will need to have extraction rules, exclusion rules and navigation rules for both target and archive.

- **Timing rules (or triggers)** – Data extracts have to start sometimes on a timing trigger, but more often on a processing one. So, for instance, you might run a series of extracts at 1.30 am, after the last batch update job has completed, or after a previous extract has completed. Information when to start and stop processes will come initially from the KDSHs in the form of windows of opportunity in the SRPs and from the technical data experts. These will form the architectural basis of your design, which will be confirmed in the tested detailed design that emerges from MDE.

- **Validation** – You will, of course, rerun all the validation rules defined in LA, and also the new ones added by your knowledge of the target gained during target gap analysis and by the delivery of the target model. You have been running this battery of rules regularly as part of data quality monitoring as a service, so you will know the percentage of units of migration that will fail. These will have been signed off as acceptable in the DQR process. Also you will have 'fall out in flight' DQR fixes from the DQR process. However, even if you are predicting a zero fall-out migration, you still run a validation.

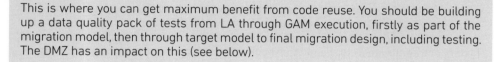

HINT

This is where you can get maximum benefit from code reuse. You should be building up a data quality pack of tests from LA through GAM execution, firstly as part of the migration model, then through target model to final migration design, including testing. The DMZ has an impact on this (see below).

- **Transformation rules** – You almost always have to perform some degree of transformation after 'extract' and prior to 'load'. You will know what transformation is required from the 'fix in flight' DQRs that were generated as part of gap analysis and also from testing, which is part of MDE. Standard transformations include the use of external data (or data enrichment), use of look-up tables or MDM created in LA, data parsing and combining (which I look at in more detail below) and data typing (e.g. changing the data type of a coded value in flight from Long to Int). The simplest transformation rule is defaulting, that is putting a uniform value into a field (e.g. putting the value 'Y' into the Employed field on the target system Employee record to show that they are an employee when there is no matching field in the legacy).

- **Loading rules** – Obviously, you have to show where the data will go. Again, available software packages will perform this task differently, but generally you will link source to target at the lowest field level after having taken account of the transformation rules. Whether that source is a staging database or LDSs, and whether that target is the final destination or a staging database, are dependent on where you are in relation to the DMZ (see below). The detailed destination fields will be determined by the target data dictionary and the source by the target model gap analysis. Data has to be loaded in the correct sequence (e.g. you might have to load Customer master records before you can load Orders). The target model, the target data dictionary and the target technical data experts will tell you the requirement. You will also get the connection information from your technical colleagues (often on both sides of the DMZ). Loading rules include sequencing rules, as well as telling you where data items will be placed.

DATA LINEAGE, DATA AUDIT AND THE 'ONE-WAY STREET' PROBLEM

In the following I have included data audit and lineage with parsing and combining because of the way they contribute to the 'one-way street' problem, but first I need to clarify some more terms as I use them here.

- **Data audit** – You need to satisfy the business owners that all the units of migration that they wanted you to move from the (soon to be decommissioned) LDSs made it to either the target or the archive solution. The degree of audit will be captured in the SRPs, forming one of the key requirements statements for the data migration.

- **Data lineage** – Sometimes (but rarely, and usually for regulatory reasons), you need to track the specific extraction, exclusion and transformation rules as they act upon individual units of migration as they pass through the migration process.

ANECDOTE

I have only had to perform full data lineage on less than 10 per cent of the data migrations that I have been involved with. A memorable one was in a heavily regulated commodities trading system where it had to be possible to trace all the trades and history of trades with a clear audit trail back to the originating activity on a trading desk. All copying of data and transformations had to have a 'before and after' image retained with accompanying transformation logic explanations.

- **Parsing and concatenation** – In an overwhelming majority of cases, mapping involves a one-to-one match of LDS field to target field. However, it can also involve splitting a field in the LDS into a number of fields in the target (i.e. parsing). A common example of this is the splitting out of combined Name and Address fields into Title, First Name, Surname, First Address Line etc. Conversely, it can mean combining multiple values from the LDSs into one value in the target (i.e. concatenation). Putting individual Name and Address lines together into a combined Name and Address field is an example of this. The worst case is where multiple values from an LDS need to be combined and split over multiple values in the target. This is thankfully rare when considered against the hundreds (or thousands) of mappings that you will perform and it is usually caused by differences in reference data tables.

ANECDOTE

I worked on a central government data migration where I was moving personnel data. Each record had a Racial Origin field for diversity monitoring. The LDS had 17 entries. The target had 21 and only 10 were common entries. There were others where two from the legacy would become one on the target, and vice versa.

Appendix A5 gives a worked example that goes through this type of data mapping issue in more detail.

These relationships are usually expressed as a ratio of the form number of source fields to the number of destination fields, so that:

- o 1:1 means one source field to one destination field;
- o 1:M means one source field to many destination fields;
- o M:1 means many source fields to one destination field;
- o M:M means many source fields to many destination fields.

HINT

Be wary, nomenclature can vary. Often the letter 'N' is used in place of 'M' (meaning 'a number of'). If in doubt, ask.

Clearly 1:1 mappings need no further transformation rules. They might still have complex extraction and navigation rules depending on the data structures you are dealing with. Anything with an M in the relationship, however, will need rules explaining how to split or consolidate values.

The 'one-way street' problem

It is perfectly possible to perform the transformation in such a way that it is not possible to get back to the original values. It might appear counter-intuitive that it is possible to alter the data as you migrate it so that it is impossible to go back the other way and recreate the original values. But it is. Anyone familiar with one-way encryption will be aware of how this can happen. M:1 or M:M mappings are a simple example of how this can happen. If you try to reverse a M:1 mapping, you have M choices. If you have not retained some way of identifying which choice you made, then you are stuck.

ANECDOTE

The 'one-way street' problem caused me considerable pain on one project where it was requested that an accounts structure be reorganised. It can be tricky to explain for a simple example, but for more complex scenarios, where there are a dozen or more steps in the transformation and the subsequent reverse navigation, it can be very difficult to see what has happened. Proving that something cannot be done is far harder than proving that it can.

The 'one-way street' problem can be an issue for fallback as I will show when I discuss MDE. It can also be a challenge if there is a change of heart in the bigger programme about the way some part of the data is structured and you are requested to part unload/reload data.

HINT

A common belts and braces solution for this is to hold the key to the unit of migration in some unused field on the target with the legacy data archived in total somewhere just in case. It can also be resolved using some form of data lineage. Retaining a pointer back to the original unit of migration is not full data lineage, however, because it does not explain the logic of changes that have been made to data en route.

It is unlikely that you would encounter this issue in a big-bang implementation. In this case, either the new system has not gone live and you can start again, or if you are already working in the target system, structural changes will have taken place by moving forward with the new system. It is an issue when you are pursuing either a phased-delivery or parallel-running implementation.

In a parallel-running implementation, where transactions have been processed by both the new systems and LDS, reloading from scratch might not be an option because it might not be clear against which reloaded entity transactions that take advantage of new functionality should be recorded. It is even more of a problem with a phased delivery. At least with a parallel-running implementation, if you are prepared to lose the novel updates you can fallback and start again. With phased delivery there might be no way to fall back and roll forward without a considerable manual effort.

You should factor all these issues into your fallback and migration forms decisions. There is unfortunately no scientific answer on how to proceed. Being able to maintain an audit trail that covers every update is, as I will show, very software dependent. In essence, wherever the data migration exercise encounters a M:M or M:1 condition there is always a risk that if you do not take sufficient precautions you will be stuck at the wrong end of a one-way street!

HINT

Another reason for warning you about this is that you might be invited (without notice) to a meeting with senior executives where you will be asked about the feasibility of falling back for restructuring. It helps if you can lay down a marker for the future by saying that you will need to investigate further to safeguard them from the 'one-way street' problem. It might not make you popular at the time, but this is where you can leverage the support of the virtual team.

If you are finding all this a little hard to digest, the worked example in Appendix A5 might make things easier to understand, but the key point to take away is that the process of migration can render the audit trail from source to target impossible to reconstruct. You need to know in advance what degree of audit and data lineage you require and either buy the software tools that support you or construct the architecture accordingly. You will get audit and data lineage requirements from the SRP.

IMPACT OF THE DMZ

The DMZ is a fact of life in most enterprise application migrations. Normally, there will be a software vendor or a reseller installing and configuring the target for your use. They will, nearly always, perform the final lift and shift of data into their application. You will, nearly always, have to perform the initial LA and data preparation. You will meet somewhere between those two points. Breaking down the steps into different rule types etc., as in the above example, makes it easier to see who will be responsible for which piece. It is the responsibility of the data migration analyst to put this altogether in one coherent architecture, as I will show in Chapter 11 on the migration design and execution module. This section concentrates on data mapping.

What follows is a description of how the division of labour between client and supplier is generally applied; however, each project is different and it is the data migration analyst's responsibility to define for their project where the DMZ(s) lies. This should be captured in the data migration strategy, reflected in the supplier contract and worked through into the rules of engagement between the parties. What follows is the plain 'vanilla' version.

Although most of gap analysis and data mapping occurs on your side of the DMZ, there are significant contributions that are required from the supplier.

- **Gap analysis** – This is always the client's responsibility. The supplier is responsible for providing the target model. It is the client's responsibility to provide the migration model and the proceeding data analysis, and it is nearly always down to the client to resolve the gaps. *PDMv2* expects this division of labour. Gap resolution is carried out by a joint supplier/client representation on the DQR, so it is inevitably the client who is ultimately responsible.

- **Data quality monitoring as a service** – Generally this is the responsibility of the client, but it is sensible to see which side of the DMZ is better positioned to provide it. It might be the supplier, given that they tend to have more experience in the tools and resources for data quality management, plus they have to duplicate the validation anyway. If you do go down this route, expect it to be in addition to the basic service provided by the supplier because they will have to perform 'what if?' and quantification analysis in addition to pure validation.

ANECDOTE

On a project for a national telecom provider it was agreed, given the sheer scale of the data involved, that duplicating the validation and query function was not financially or technically sensible. A perfectly sound solution was found that allowed a bank of rules to be built up using the specialist services of a third party who served both sides.

- **Extraction rules** – Delivery of these are normally the client's responsibility based on the products developed during LA and, crucially, the target model. This has implications for configuration and release management (see below).

- **Exclusion Rules** – Definition of these is normally the client's responsibility based on products developed during LA, DQR, testing and migration run time. However, it might be that some of them are incorporated into the ETL software developed by the supplier, depending on the technology options and migration architecture.

- **Validation** – Both the supplier and the client will originate validation rules, but, in principal, the supplier specifies the rules that they will be using to accept or reject client data, even where the rule is one that reflects a client-side and not a supplier-side requirement. In other words, where the client has requested validation beyond that normally supplied, to fulfil business requirements, this is normally included in the ongoing validation built into the target, and so has to be true of the data supplied at start-up.

- **Transformation rules** – Depending where these originate, from DQR or as part of gap analysis, they might have been suggested by the client or the supplier. Transformation rules might be incorporated in code on either side of the DMZ, so it is important that there is allowance in the contract for some transformation.

ANECDOTE

I was working at a large utility that had a number of projects running. The supplier had a very tight contract on a parallel project that prevented them from performing any data enhancement. What they got from the client is what they loaded. This extended to them refusing to even put default values into a field when it was blank, at load time. Sometimes, given the way you bring data together from disparate sources and load it, often weeks apart, it is only when the data all comes together at the point of load that the correct values for derived data can be ascertained. Make sure you have a budgeted allowance for it in the contract.

The supplier might also specify transformation rules in their own 'final mile' ETL for particular data structures that the target needs, but which are difficult to reproduce.

- **Loading rules** – Loading rules are normally the responsibility of the supplier who understands what the target needs. These are passed to the client to prepare the data for passing through the DMZ. Sequencing rules are always the supplier's responsibility.

- **Data lineage and data migration audit** – As I have shown, data lineage and data migration audit principally originate on the client side and are captured in the SRPs unless they are going to form part of the architecture for fallback or for precautionary reasons. They might be implemented on both sides of the DMZ, but they are most likely to be on the supplier side to capture how the data was written to the target.

Configuration and release management

As you can see there are a lot of rules originating on either side of the DMZ that have to be managed if you are to have a holistic framework.

The rules can be problematic for the supplier. Many of the data rules they are implementing originate in business requirements from the client, and then the client's IT department passes them data that does not fit their own rules. It is easy to see why they are confused, but it is better if you keep the data migration project isolated from everything else that is going on and pass requirements back and forth across the DMZ in a known and agreed way. As you have seen in Chapter 4 on migration strategy, *PDMv2* expects that you will have developed a robust mechanism for controlling these rules. How that mechanism works is dependent on your technology choices.

SOFTWARE SUPPORT

Technology is changing fast and so the following is a general picture of what is available. I have shown you that in LA, gap analysis at the model level can be performed visually. You can then use query or data quality tools that instantiate that model at lower levels to qualify the model. An alternative approach is to use semantic analysis tools to compare data structures.

This is often supplier-led when it comes to recording data mappings. If the supplier has a preference for presenting their clients with a data dictionary represented in, say, spreadsheets or csv files, then their response is often to provide data mappings in the same format (much like the worked example in Appendix A5).

Although this is still, probably, the most common representation, it is no longer as dominant as it once was. There are, currently, two flavours of disruptive technologies that are increasingly challenging this approach.

The first, and more established, is the use of ETL software. This reads legacy data source and target schemas and allows the user to link data by dragging from one side to the other, so it dispenses with the need for data mapping spreadsheets. However, there is still the issue of the DMZ and the migration architecture. If you are going down the increasingly normal route of using a staging database between client and supplier, then you still need to communicate any transformation logic that needs to be in place on the supplier side of the DMZ in an agreed format. They, in turn, will need to communicate the destination fields to you so that you can confirm they are acceptable to the users.

On the other hand, if you are going to perform the whole journey in one set of ETL mappings without a staging database, then you need to agree who is responsible for defining and implementing the various rules.

There is also semantic model-based data migration software. This software is well served by *PDMv2* with its recommended use of data modelling. Here, however, it is the data structures that are mapped, not the fields as such. A full set of data mappings is unnecessary except, of course, that the initial selection, validation and exclusion rules need to be specified to the migration software builders. There also needs to be an agreed path to accommodate the 'fix in target' DQRs, because the semantic model might need to be modified to allow certain units of migration through that would violate model rules.

These are really issues for Chapter 11 on the migration design and execution module. The point to take away is that whatever the technology being used, the format, storage, change, configuration and release management of the communication of rules and DQRs need to be agreed in advance as part of library services in the data migration strategy. As I have shown, these are partially determined by both the architecture and the position of the DMZ. This is why I suggest that you have an outline architecture in the data migration strategy. If this is really not possible because you are undecided at the time the strategy is created, then when it is decided, you need to revisit the library services and DMZ definition to realign these to the agreed design.

HINT

This is really not as difficult as maybe I have made it seem. I'm trying to cover all eventualities here. In most cases the architecture is obvious and who does what and where are also obvious (although you still need to document it). The conceptualisation of mappings into their different component rule types helps to explain the differences that different architectures and DMZ agreements cause. They give you some generic terms you can lay across your migration and check that you have thought through and documented who does what and where. There should then be no misunderstandings.

CHAPTER REVIEW

In this chapter I have reviewed types of gap, types of fix, and the use of models. I showed you how target gap analysis leads you into data mapping. I looked at how, within *PDMv2*, data mapping is broken down into a series of rule types and that, depending on the architecture and the position of the DMZ, these different rules types might be instantiated in different places in the ETL flow.

11 MIGRATION DESIGN AND EXECUTION

PDMv2 *migration design and execution is made up of the following sub-modules:*

- *migration end-to-end design (E2E design);*
- *extract, transform and load (ETL design);*
- *detailed decommissioning design;*
- *migration build, test and execute.*

I will look at the role of each of these in turn, assessing the impact of technology options and the DMZ, and show how all the PDMv2 *artefacts I have created so far are brought together to create an ideal zero-defect data migration.*

MIGRATION END-TO-END DESIGN

Migration end-to-end (E2E) design is an overview, or architectural design, that describes the migration from the moment the first extract of framework data is taken through to the moment when the last LDS is decommissioned and the last transitional business process is ended. On smaller migrations you might not need a separate E2E and ETL design. The principal reason for it is to maintain overall coherence of design given the impact of technology and the DMZ.

The impact of technology and the DMZ

Different types of software (e.g. DIY, ETL, semantic) require different inputs and, to an extent, perform different parts of the whole better or worse, or not at all. It is also true there are marked differences even within each community of software. To get the best out of the software you choose, you need to optimise the specific inputs and ways of working that your software needs. However, outside of the activities closely coupled to the software, the processes of choosing the more appropriate LDS, LA in general, data preparation and capturing user requirements of the migration are always the same.

ANECDOTE

I have advised some of the biggest names in the data migration software space and helped devise best practice recommendations that match their software and will easily hook up with *PDMv2*. Some have even gone so far as gaining *PDMv2* compliance for their software implementation practices. There is no contradiction between optimising the operations closest to the technology and using standardised techniques for activities further away from the software.

To an extent, therefore, the technical design and build of the migration is not prescribed by *PDMv2*. Provided it supports all that follows in this chapter and, as I will show, there are sufficient checks in *PDMv2* to ensure that it does, then you can allow the supplier to operate in a manner that maximises the benefit of the special features of their chosen software.

From a supplier perspective this is also attractive. Provided your preferred approach can support some essential components, like being able to send records that fail to load to an agreed location to be picked up by the DQR process, then you are free to make best use of your skills and experience with the software and target you are expert in. You will benefit from a timely response and the most appropriate data, prepared to the appropriate quality with a clear set of requirements for audit and data lineage. Your solution will run to time without the distraction of the finger pointing that bedevils other projects.

Impact of the DMZ

The existence of the DMZ divides the implementation of the data migration, and therefore its design, build, test and execution. It is also a fact that different organisations will have different policies for their design packs. *PDMv2* does not dictate the detail of what a program specification should look like. Rather it controls the project by issuing high-level design documents and controlling the inputs and outputs from activities to make sure that they align to requirements.

If you look at the elements needed for a successful data migration and lay them against a standard data migration scenario, then you find that you often divide the design and execution into the following:

- **Extraction including cleansing and preparation** – This is nearly always the client's responsibility. When choosing the LDS source, through data preparation and gap analysis to mapping, it is the client who has to lead and deliver.

- **Transformation** – The responsibility for this is split between client and supplier. Sometimes the supplier performs a significant amount of transformation coding. More often, the client has to transform the majority of data before it hits a staging database leaving the supplier with a minimum amount of activity. In either case, the supplier is normally only interested in designing for the target and not the archive, and you need a design that caters for both.

- **Testing** – This too is a joint supplier/client responsibility. As I will show when you come to look at testing later in this chapter, you expect that the supplier will perform unit testing, participate in integration and end-to-end testing, and be a leader in mock load testing. Again, though, this is only for the target and not for the archive solution.

- **Load** – The detailed load design is nearly always the supplier's responsibility, leaning, however, on the support of the local technologists for infrastructure support.

- **Orchestration** – This is the organisation and management of the wider business to support the migration and to mitigate the disturbance caused by an enterprise application migration. This is always the responsibility of the client.

- **Fallback** – I have yet to cover fallback design in detail, but it is a key part of any data migration design. It is usually a joint supplier/client responsibility.

- **Legacy decommissioning** – This is always the client's responsibility. Even where a business might employ third-party providers, for instance, to perform a sweep of the desktops for licence recovery, the responsibility, design and control always remains with the client.

To bring all these disparate designs together you need to have an overall design that ensures they are all linked up. However, as noted before, if your migration is small and of a sufficiently short duration, you might choose to go straight for the ETL design, provided you are confident that you have covered all the items below and you are not risking uncovering gaps and omissions caused by misunderstandings between supplier and client.

Content of E2E design

The following is a guide to what you would expect to find in an E2E design.

- **Scope statement** – I believe that all documents should be sufficiently stand-alone to allow them to be read without going back to other documentation. A simple scope statement (probably cut and pasted out of the migration strategy document), no longer than a page, will suffice.

- **Migration form** – By now you will have decided on the migration form (if it was ever in doubt from the beginning).

- **Key business data areas** – Explain what the key business data areas are. This will make the rest of the design meaningful.

- **Units of migration** – Both the business and the technical designers need to know what unit of migration they are working to. Fallout, fallback, data audit, data lineage and reporting all work at the unit of migration level.

- **Audit and data lineage requirements** – These will come from the SRPs and might need to be expressed at a summary level with a reference to the relevant SRP.

- **Migration reporting** – This is where you describe the level of report detail you will expect from the extraction, transformation and load steps (and whatever intermediary steps you intend to create). In the E2E design, this is expressed more as a set of requirements than a statement of design.

- **Technology overview** – This should have an architectural diagram that shows the position of the DMZ. This could be a 'swim lane'-style diagram or even colour coded to show who is leading on each step. Bear in mind that the work within the supplier might not be too visible to the client (the other side of the DMZ can be a series of black boxes). However, where it is allowed to be known, this should be accompanied by a description of the:

    o **Data transport software** – This shows how you are going to move data around and who will be responsible for providing the transport.

    o **Migration software** – This is your profiling, data quality and ETL software overlaid on the architecture diagram.

    o **Transitional data store software** – If your solution requires these (and this should be clear by now), then they should appear on the architectural diagram.

    o **MDM software** – If this is appropriate.

    o **Archive software** – This is very important. At the foremost of your mind should be that you need an archive as well as a target solution.

- **High-level cutover timeline** – This should include the resource implications for the extraction, transformation, load and decommissioning. If this is to be a phased migration, then a generic cutover timeline is needed. Remember, the timeline can often start with some preliminary transitional business rules (for instance, the shutting down of as many in-flight transactions as possible) some way ahead of LDS shutdown and initial data extract. It should include an indication of where the agreed sign-off (go/no-go) points are going to be. This will help in getting access to the correct people at the correct time. There should also be a statement of timelines alignment to both technical- and business-side windows of opportunity.

- **Outline testing strategy** – I will cover testing below, but within the E2E strategy you should be clear about who will be performing which tests and when they will be performed.

- **Main sources and target data stores** – These might not be fully decided, given that this deliverable will be produced before the full design is ready and therefore before all the gaps are known. In large data migrations, where the numbers of LDSs that are accessed can run into the hundreds, it is acceptable to bunch some LDSs together (for instance, 'Pricing spreadsheets' as a single LDS in the E2E design).

The production of the E2E design coincides with the latter stages of mapping, so it is often produced in advance of the final target design being available.

HINT

In my experience, almost without exception, the final design of the target is late. More often than not tweaks are being made to it right up to go-live. However, there is a peak in activity on target design and build. Plan to time the commencement of E2E design to coincide with the end of this peak when there will be technical resource available on both sides of the DMZ to engage with and there will be more concrete knowledge and less speculation. On very large projects it might be advisable to have an architect working on the E2E plan from the commencement of the project given the need to engage with so many non-project resources, but still expect to ramp up as the target becomes more fixed.

Relationship of the E2E plan and SRPs

The first-pass SRPs are a key input into the E2E plan in order to maintain the relationship between the data migration project and the impacted business areas. You will get the following from these SRPS:

- **Training requirements** – Specifically the training lag that might impact the data migration form choices. The migration date has a dependency on the successful completion of the training plan.

- **Testing** – Obviously UAT requirements are captured in the SRPs, but the plans will also express the degree of other testing that has to be reached before the data owners can sign the decommissioning certificates.

- **Data retention** – It is crucial that you get agreement between the bigger programme and the data owners on the units of migration that will be in the target, those that will be in the archive and those that will be lost forever in the migration. The sooner this discussion is engaged in the more likely you are to come to a conclusion that is acceptable to all parties.

- **Audit and data lineage** – All too often data migration auditing is seen as an afterthought defined by the testing team. You capture it in *PDMv2* as a requirement from the business domain experts who know what is important and what is not, prompted by the data migration analyst. As I showed in Chapter 10 on the GAM module, data lineage can be a business-side requirement. If so, it will have been captured in the SRPs.

- **Go-live restrictions (windows of opportunity)** – The business-side go-live restrictions will have been recorded in the SRPs, and they must be planned around, starting with the E2E plan.

- **Customer experience** – This is more for the ETL and detailed decommissioning and migration design where all the mappings are in place, but it is useful to check that you are not making any mistakes in your high-level design.

- **Resources** – This very much relates to the sign-off and user acceptance criteria.

- **Unit of migration** – Although these are initially defined in the SRPs, by the time of the E2E plan it is beginning to be come clear if they are possible or need to be renegotiated.

ANECDOTE

I was working on the migration of a core system for a company with an international branch network. Although, at first, it felt that I would set the unit of migration at branch level (i.e. if a single significant item within a branch failed to migrate the whole branch would be rolled back), it became clear that this was unreasonable and I settled on Customer within Branch.

Part of the process of developing the E2E plan is to enter into a process of negotiation mediating between the demands of the business and the possibilities of the technology (and the budget). Both the E2E design and the SRPs should be updated as a consequence.

Other inputs to E2E design
Other significant inputs to the E2E design come from the data migration strategy, especially the scope and policies. LA provided a list of LDSs and the topography that you might need to maintain (especially in a phased migration). The DQR process determined which of these DQRs you are going to use to extract, enrich or validate data. They will also provide you with your 'fix in flight', 'fall out in flight' and 'fix in target' DQRs. The mappings will decide the extraction, inclusion, navigation, timing, validation, transformation and loading rules as you create the E2E design. Although both the mapping rules and the individual DQR are at too low a level to be included in a document like the E2E design, it is worthwhile noting where they might be applied and who is to apply them because, as I will show when I move on to the more detailed design, you need to ensure that everybody is aware of what is to be expected of them in the detailed design cycle.

Finally, never forget that you can always reach out to the virtual team you have built up of both technical and non-technical resources to validate your assumptions and look for solutions.

Outputs from end-to-end design
The output from the E2E design will be an E2E design document signed off in line with the sign-off criteria you agreed in the data migration strategy. This sign-off can be with caveats for where there is still ongoing discussion. The most common areas for discussion are around the units of migration and the amount of data that is going into the target as opposed to the archive solutions. The E2E design is an internal project document and you do not want to hold up the data migration project waiting for some of the detail to be agreed, especially when detailed design work might clarify assumptions and make decisions easier.

You will use the E2E documents to update the project plan because it will have the detail of who will be designing each part of the lower level designs with enough indications of scale to allow for close estimation. There will also be a confirmation of the timeline of the migration.

HINT

When I say 'update the project plan', I am anticipating that this also includes the issuing of work package agreements, work schedules and whatever other documents the project management methodology requires.

Finally, the process of getting compromise agreements about units of migration, testing, data retention, audit and data lineage will result in updates to the SRPs. Although you do not generally consider this to be one of the sign-off points for the SRPs, you can consider it if you feel there will be substantial changes to plans at this point.

EXTRACT, TRANSFORM AND LOAD DESIGNS

Unlike the E2E design, it is unlikely that the ETL design will be a single document except on the smallest of migrations. Where a supplier is involved there will be at least two sets of documentation. All the documents must align to the E2E design.

You also need to include some non-functional analysis and design at this point for input into the detailed design.

Non-functional requirements

No two IT departments or consultancies can quite agree on what constitutes non-functional requirements. The following is not an exhaustive list and strays into areas that are not really the domain of data migration. Do not be surprised if an additional non-functional requirement is added to the list in your environment. However, there are some aspects peculiar to data migration that you will be expected to deliver to the system designers and programmers. These include:

- data sizing;
- run times;
- sequencing;
- hardware and network considerations;
- fallback.

Each is expanded on below.

Data sizing

Data sizing is the amount of data to be loaded. How much data you have to move is significant to the design of a data migration event. It is the biggest single determinant of the run times (see below).

Data size is normally expressed in bytes, kilobytes, gigabytes or terabytes (in increasing order of size); however, you can also measure data in terms of the number of records to be read and written. The number to be read is often far more than the number actually written, and reading takes time too. Complex data navigation can involve a score of logical reads and ten times as many physical reads before a single record is extracted.

You will have captured the gross numbers of records in each data store on the LDS definition forms. The data mappings tell you the navigation involved and the consequent number of intermediary records you will be hitting. The system retirement policy and the new system definition will tell you how many records you expect to load. You will be able to calculate the size of the data load from this information.

HINT

It is rare these days to perform a formal access path calculation. You work on good guesses to assess the time it will take, but all the factors mentioned above are fed into that guess.

It is not only the run times that need this input. Any transitional data store, the target system and the ETL process will all use hardware space. Temporary tables will be created, temporary indexes need space etc. You need to know both the size in bytes and the number of records to pass on to the programmers and database designers to help you to estimate, then tune, the process.

Run time

When you plan a data migration, the time it will take to run is key to defining the windows of opportunity, and even, possibly, the data migration form. The biggest single factor determining the run time is the data sizing. However, it is not the only determinant of how long the migration will take. The software used makes a big difference. ETL tools are normally significantly slower in execution than optimised, bespoke code. Their advantage is that they are easier and quicker to write, but what you gain on the development side you lose on the run times.

Different computers have different processor speeds and some operating systems are faster than others, but some of the biggest timing issues come from 'commercial off-the-shelf' (COTS) packages. Some have very efficient load utilities, but often you are constrained by having to use an application program interface (API) provided by the target system software supplier that is designed for transaction-by-transaction updates, not bulk loads. These can be extremely slow.

ANECDOTE

Since I wrote the first edition of this book, I have worked increasingly on target software packages where all the data had to be entered through an API. These were almost equivalent in speed to that of the old keyboard emulators. If you try to reach around them and update the underlying database directly, then you invalidate your warranty so that is really not an option.

Whatever software you choose (even manual data entry takes time, but you do not usually call that run time), the same software can be written well or badly. It can take maximum advantage of features in the software or it can be written very inefficiently indeed.

ANECDOTE

I was consulting on one project where, by employing a skilled database administrator (DBA) for one day, I reduced the run time of one piece of software from eight hours to 45 minutes. The moral is, find the appropriate technical data experts for both the target and the LDSs.

Software run times are not the only consideration in determining the time you need for your window of opportunity. Do not forget all the manual preparation that you expecting to occur: the time taken by your go/no-go meetings and often the time taken to courier data physically from its source to a processing centre.

ANECDOTE

The introduction of cloud computing has reintroduced the need to courier data around. Internet interfaces are often not the best way to move large quantities of data into a new application, so just as I thought they were a thing of the past, we are again employing couriers. Only this time to get data to data centres owned by cloud providers.

Sequencing

Sequencing is the ordering of update processes into a tenable progression. There is usually a sequence of updates that must take place in a known order (as I covered in Chapter 10 on the GAM module). This dictates the sequence in which the data must be loaded. However, there are other considerations that can reduce run times at the point of cutover. Churn is one of these.

DEFINITION

Churn is the relative frequency with which records of different types are added, amended or deleted from a data store.

You will get a first good estimate of the volatility (or churn) of each data item from looking at the LDS definitions. However, you must also consult with the target technical data experts. The target will have its own way of processing and might alter churn. If there are very low churn rates among some data items, then you might consider loading them in advance of the main load. You will need to institute data transitional rules to make sure that if there are changes these are reflected in the target.

Of course, if you have elected to use software that supports forward or bidirectional synchronisation, then slow input speeds are not such an issue. You can load pretty much any time, but you will usually restrict yourself to times of low business activity to prevent the load on the production servers slowing down the extract and interfering with the business service.

The use of synchronising software also, normally, takes account of churn. Again, to reduce the amount of data travelling over the network, you should aim to take the low-churn items first and the high-churn ones as close as possible to the cutover point. Units of migration all have their own churn profile. It is usually the newest items that are the most volatile, and there are business processes that work to different cycles.

Another set of data items that can be loaded in advance of the 'big day' are those that are peculiar to the new system. These are typically code items.

Commercial or other reasons can also influence sequencing. Not all business cycles run to the same timetable and some data items might be available for moving before others.

Human resource and physical constraints can also affect sequencing. If the same set of business domain experts is needed to perform more than one manual audit, then the two audits will need to be separated. As I noted above, there has been a rise in data migration-related courier activity recently and data travelling furthest should be scheduled later in your plan, if possible.

Finally, just as some data items can only be loaded according to a strict sequence, others can be loaded in parallel. You might add these in, just because you can, where processing is light.

All these considerations need to be investigated and will alter the sequence you employ in the data migration design.

Hardware and network considerations

Few of us will ever have the luxury of deciding what hardware and network software you will be working with. Most of us are stuck with what we are given, but each combination has its strengths and weaknesses. As you will, by now, be aware, once you have compiled the LDS catalogue, you (and your managers) might be amazed at the variety of data stores out there.

You will have recorded the hardware and software types on LDS definition forms, where you will also have identified the technical data experts best equipped to help you. When it comes to getting the best out of the enterprise's data, you will be in a strong position. Once again identifying the best technical resources to get the best out of the situation you find yourself in is crucial.

Fallback

Strictly speaking fallback is not non-functional. It is very much functional. However, I am including it here because it is one of those technical requirements that might have to called from anywhere in a migration flow, even though the design of each piece might be the responsibility of a different party on either side of the DMZ.

DEFINITION

Fallback is the group of steps that will be taken to get an enterprise back into the position it was in prior to a data migration.

After having read this book you will, of course, be confident that nothing can go wrong with a migration, so why plan for something going wrong? Well the reasons are multiple.

- It provides reassurance to your sponsors and data store owners that you have an alternative strategy.

- It might be a stipulation in a system retirement plan that normal functioning must be restored within a certain length of time. Having a fallback option allows you to guarantee that this obligation will be met.

- Software and hardware can go wrong.

- Unforeseen circumstances can overtake the project.

ANECDOTE

In one of my earliest go-live experiences (not as a data migration analyst) the power to the new computer room was cut by contractors working in the road outside, causing us to hold up implementation by two weeks until power was reliably restored.

- Regulatory or legal requirements might mandate it.

ANECDOTE

This was especially the case when I was consulting to a company in an industry where a formal safety case had to be made, including fallback, before the go-ahead could be given for a new system to go-live.

So whatever reason you cite for getting the budget for creating a fallback plan, make sure you do it.

HINT

Fallback, like car insurance, is one of those items that you pay for and hope never to use. Use the power of the data store owners to create enough valid reasons to fund this necessary expense.

Of course, when everything goes right on the night, you will hope that the overwhelming feel-good factor, and the fact that the virtual team across the enterprise will be celebrating too, means that this redundant expense will be forgiven, if not forgotten!

ANECDOTE

I have yet to execute a fallback plan while I have been working on data migration projects, but I recognise that one day I might, and I would never go into a data migration without one.

What should a fallback plan contain?

Fallback planning goes way beyond data migration. It includes human resources, physical implementation, office space, and legal and commercial issues. It also has business continuity and commercial implications. So, as with much else in this book, I will limit what I have to say to the areas affected by data migration.

Data fallback, in essence, is the reverse of a data migration (i.e. taking data from the new system and rewriting it to the LDSs where it came from). The scope of planning needed is affected by a number of factors:

- the data migration form;
- the window agreed before the new system becomes accepted as being fully live and cannot be fallen back from;
- whether there has been a partial or full migration from the LDSs;
- where you are in the ETL cycle.

The plan should contain certain common features:

- **Check points** – If you have done gap analysis and the follow-up DQRs work properly, then you will be able to predict accurately the numbers of units of migration that you expect to see at each of the natural break points in the migration flow. You use these, especially in the extract and transform phases of the migration, to inform check points.

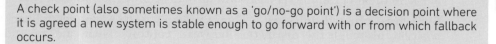

DEFINITION

A check point (also sometimes known as a 'go/no-go point') is a decision point where it is agreed a new system is stable enough to go forward with or from which fallback occurs.

When you reach the load and post-load stage, you use the SRP UATs, in addition to the migration audit counts, to show whether the migration has been a success.

Check points are best carried out by having a formal, minuted meeting between the relevant KDSHs. From the enterprise side, the data store owners should be represented and to aid them, possibly, the business domain experts. From the programme side there should be the technical data experts and the programme experts. On hand, although not necessarily at the meeting, there should be a clear contact line with the corporate data architect. The data migration analyst needs to be there, of course, to mediate and facilitate.

The meeting should discuss only the checks in the SRPs (from a data migration perspective, but the programme and technical data experts might bring issues in from their own viewpoints).

This is not the time to introduce additional checks or allow vacillation. Provided the criteria in the SRPs are met, there should be no question about signing off the check point. If, for some reason, the SRP requirements are not met, then the meeting must decide if it is safe to proceed (always being mindful of Golden Rule 3).

If the decision is not to proceed, then it is time to initiate the fallback procedure. Otherwise, you proceed to the next check point.

- **Forms of fallback** – Just as there are different migration forms, so there are different, although to an extent matching, fallback forms, influenced to a degree by the form of data migration implementation.

  o **Partial fallback** – This is where you fall back as far as the previous check point, fix the problem, then attempt to reload. This is the commonest form of fallback, and is often caused by some unforeseen software or hardware challenge, like the filling of index tables that will need to be cleared, resized, then rerun.

  o **Full fallback** – This is where you completely abandon the migration exercise and restore the LDSs to full working use. You would only do this under the most pressing of circumstances. It would mean that the whole migration was a failure.

  o **Continue with caution** – It could be that the failure is minor or easily fixable, therefore you can continue while acknowledging that additional work will have to be done. Getting enterprise agreement to this is much easier if the business is part of the virtual team. It will have learned to prioritise from the DQR process, so it will be more amenable to considering a compromise. It is very important that at this point you are guided by Golden Rules 1 and 2, but there can be conflict between the data stakeholders. This is where the programme sponsors will have to be brought into the debate.

o **Switch to phased delivery** – This is unlikely to be a planned fallback position, although the distinction between 'continue with caution' and 'phased delivery' is really a question of degree. It tends to suggest expediency (e.g. you might be trying to load data that you are unsure about). I strongly advise against this approach. It leads more often to disappointment and ruined IT–enterprise relations than success. Do your utmost to resist the 'chance your arm' approach to data migration.

HINT

You would be surprised how often this risky option is suggested, usually late in the timeline and usually to accommodate some late change. Get it discussed as widely as possible with the other data stakeholders who might be negatively affected. Given your strict adherence to Golden Rules 1 and 2, you will always bow to the wishes of the enterprise, but the way I see it, if the enterprise is prepared to live without the data loaded, then wait until you can be certain it will load.

o **Fall forward** – There are occasions (e.g. de-mergers, where the previous owner will be removing access to their computer systems by a given date) when falling back to legacy is not an option. You then have to plan for how to 'fall forward'. In other words, a bit like business continuity planning, you have to work out mechanisms that will support the company whatever happens. Look for the processes that you absolutely have to have in place. How can you support them? What is the minimum functionality you need? The minimum dataset? How long can you operate with transitional business processes working off partially delivered systems backed by spreadsheets and manual reports?

ANECDOTE

I first came across a 'fall forward' requirement when I was invited in to a project that was in full flight. They had a cutover plan that did not include a fallback plan, but the project was running behind its original schedule (which is why I was called in) and had to be delivered on the weekend scheduled or else it would fail regulatory compliance with consequent large fines. I created a 'fall forward' plan that was messy and would have involved a lot of overtime, but was tenable and compliant. And guess what? The next project I went to was a de-merger, so I took that learning with me, but this time built a 'fall forward' plan that was far more elegant.

Of course, if you are using bidirectionally synchronising software, and therefore running a fully automatic form of parallel migration, then fallback is easier, although you might still be constrained by a window of opportunity that is linked to a significant event in the business calendar.

- **Fallback window** – This is critical to the complexity of the fallback process. There is a necessary contradiction here. On the one hand, there is the heart-felt need to keep a fallback position in place until you are really confident that the migration has been successful and the new system is satisfactorily up and running. On the other, the more transactions that have been allowed to run through the new system, the more difficult it will be to reverse the new system data through the data migration transformation process.

DEFINITION

A fallback window is the length of time between starting up a new system and taking the final check point that allows for the full decommissioning of LDSs according to the SRPs.

There is a common misconception that if you can go one way through a set of algorithms, then you can go always go the opposite way just as easily, but I have shown from the 'one-way street' problem (see Chapter 10) that this is not the case. Each part of the technical design has to have a design for fallback, and as I have explained, that might include putting data lineage into the migration design to support it and prevent the dreaded 'one-way street' problem.

- **Fallback audit and data lineage** – Just as you have to consider audit and data lineage for the migration to the target, you also have to make sure you can account for it in fallback. Obviously, the simpler you can make a fallback design, the less attention you need pay to it. Fall forward, on the other hand, has to be as accurate with its data lineage and auditing as the target migration. This is one of the many reasons why fall forward planning is more complex.

Technical design

The objective of an ETL design is to produce a tenable flow from LDS to target, taking account of the preceding analysis and requirements documents, and the non-functional considerations. Once again, the plethora of different data migration software options that *PDMv2* must operate with makes it impossible to be too prescriptive about how each step should be defined, but what you need is a coherent, integrated set of designs. The designs might be contained in UML products, old-fashioned documents or via closely coupled Agile activities, but they still have to arrive at solutions to the same challenges.

HINT

I intend to use the ETL paradigm to describe what these designs look like because it is still the most common architecture and it is easy to see where the standard DMZ would fall. You must work through your particular circumstances and work out the break points that apply to you.

Extract design

The extract design has to describe how data will be lifted from the LDSs in a timely and orderly fashion. It will use the LDS documentation originating in LA and the mapping specifications, specifically the extraction rules, exclusion rules, validation rules and, depending on the architecture, any data lineage rules.

Extract design:

- will manage fallout and contain a fallback plan, although obviously at this stage, fallback is generally simply a case of stopping the migration and restarting it when the problem is fixed, provided nothing has been loaded yet. Of course, given that it is possible to have loaded ahead, as I have shown from the non-functional requirements, it could well be that a more sophisticated rollback is required;

- will include retention of audit data to support the data migration audit in line with SRP requirements;

- must contain a description of the software used for the extract itself and con- nectivity to LDSs and to the transformation stage;

- will specify the data transport mechanism and the personnel, both technical and non-technical, who will be involved;

- must be planned to perform sufficiently well to fit in the window of opportunity.

Impact of the DMZ – Extract is principally the responsibility of the client (although it is not unknown to hire in temporary staff with ETL software skills to write and configure the software).

Transformation design

Transformation design is the reformatting of data that occurs between extract and load. It will principally use the mapping rules, specifically the transformation rules, generally validation rules, and possibly data lineage rules. Validation rules are often rechecked for due diligence, where the transformation logic is being applied on the supplier side of the DMZ, but also because it might be only after transformation that some validations can be performed, especially the ones relating to matching target model rules.

Transformation design:

- will include fallback and fallout provisions and will have the necessary audits, check points and reporting;

- will specify the data transport mechanism and the personnel, both technical and non-technical, who will be involved;

- must be planned to perform sufficiently well to fit in the window of opportunity;

- will have designs for connectivity that will allow it to connect with any MDM, transitional data stores, third-party data or LDSs for validation and enrich- ment as specified in the transformation rules;

- will retain audit information in line with the SRP (this is especially true where the transformation will make simple 1:1 counting impossible);
- will support the data migration reporting requirements.

Impact of the DMZ – Transformation is performed on either side of the DMZ and so involves both client and supplier staff. Fallback, even if it starts on the supplier side of the DMZ, always has implications for both client and supplier.

HINT

Suppliers are understandably reluctant to get involved with managing fallout other than to return records that have not loaded back across the DMZ. Similarly, with fallback, the major onus is on the client to restore their operational systems. It is unreasonable to expect a supplier of one system to help restore the workings of another. On the other hand, it is acceptable to include support for audit, fallout and fallback (e.g. a data lineage requirement) in the supplier work package.

Load design

The load design will specify how the data is loaded into the target. Often this will be by invoking an API. It will need to link backwards to pick up data from the transformation design. It will be principally based on the mapping load rule, but it will often have some validation rules for due diligence reasons and it might have data lineage rules depending on the architecture.

Load design:

- will include fallback and fallout provisions and will retain the necessary audit data and check points for reporting;

HINT

Reporting while the migration is running is essential. There is nothing more worrying than being several hours into a migration run on a tight migration timetable and having no idea how many units of migration have been processed and how close to completion you are.

- will specify the data transport mechanism and the personnel, both technical and non-technical, who will be involved;
- must be planned to perform sufficiently well to fit in the window of opportunity;
- will have designs for connectivity that will allow it to connect with any MDM, transitional data stores, third-party data or LDSs for validation and enrichment as specified in the transformation rules;

- will obviously be designed to connect to the target;
- will be designed to produce an audit report in line with the SRPs on completion of data migration using migration metadata on units of migration captured in the extract and transformation steps.

HINT

In other words, it must be designed to produce the reports that will be fed into the final decommissioning sign-off.

Impact of the DMZ – Load design is performed on the supplier side of the DMZ. The supplier might be operating to a different set of documentation, operational, software and procedural policies than the client. This is not an issue, provided the above conditions are met. As part of the initial establishment of the DMZ as the supplier comes on board, it is necessary to agree the extent to which the supplier will be responsible for supporting audit, fallout and fallback. Load design (and transformation design, to the extent that it is performed on the supplier side of the DMZ) is where the DMZ is physically defined.

HINT

In my experience, all suppliers expect to support fallout (at least to the extent of putting records that fail to migrate back across the DMZ). They might support fallback at least as far as stopping the migration, dropping the target database and restarting the migration process later. Audit is a feature that they might not have supported in the past. It is possible to perform an audit after the migration has occurred. It is more of a challenge when units of migration have been through anything other than a 1:1 transformation.

Just as with fallback that occurs within transformation logic on the supplier side of the DMZ, fallback design within the load will be a joint client and supplier responsibility.

Transitional interface design
If you are engaged in a phased migration, and these are increasingly common, then the data migration team might be responsible for creating and managing temporary interfaces to LDSs that will be themselves migrated later down the timeline. These should be designed as part of the ETL design pack and are generally a client-side responsibility.

Transitional business processes and in-flight transactions
As I covered earlier, on most data migrations, business processes are put in place specifically for the migration. The commonest of these handles in-flight transactions. In-flight transactions are business events (e.g. the request for a quote) that were

started in LDSs, but were not completed prior to the window of opportunity. Generally, open business transactions are very difficult to migrate because of the number of conditions that might or might not be in place, and the different processing on the target system. The commonest solution to them is to allow them to complete in the LDS, and then perform a subsequent small migration of the newly completed transactions. Usually, after a set period of time, it is agreed that the remaining open transactions will be closed down in the old system and started afresh in the new. There is usually a concerted effort to close down as many open transactions as possible prior to migration.

Both the drive to close down in-flight transactions and, if you go down the route of allowing them to complete in the legacy, the fact that you will be operating for a time with production data in two places, require transitional business processes. Call centres, for instance, will need to be informed that for N weeks after go-live they either need to ask if there is a quote outstanding or to search the old and new systems for client data.

HINT

As preparation for dealing with in-flight transactions, run a set of DQRs to find the spread of durations of business transactions that are in this category (i.e. not instantly opened and closed). It is normal to find a median duration and one or two outlying transactions that have got 'stuck'. As part of the DQR process, agree when it is reasonable to close down these transactions for reopening on the target.

Although this is the most common transitional business process, there will be other offline data checking, data preparation and business management tasks that are run to manage the disturbance caused by a data migration. Transitional business processes need to be briefed out and are different in that they have an end date after which they will be closed down and withdrawn.

Impact of the DMZ – Transitional business processes are required by both the client and the supplier, although it is generally a client-side responsibility to specify, brief out and train for them, if necessary. It will be a client-side responsibility to see that they are closed down to time.

Outputs of ETL design

The ETL design is bigger than the sum of its parts. It will take the architecture in the E2E design and meld it with the technical design elements above into a single design. Once again, *PDMv2* does not specify how this design is documented, that is something that should have been resolved in the library services section of the data migration strategy. The design will, however, contain the following:

- **ETL designs** – These should be detailed, physical designs.

- **Fallback design** – A detailed physical design that links the fallback designs in ETL to the transitional business processes and LDS operations that will be needed to provide business continuity in the case of migration failure.

193

- **Fallout design** – A workflow design showing how the fallout from ETL design will be reported on and managed.
- **Audit design** – Linking together the audit metadata collected by the ETL designs with the data collected by the DQR process on the expected number of units of migration to produce an audit report in line with the SRPs.
- **Transitional interface designs** – Where these are required.
- **Migration reporting designs** – Dashboards, drill downs and detailed reports, email alerts and sign-offs, including designs for handling fallout, audit and data lineage (if required).
- **Cutover plan** – A fully detailed timeline including technical and non-technical activities and personnel with check points, system close downs, transitional business processes, ETL start and finish times, final UAT and go-live times.

HINT

I have produced plans broken down to 15-minute intervals specifying exactly when I expect to have each step completed. This level of detail is a great comfort in the stress of a potentially business-breaking system change. Use the virtual team as extensively as possible in their production. This will help you spot the small, especially non-technical details that can scupper an otherwise perfect plan.

Make sure that you check that all the set-up operations for the target are in someone's plan. Often things like establishing user access permissions are batted about between the bigger programme and the data migration team because, although the structure of access permissions is a target design task, the current users of the LDSs can be seen as data like any other, potentially with mappings.

ANECDOTE

I very nearly fell foul of the above in a business-to-business application that was moving to a web-based service. With two weeks to go, no one had thought to contact the other partner businesses to allocate user IDs. Well, actually both the migration team and the target design team had thought about it, but they had thought each other responsible. It was a close run thing.

- **Business transitional processes** – These should be detailed and formatted in agreement with the client's training policy.
- **Signed-off SRPs** – The ETL design is one of the key sign-off points in the business engagement workstream within *PDMv2*. It should satisfy every business-side data migration requirement from audit to data retention to customer experience. It should include a list of the transitional business processes.

Impact of the DMZ – As explained, the extract design is normally the responsibility of the client, the transform design is often shared, and load design responsibility lies with the supplier. Transitional business processes originate with both client and supplier, but are best collated, managed and briefed out by the client.

The fallout and audit process designs are normally the client's responsibility, but it is implemented in the ETL designs. Responsibility for a coherent fallback strategy lies with the client, but is implemented in part in the supplier's transform and load designs. Transitional interfaces are generally designed by the client. Migration reporting is nominally the client's responsibility, but in practice and, given their greater experience of what their tools and processes best support, is often provided as a service by the supplier.

The cutover plan creation is generally led by the supplier, heavily supported by the client. This is because it is normally the contractual responsibility of the supplier to perform the delivery of a fully functioning target, but, as I hope I have shown, there are areas that are dependent on local support. On the other hand, it is the client's responsibility (and therefore the data migration analyst's) to ensure that the whole ETL design is going to work. The client, therefore, takes on the architectural responsibility (if you have not taken my earlier advice to get a dedicated migration architect involved from the creation of the E2E plan onwards).

DETAILED DECOMMISSIONING DESIGN

In *PDMv2*, as I showed with the E2E design, you do not conceptually separate the migration to the target from legacy decommissioning and archive design. In fact, you make a virtue of system retirement and use it as one of the key levers to gain business engagement. The other side of this contract with the business is that you have promised that any data agreed with them with which they have a genuine business need for in the future will be available to them within appropriate timeframes. You have to make good on this promise. It is part of the SRP process. However, the DMZ dictates that this is mostly a task for the client. To fulfil this you need an archive design with an accompanying migration design and a physical decommissioning design.

Archive design and migration

Archiving can involve a larger migration in terms of absolute numbers than the target migration; however, it is normally less time critical (this does not mean it can be postponed indefinitely, but that it is not the first priority to be up and running on day one).

Like any good design, you should start with the SRP requirements. They have recorded the data history that the business needs. You have looked at access requirements and therefore you know what data needs to be online, near online and offline. You know the volumes. You know from the policies in the migration strategy if there is a driver to remove the old LDS and all its hardware and licences.

As an aside, it is often assumed (if the event is given any consideration at all) that you will keep a whole version of the old database with maybe one licence and if you ever need to get old data out you go back to it. There are a number of problems with this:

- The 'one-way street' problem might make backward access awkward.
- If there is a regular and repeated need for access, then one licence is not enough.
- If you have more than one licence and retain all the legacy data, including units of migration that have been moved to the target, you risk having two sources of business information with all the problems that generates.
- You might need to retain data for years and so need to keep legacy skills ongoing when people retire or move on.
- The legacy will be running on increasingly aging hardware and software that will go out of warranty and eventually become impossible to maintain.
- Data might (almost always is) spread over more than one LDS. Do you keep copies of all them? If you do, the above problems are multiplied by the number of LDSs you choose to retain.

Often, keeping an old version of the main LDS is the best and most sensible solution, but challenging it is no bad thing. The rise of cheap data warehouse solutions and the abundance of skills in data warehousing in most large IT shops is making it an increasingly popular alternative.

ANECDOTE

I have seen a number of clients whose requirement for long-term data retention (insurance companies might have to keep data for the life of a customer plus 20 years) means that as I am migrating off the current legacy, there is, sitting in the server room, an aging mainframe with the archive data from the migration on what is now my prime LDS. In one memorable example, an IT department's whole location strategy was based around not being able to relocate because of the impossibility of moving an ancient mainframe in the basement running only archived applications.

If you are going to create an archive (or archives if there are different storage requirements for different ages of data), then go through pretty much all the same steps and produce pretty much a similar set of documentation to the ETL design, although there are some differences and the main actors are all client side.

Similarities with E2E design
The archive design is essentially the same as the ETL design but it is biased to the inverse of the extraction and exclusion rules of the ETL design. You tend not to have as complex a set of transformation rules because you will optimise the archive to be as similar as possible to the LDS. Similarly the load design is simplified. You will still need validation rules or even DQRs to prepare data because most data stores are riddled with internal gaps, and the older the data the more it is likely to diverge from the LDS model. You will, therefore, also need to have fallout rules.

The biggest difference to the ETL design is that you will have to design, build and test the archive as well as the migration to the archive.

Physical decommissioning design
You need to observe certain principles when physically decommissioning hardware and software, including revoking access permissions to LDSs that are not being decommissioned, but which will continue to be used by other processes (e.g. in de-mergers).

Much of physical decommissioning is a technically specialist task. Often these days, you are not removing hardware, but, instead, allowing it to be reallocated. Make sure you have budgeted for it if it falls within your scope or that you are liaising appropriately with the correct technical system experts, if it doesn't. If it is not your responsibility, but you cannot see whose it is, as a good corporate citizen, you need to flag it to the bigger programme board as a possible gap.

Removing applications from desktops, especially cherished spreadsheets, is an onerous task, but if you do not plan to do it and follow through on your plan, then, firstly, you have the potential of old systems living on in a ghostly half-life with the potential to provide an alternative data source. Secondly, you make it that much harder to convince everyone next time around that data migration means physical decommissioning of LDSs.

Recovering licences is likely to be a necessity if you are to meet all the bigger programme objectives (which you will know from the policies in the data migration strategy). Even if it is not an articulated policy, it is still a good idea to remove unused licences because it saves the company money in licence fees if they are still paying, and exposes them to potential litigation if they are not.

Fallback is less of an issue to decommissioning because you rarely initiate it until the target has been signed off, with the exception maybe of altering user access permissions. However, if you have to fall forward, there can be just as many issues and the fall forward archive solution has to work alongside the ETL one.

Output from decommissioning design
From a *PDMv2* perspective there are not separate ETL and decommissioning designs. There is a single consistent design that includes ETL (which itself includes fallback, extract, transform, load etc.) and decommissioning. It is the data migration analyst's responsibility (aided by a migration architect) to see that the many designs from different parties come together to make a single whole. The decommissioning design should include:

- **Archive design** – Either the physical data store design with a migration design or a plan to reuse the old LDS with changes to access permissions. Either way it has to align with the SRP requirements.

- **Physical decommissioning design** – Or at least a note saying who else is responsible for it.

- **Fallback design** – Explaining how the decommissioning design links into the fallback processes.

Finally, because decommissioning design and ETL design form the complete migration design, sign-off of the SRPs cannot be completed without both designs being agreed by the relevant data owners. Without their sign-off, you proceed to build and test at risk of late challenges.

HINT

It is not a good idea to put all of a complex set of documents, some very technical, in front of data owners for sign-off. Approach it from the other end: go back to them armed with their SRPs and show them how their requirements are satisfied in the design.

MIGRATION BUILD, TEST AND EXECUTE

Migration build

PDMv2 has little to say about how to build software in general and migration software in particular. This is because commercial software has been around for the last 50 years or more and it is, by and large, pretty good by now. Providing the specification is correct, you are not trying to do anything cutting edge, the testing is adequate and you follow industry best practices, then you can even write perfectly fit-for-purpose software. You can certainly write pretty good single-use software, which is what data migration is all about. There is plenty of great pre-written software out there to make your life even easier. What you need are clear, unambiguous specifications (that actually specify what the user needs) and the time to create the software. This is the thrust of *PDMv2*. Given that you have 'front ended' as many tasks as possible, thereby gaining as much time as possible, that you have spent time understanding the KDSHs' requirements and articulating them in a way that is easily communicated, that you have analysed the source data exhaustively and understand the data readiness to within a single per cent, then you are ready to code and test.

This is not to say that some of the data lineage, fallback, transformation or navigation logic is not awesomely complicated, because it can be, but that is what software engineers are good at and enjoy. Optimising large data transfers is what database administrators, network engineers and software engineers do for a living. Give them the tools and let them get on with it.

On the other hand, the very diversity of the technology you encounter in a data migration is part of the fun. You get to use profiling tools, the output of which you use to populate the data quality and ETL tools. You get to build whole new data stores from scratch either as transitional data stores to hold survey data, or MDM hubs to hold reference data or as permanent archive repositories where you might use data warehouse technology. There is probably nothing like as broad a set of technological opportunities anywhere else these days.

This breadth of possible software, of course, also makes it next to impossible to be too prescriptive on how to build it. *PDMv2* looks at inputs, outputs and deliverables.

You therefore expect that the migration build will deploy:

- an extract build;
- a transform build;
- a load build;
- a fallback build;
- an audit/data lineage build;
- an archiving build (if required);
- a migration reporting build.

Each build will be built according to the appropriate specification against which you test.

Data migration testing

As with writing software, testing software is now a mature discipline in its own right. There are hundreds of books available on the subject. I do not intend to create another one. What I will do here is show what I mean by testing within *PDMv2* and confront a few myths that betray a misunderstanding of how to go about data migration in the first place.

The client usually has policies in place around software testing and these should have been captured in the data migration strategy. What follows are the generic types of test that you, as project manager, would expect to see:

- **Unit testing** – Does the software work as per the specification? This is increasingly becoming redundant in the data migration arena where the use of point-and-click ETL software can be used while sitting alongside KDSHs, so you effectively create both the software and the specification at the same time.

- **Integration testing** – As I have shown, the extracting, transforming and loading of data can be built by different parties at different times (and with the increased use of offshore workers, even on different continents). You need to test that it works from one end to the other. This is testing the technology and whether it links together, and it can be performed with subsets of data against a dummy target.

- **Load testing** – This is the full end-to-end test from initial extract to final load-to-target with all the validation, fallout, reporting, auditing and data lineage switched on. You often perform this as a mock load (but see below).

- **Fallback testing** – It is difficult to replicate the exact circumstances of a disaster that might invoke fallback, but you need to test its functionality, including communication and briefing channels. Test the technical functionality first, then think about including the briefing elements as part of a mock load.

- **Decommissioning testing** – At least up to integration testing. The data volume often prevents a full archive dataset being loaded. This should include post-implementation functionality (can you get the reports the business needs out of the archive in the times they need them?).

- **Audit and data lineage testing** – Although this is part of load testing, it is so intrinsic to validating the competency of the migration that you will probably not have time in the load testing to see that it does what the data owners want as opposed to that it works to specification. It is worth setting aside separate testing situations where a more considered review can be carried out.

- **User acceptance testing** – In addition to audit you will have been given some UATs in the SRPs (usually the 'sanity check' by business domain experts eyeballing the data as it appears in the target). Mock testing is a great place to run some of these, but expect that you will be asked to allow users to perform them on day one of go-live. (Actually expect that they will whether you allow it or not!) UAT might call for some support to help build test data, and testing the archive solution (where it is not the old LDS in mothballs) might require additional support. This will be clear from the SRPs and the archive design.

Test the migration, not the solution

You should be clear that you are testing the data migration, not the target design. In other words, it is your responsibility to extract, prepare and load data that fulfils the requirements of the target model. It is not for you to determine what that model should be (obviously, as a good corporate citizen, if you spot an error, then you should bring it to the attention of the target system designers). This is why you should insist on clear configuration management between yourself and the providers of the target model. This is not always as easy as it might seem and you can slip quite quickly into trying to correct a system design flaw with a data migration fix.

ANECDOTE

A great example of the above is when I have been involved in migrating accounting solutions (and most commercial enterprise applications have an accounting element). When there is a change to the structure of the accounts (the chart of accounts as it is known) the data you migrate is both the value and the structure. If the account balances are not what is expected then is it because the mappings were wrongly coded or was the new chart of accounts wrongly specified? It might seem like a 'how many angels can dance on the head of a pin' question, but it is significant commercially and for the project. Commercially, if it is a flaw in the design of the chart of accounts, then the potential cost of fixing it lies with the team who got it wrong. From a project perspective, there is high risk in fixing the data mappings if the underlying chart of account structure is wrong.

The other side to the issue of what constitutes a test is that the role testing ought to play in system design and implementation. Testing is there to find defects in the code. If there are errors in analysis and design, then testing, coming as it does at the end of the timeline, is the worst and most expensive place to find them.

HINT

Remember, my motto here is that you test defects **out**, but you design quality **in**.

Data migration is no different in this regard. You might find bugs in the mapping code, especially given how complicated it can be, but you should not be finding errors in the analysis. It is for this reason that you perform rigorous gap analysis and make sure you fully understand the migration from the business's point of view via the DQRs and SRPs. A common example of this is confusing a data migration audit with system testing. A data migration audit requirement is a standard part of a data migration. You think about it and plan it in from the very first conversation you have with data owners. You understand their requirements and design the migration around it. You test that the audit does what it is supposed to and the audit proves that the migration has worked. It is not a *post facto* notion overlaying a finished design.

Mock load testing

There is a second example of poor practice and that is an over-reliance on mock load testing in lieu of early detection of data issues that *PDMv2* is built around. There are a number of problems with this approach.

Firstly, there can be restrictions on the use of pure legacy data because of data security issues. These mean that you have to engage in data masking, but as soon as you mask, then you are no longer using the real data, so issues can be hidden and only appear in the live run. An example from the UK would be postal or zip code data. If you are masking identity, then obviously the postcodes (which can potentially uniquely identify a customer) would need to be masked. However, it is likely that the masking would create 'dummy' postcodes that would pass testing, so any invalid postcodes get masked away.

Often, there are also issues of scale. Do you have the spare server capacity to take a full cut of the live system, run it through a full copy of the migration suite and load it onto a fully working version of the target? Anything short of that and you risk finding out the truth only at go-live.

Then there is the issue of timing. For realism, the test run has to be against a working version of the target. This means completing development, waiting months with all the consequent licence and development staff costs, while the first few mock loads run through spitting out maybe half of the legacy records. And this is if you are lucky. I've seen many migrations where on the first cycle zero records migrated. This was not down to connection issues (the run was not abandoned before it had properly started), it was down to data gaps and validation failures. This issue is exacerbated when the recursive nature of this kind of approach is considered. One data issue can be masking a second which masks a third and so on. The first migration cycle uncovers the first set of issues. These are fixed, but then all the legacy records fail to load subsequently.

You either allow a considerable elapsed time in your plan after the main work of the programme is finished and before go-live or you risk the almost certain failure of the programme to meet its deadlines.

However, mock load testing is an approach that is often recommended in proposals as the mainstay of the testing strategy. However, I don't want to give the impression that performing full trial migrations is a bad thing. On the contrary. They are an excellent way of proving that the migration is going to work and for removing niggles.

Niggles are all you should have. After the integration test, the first migration cycles should flow through with minimum defects and not have data spilling out all over the place (which would have reassured no one).

Test execution

Tests either pass without exceptions or, more normally, there are some exceptions. The library services, as defined in the data migration strategy, should be configured to handle the fault reports. Fault logging is a standard IT development activity. Faults are logged, assessed for criticality, and given an estimated fix date or release number. With a *PDMv2* data migration they are then passed to the appropriate resource. A typical set of scenarios would be:

- **Cosmetic fault** – No action will be taken where an exception is considered to be low priority.

- **User acceptance failures** – Decide if the error is down to a design and build issue in the target. If so it belongs on the target design's fault logging system. Exception to this are faults with the archive solution, which is designed by the migration team. In this case the error will go to the data migration analyst who will perform an initial investigation, then engage with the technical design and build team.

- **Data quality issues** – These go to the DQR process.

- **Mapping faults** – These go to the mapping teams to check. If they see that the result does not match the mapping, then it would go to the ETL teams, depending on how the project is divided and who checks that the ETL code matches the mapping.

- **Process faults** – These typically emerge in a mock load and show either disconnections in the migration software or in manual processes. If they are in the software interfaces, then they go to the appropriate development team. If they are in manual processes or the process flow, they go initially to the migration architect to decide how to fix them and who to engage.

- **Performance issues** – Connectivity, speed and other non-functional issues would initially go to the migration architect who would then decide which technical data stakeholders to engage.

Test success

Once you have been through all the tests and either fixed the exceptions or mitigated their impact (if you are mitigating the problems, you might have to enter into dialogue with the data owners to get their consent to changes to the SRPs), then you can declare the tests a success. You will then get the third sign-off of the SRPs to say that all the tests have been passed, all the conditions in the SRPs have been met and you are ready to migrate. Depending on how you have decided to use the SRP process, this could be the final decommissioning sign-off or that might occur after the load has completed and the audit reports have been examined to confirm that the migration went ahead as planned.

Migration execution

Given all that has gone before, this is a surprisingly small section of this book, but then that is probably a true reflection of the relative effort involved in a data migration.

ANECDOTE

On one of the earliest data migrations I was involved in, as an act of shear bravado, the software company I was working for declared itself so confident that we went ahead with a 'lights out' migration. Over one weekend, the migration scripts were triggered and left to run unattended. We turned up on the Monday morning and over a million units of migration had successfully migrated. We had a fallout of less than 200. This is not an experience I recommend or intend to repeat, but it does show that with the correct planning and preparation, cutover does not have to be a white knuckle ride.

The sign-off of the SRPs after testing is the green light for migration to go ahead. You run though the cutover plan (by this point I am often referring to it as a cutover script to emphasise how confident I am that I will be following it exactly).

Within the cutover plan, you have all the system close downs, batch runs, taking of back-ups, running of ETL software, checking of audit logs at the planned check points, check point meetings to follow and transitional business processes to kick off and terminate. When the last unit of migration successfully hits the target and the final audit report is run, you allow the gold users onto the target to perform a final sanity check before declaring the target open for business and moving on to legacy decommissioning.

The whole time you have the fallback (or fall forward) plan in your back pocket just in case, but you don't have to use it. You inspect the fallout, but find only the records you expected (the ones identified in the 'fallout in flight' DQR). You will be dealing with them as part of legacy decommissioning.

You then go off to have a cup of tea to celebrate.

ANECDOTE

Immediately prior to writing this chapter I was consulting to a utility company who were moving their outsourced customer billing system to an in-house SAP® system. We had calculated that from a population of over 2 million customer units of migration, 99.6 per cent would migrate. The rest were 'fallout in-flight' DQRs. When the migration was over we were exactly right. My friends there had given me a scare the previous week because no one was answering the phone when I called. It turned out that they were so confident that they had all taken off the week prior to migration. That is the position you should be in. Use *PDMv2* and you will be.

CHAPTER REVIEW

In this chapter I looked at the migration design and execution module within *PDMv2*. This includes an end-to-end (E2E) design, an extract, transform and load (ETL) design and a detailed decommissioning design.

I also covered data migration testing and migration build as being part of the MDE module.

Finally, I showed how all the elements can come together to produce a zero-defect migration.

12 LEGACY DECOMMISSIONING

In this chapter I will look at how you carry out legacy decommissioning, the 'long tail' problem, and how, in project close down, you create products that are of value to the enterprise.

EXECUTING THE DECOMMISSIONING DESIGN

Officially, decommissioning activities start as soon as the final decommissioning certificate is signed in the final SRP. In reality, it is kicked off as part of the cutover plan. At some point in that plan, which has to reflect both the target migration and the decommissioning design, there is a trigger to start the decommissioning design extract. Once the target migration has achieved its objectives, control is handed over from the supplier to the client and you commence implementing the decommissioning design.

You will be expecting to:

- **recover licences**;
- **recover hardware**;
- **remove LDSs** – You can identify these from the LDS catalogue and you will have a signed-off SRP;
- **implement archiving design** – This too will have a cutover script, but it is fair to say that the pace is usually not as hectic and the attention of the senior management is not so focused on you. However, you need to complete the archiving strategy if you are to keep faith with the virtual team of business colleagues;
- **initiate project close down** (assuming that this is the only or final migration in a phased migration).

ANECDOTE

With the exception of setting up and archiving non-migrated data, I have not had to perform the hardware or software recovery roles for some time. However, the more far-sighted clients have accepted the need for a project close-down activity, especially when they considered the benefits.

Project close down

You should ensure that certain project activities have occurred. You need to clean up after yourself.

- You should make sure that any software components that were installed (such as the database log checking software used for synchronisation) are removed from production databases, or that messaging flows used to route migration data are removed.

- You should ensure that the transitional data stores you created are removed (unless you decide that they might be useful).

- You should recover the ETL software licences that you have installed.

- You should close down transitional business processes, but here you come upon the 'long tail' problem.

The 'long tail' problem

Although you should close down transitional business processes, some of them are slated to run for quite a long time.

ANECDOTE

I was performing a data migration for an engineering company, some of whose routine maintenance cycles were over a year long. One of the 'fix in target' DQRs involved picking up additional information on routine inspections. This meant I had a DQR that was going to run for at least another 12 months. The project was long disbanded by then. I have never checked back, but I would not be at all surprised if this business process is still running.

Most enterprises do not have a business process management function that allows them to close down transitional business processes as they should.

Reaping the benefits

It always makes sense to hold a project close-down session. There are some specific benefits from carrying out a *PDMv2* migration (aside from a zero-defect migration) that you can leave behind you, if you can find someone to pick them up. These include:

- **The DQR list** – Data migrations in general, and the use of *PDMv2* in particular, will discover more data quality issues than they can solve in the course of the project. You know this. This is why you have to ruthlessly prioritise the DQRs. Just because you choose not to act on a particular problem, however, does not mean that it is not having a material impact on the well-being of the enterprise. It is just as likely that there were other problems that had a higher priority because you could not migrate unless you fixed them. The DQR list is a data health check on whatever part of the enterprise you have been dealing with. It will also contain insights into other areas that were tangential to where you were working. The DQR list should be picked up by someone.

- **The DQR process** – This is a process that really works. You will have built up a virtual team that has bonded over the shared need to deliver the best data it could with the time and money it had available. Many companies have a data management team or the desire to form one. I always regret leaving this willingness, skill and pool of knowledge in the certain knowledge that it will wither away.

- **Master data management** – This is another benefit that the shrewd could make use of. You do not often have the need to create a full MDM function in data migration. You have no need for data replication or federated data stores. However, what you do with MDM 'lite' is to overcome one of the biggest obstacles to achieving an MDM hub: resolving the semantic issues that bedevil the establishment of MDM platforms. You have the compelling event of imminent decommissioning of an enterprise application to concentrate minds and drive consensus. You have to resolve ambiguities and de-duplicate in time to load the data. This can be picked up by any nascent MDM project as the starting point for a full MDM implementation.

HINT

The previous point is very true. If you assume that major systems are replaced every 10 to 15 years, ask yourself what you were doing 15 years ago and what you are likely to be doing in 15 years' time. What will the technology be like by then? The chance of reusing mapping components is therefore unlikely.

- **Mapping components** – Most data migrations are a 'once in a business life-time' activity for clients, so the prospects of reuse are slim.
  However, not every organisation is like this. Some companies are frequently absorbing others in mergers. They would benefit from retaining some mapping metadata. From the supplier's viewpoint, data migration is a 'business as usual' activity. Retaining mapping components therefore starts to make sense.

- **Lessons learned** – We all say that a project wash-up meeting should focus on lessons learned, but it generally descends into friendly back-slapping and anec-dote swapping exercise. However, if you have followed *PDMv2* to build virtual teams to solve problems and you see your colleagues as potential allies with vital knowledge to contribute to your tasks, and if you have seen the benefit of creating Super SMART Tasks wherever you can, then they are the lessons you can export to your next project, be it a data migration or otherwise.

Impact of the DMZ

All activity in legacy decommissioning is the client's responsibility, even if some hardware and software recovery might be outsourced.

ANECDOTE

Even as I write this I am aware that a major software vendor is about to announce an archiving solution that will allow LDSs, or at least those that are platformed on the more common databases, to be semantically analysed and stored in a compressed format that can still be queried, but I have yet to see this delivered. Who knows by the time you read this it might be commonplace. So I guess the key point to take away is: always work out for yourself where the DMZ lies on your own project.

CHAPTER REVIEW

In this chapter I have look at the typical activities that are part of legacy decommissioning: recovery of software and physical assets, and the instantiation of the archive solution. I also looked at the benefits that a tidy handover gives you in terms of preserving items of value and resolving the 'long tail' problem.

SECTION 3:
FAILING DATA MIGRATION PROJECTS

SECTION 6
REAL-LIFE DATA MIGRATION PROJECTS

13 RESCUING FAILING DATA MIGRATION PROJECTS

This chapter gives you a step-by-step guide to straightening out flawed data migration projects. It makes use of concepts introduced earlier in the book and you are advised to re-read those sections as appropriate.

INTRODUCTION

First of all, you have my sympathy, but be of good hope. This is not an isolated incident. At least half my career has been spent parachuting into data migration projects that have gone wrong and trying to get them up and running again.

I shall be brief and to the point: if you are reading this in anger you will not want expansive prose.

You need to work through three phases of activity:

- **Stabilisation** – Stopping the situation getting worse, controlling the fire-fighting and creating an environment where a more considered approach can be adopted.

- **Planned activity** – Working in a more controlled way through a series of releases or iterations that will deliver measurable and perceivable improvements to the situation.

- **Post-implementation mop-up** – Taking care of those things that, in a well-delivered migration, would have been completed as a matter of course, but that in the present circumstances are probably best put on the back-burner.

ANECDOTE

Typical of my experience was the well-known high-street name that was two years into a six-month migration project! The management were making a last-ditch effort to get something delivered. At the same time the lawyers were being consulted with a view to suing the principal supplier. It all looked very messy and about to get even messier in public. Fortunately, common sense prevailed and a staged migration was achieved to a new plan, but only after a significant amount of pain.

STABILISATION

Your first task is to stabilise the situation. There is often the temptation just to carry on doing more of whatever you were doing before. Resist it! Follow the points below to get out of the mire and back onto the sunny uplands of a well-managed migration project:

- **Read this book.** Come on now, I know that in panic, or desperate hope, you have picked up this book and gone straight to this chapter. I know I would. Well, you need to understand the Golden Rules and the key concepts covered in Section 1. Maybe you can skim over the rest of the book, but when I start talking about data stakeholders and data quality rules, it will help if you understand where I am coming from.

- **Buy some time to replan.** The urge to 'do something' is as understandable as it is misplaced. The project will almost certainly have compromised Golden Rules 1 and 2. You need a plan that will get the enterprise back in charge and the technologists back in their supporting role. You need to communicate that plan to all the interested parties.

  A useful way of getting this time is to enact the next two points immediately. They are necessary and will almost certainly have been overlooked. Use all the political clout you can muster to reappraise where you are and how you get to where you need to be.

HINT

A direct approach is unlikely to be successful at this point. If the enterprise has ceded responsibility for the success of the migration to the technologists they are unlikely to rush to re-embrace that responsibility when it is all going wrong. A little more subtlety is required that will draw the enterprise into the ownership roles. The best you might achieve will be that they are willing to lead, but not to accept formal responsibility. See below for some ideas on how to achieve this.

- **Get the list of LDSs under formal change control.** I have never arrived on a data migration that is under threat of failure where all the potential LDSs are documented and under control. Often the programme has succumbed to the 'group-think' that the major LDS being replaced is the only source of data. As Chapter 7 on LA shows, this is almost never the case. Do not allow the fact that one major LDS is under formal change control blind you to the requirement to catalogue all the minor ones. It is at this point of crisis that you might have the best chance of convincing the power brokers in the enterprise that the project has to be allowed to look further afield for valid data items. You will almost certainly not have time to complete a formal profiling or gap analysis to the degree of rigour you would like, but each potential LDS needs to be identified, assessed and placed under change control.

HINT

You will at this stage be confronted with a bunch of irritated business domain experts and data owners all saying: 'I told you so.' This is to be welcomed. Do not be defensive, with intelligence and sensitivity you can turn their frustration to your advantage as a lever to reinstate the business as the controllers and owners of the migration process.

Golden Rules 1 and 2 will almost certainly have been violated, or else why is the enterprise in this mess or why are you in this mess? Put your hands up and say, 'mea culpa' (or, 'yeah, you are right, we are responsible', if your Latin is not up to it), then add, 'but now we are in this mess, how do we get out of it?' Get the enterprise to share responsibility for the solution if not for the problem.

- **Get the list of outstanding data issues under formal change control and start creating DQR documents for them.** All well-run projects will be maintaining an issues register, but often it will only be for the most significant issues that need to be considered at programme board level. Therefore you might or might not find the individual data quality issues logged. Either way, it is time to get the programme to rethink along DQR lines. Each data issue needs a DQR and each DQR needs data owner and business domain expert involvement. This will start to get you out into the enterprise to seek solutions.

HINT

Whenever I go into a project that is in difficulties, I always ask the same two questions:

- What is your migration readiness percentage? In other words, what percentage of your units of migration are ready to migrate and what percentage will fail?
- Where do you hold your single list of data quality issues?

The answers I inevitably get are, respectively:

- We don't know for sure.
- Well, some are in the issues log, some are in mini-projects, some are being dealt with by the supplier in mappings and some are with the project team waiting to be allocated.

In other words, they have no equivalent to the DQR process and so have no hard facts on how ready they are to migrate and when they will be ready to migrate. Consolidating all the data preparation challenges into one list in one place being managed in one way is the quickest and most effective early step to get a grip on the project.

- **Create your own key data stakeholder (KDSH) list.** There is no getting away from it. If you are going to rescue the project you need the help of the people who know both the data and the correct order of prioritisation.

Unfortunately, this list might be something that is best kept within the confines of the project. You will be wasting your time trying to get formal sign-up to all the responsibilities of data ownership with a visible disaster awaiting the recipient. I know I would not willingly take on that responsibility. Would you? Remember the analogy of the plane journey and the quest (in Chapter 1). You are at risk of changing metaphors regarding the KDSHs. So although you must know who the KDSHs are, use a little subtlety in getting them to own the solution.

- **Stop fixing and start consulting.** Rein in the reaction to fix every problem as soon as it appears. You will not have time for the formal gap analysis. You will have suffered considerable agony as your project trips over the bigger data gaps that you did not find out about in time. Explain to the business that the process will be iterative. Accept that you are in the unenviable position of not knowing where all the data gaps lie. Expect to find more as you go along, and plan for it.

PLANNED ACTIVITY

Once you have taken on board the preceding points and have a better feel for the shape of the problem, you will be in a position to put together a plan that will involve the correct data stakeholders in DQR and prioritisation exercises. The plan will inevitably be iterative and release-based, so you can move on to the next steps:

- From the newly created DQR list, start prioritising the DQRs and create realistic estimates of how long they will take to correct.

- Institute a tight release and configuration management strategy. In the hurly-burly of a struggling migration there is always the temptation to bypass normal controls and fix things on the fly. Once you become aware of previously fixed bugs reappearing you will know that the configuration management policies are compromised (that is if you have any, of course). Step in before this happens, they hugely discredit any deployment exercise. The published releases will tell the business what is being fixed and which releases they will be in. The components of each release must be under the control of the KDSHs, both within the programme and within the enterprise. Set up a suitable forum where these decisions can be made.

HINT

In these circumstances I usually institute a weekly release strategy with a weekly meeting of KDSHs to agree the release policy. This can become fortnightly, monthly etc. once the major issues are resolved. Extreme formality is required. The releases should be documented in terms of the DQRs they implement, the date they will be implemented and given a formal release number. Keep the meetings focused and short! Less than one hour is best. They are not designed to fix the problems, but to prioritise the solutions.

I also institute the use of proper configuration management tools if these are not being used already, but the tools only work where there is discipline in place.

- Be aware of Golden Rule 3. You are now very much at risk of loading that which is expedient as opposed to that which is necessary. It might be that for political or practical reasons less-than-optimum data needs to be released, but more than ever you need compromises led by the enterprise and accepted by the enterprise. If less-than-optimum data is released, do you have a plan for correcting it in a later iteration? Has the reason been sufficiently well communicated to the other data stakeholders?

The situation should now be under control. I am not saying that you will be popular with the programme sponsors or the enterprise or even that you will hit your deadlines, but you will have a rolling release plan that will inform the enterprise of when a stable deliverable of acceptable quality will be reached. You will be managing via DQRs. These are designed to be built up into plans. You will be identifying the KDSHs and bringing them into the project to lead prioritisation decisions.

POST-IMPLEMENTATION MOP-UP

At this stage you have:

- DQRs that cover the known data gaps;
- recognised KDSHs and given them due control over the data migration process;
- catalogued the LDSs to cover some of the data gaps;
- an iterative release management strategy in place.

It is now time to look at the other items that you will not have had time for. Use the checklist in Appendix A3 and ask which of the items you have or have equivalents for. Of those that are missing, which do you urgently need now that you understand more about the interrelated product set of a well-run data migration project? I'm guessing that the following are missing.

System retirement plans

You will not have prepared SRPs. It is unlikely, given the time pressures you are under, that you will have time to create them. It is far easier to open discussions about system retirement at the start of a project when the prospect of it happening is some time in the future than when the data owners are faced with the imminent demise of their LDSs. Compound this natural instinct to conservatism in the face of change with the calamitous situation facing the data migration project and you shouldn't be surprised that any sensible person will want to hang on to existing certainties! However, the LDSs do have to be closed down at some point. I usually content myself with raising this on the programme issue log and making sure that it gets taken up as part of the post-implementation review. It really comes down to least worst case activity. Initiated early enough, SRPs tie in data owners to the migration process. Initiating SPRs at this stage distracts, antagonises and scares, so you should probably not attempt to do so.

Project decomposition

If you are parachuted into the middle of a failing data migration project, there is rarely time to re-decompose the problem into sensible key business data areas. The force of necessity will have created obvious decompositions of activity, usually centred on physical data stores. You will have to decide if what you gain by repartitioning activities around a more data-centric division, in terms of clarity of analysis, will compensate for the time and disturbance it takes. In my experience, unless management can be persuaded to accept a substantial postponement, you are better off settling for what you find. You will, however, be aware that because you have inadequate analysis to work from, you are running the risk of discovering more migration model gaps (i.e. problems of consistency across multiple LDSs). Raise a formal risk on the programme's risk register and as a mitigation point to the additional iterations in the new migration plan.

Reality check

In most cases there is no time at all to perform reality checks for the data you are trying to load. Use the new LDSs and business domain experts unearthed in the stabilisation phase to look for existing data stores or enterprise knowledge that might corroborate the fact that the items being loaded correspond to real things out there in the business.

Be especially alert to what the business domain experts are saying. Again, log this as a risk, the mitigation being the closeness you have to the business domain experts. If matching the data to existing business reality becomes an issue there might be nothing you can do about it at this late stage. Just bear in mind Golden Rule 3 and get the appropriate data stakeholder to assess the need for remedial action post implementation.

One of the benefits of introducing the enterprise to the use of DQRs, albeit at a late stage, is that you are introducing them to a corrective mechanism that can be used post implementation (fix in target DQR). It is a question of getting the DQR process embedded in the culture and successfully transferring ownership of ongoing data quality from the programme to the enterprise.

IMPACT OF THE DMZ

Inevitably, at this stage, the supplier will be retreating behind their contract as they see trouble brewing. The client–supplier relationship will be under strain.

Normally the client will feel misled because they allowed themselves to believe that the supplier has all the skills needed to perform data migration. Now the client finds that when the supplier said 'data migration' they only meant the 'final mile': from staging database to target.

The supplier is getting worried. They have committed time, effort and money to the project and can see themselves not achieving go-live, to which a significant proportion of their payment is tied, in line with their expectations because the incompetent client cannot sort out their own data. The supplier would like to help, but not at extra expense to itself, it is loosing margin on this project as it is.

They might well have experienced staff that they can throw in who have pulled projects like this around in the past, but they would look to some commitments from the client that they will be compensated for deploying even more resources to the task.

All this is without the fact that there is no clear configuration management across the DMZ. The client is asking for changes to accommodate their unique processes, but when the supplier complies the client then complains that the data they have prepared no longer loads. How is it that they did not realise the impact of the changes they themselves requested?

Added to that, the client thinks the supplier is being awkward in not making amendments to its load validation that would allow some of the client's data through, whereas the supplier is suspicious at the amount of additional processing it is being asked to do at no extra charge.

Both sides eye one another with suspicion. Relations between the two sides just get worse.

The solution, of course, is first of all to recognise the reality of the DMZ and get some supplier, client and configuration management in place. The client then has to sort out the problems on the client side of the DMZ, while being realistic about the commercial position of the supplier. The client has to guard against being over-cynical about the efforts the supplier is making, while remaining aware of the possibility of perverse incentives kicking in across the DMZ.

CONCLUSION

Like a large ocean liner, when a programme is heading in the wrong direction it takes considerable effort to turn it around. In the case of data migration projects that are going wrong, there will be a huge weight of misplaced expectations and misunderstandings to overcome. It is more important than ever that the four Golden Rules are obeyed, but preaching them enterprise-wide might be counterproductive.

The enterprise, generally excluded in failing migrations, needs to be brought back to the centre of the solution, quality improvements must be measurable and data quality compromises made that are acceptable both to the enterprise and to the programme. The relationship between client and supplier needs to be re-established with a realistic view of each other's position.

All this in the context of a tense and conflict-ridden atmosphere, where recriminations are never far away and senior management are breathing down the necks of project managers on both sides of the DMZ.

I wish you the best of luck.

CHAPTER REVIEW

In this chapter I have covered:

- steps that will help to get your project back on track;
- items that you will probably have to jettison, at least in the short term;
- the impact of the DMZ and how to repair relationships across the client–supplier divide;
- how you can recover some of those things that you should have to hand, but probably don't.

APPENDICES

A1 CONFIGURABLE ITEMS

This is very much a starter list of *PDMv2* configurable items. Most projects have their own additional items that relate to the bigger programme. There are also technology-specific items related to the build of the migration software including the load programs themselves. Finally the constitution of the DMZ will add more configurable items.

Table A1.1 Some *PDMv2* configurable items

Configurable item	Comment
Legacy data store (LDS) list	Will have associated artefacts especially for the larger LDS.
Topography documentation	Especially in phased migrations the interfaces as well as the LDS will have their own documentation.
System retirement plans (SRPs)	Will have associated artefacts especially for the larger LDS.
Key data stakeholder (KDSH) list	Includes both the KDSHs directly involved in the migration process, but also members of the project and bigger programme governance.
Conceptual entity model	If used.
Legacy data store models	If used.
Migration model	If used.
Target model	See DMZ discussion below.
Other data models	If used.
Project initiation document	Or its equivalent in your organisation.
Metadata management repository	Like any application this covers its design; use; integration; platform; development; testing.

(Continued)

Table A1.1 *(Continued)*

Configurable item	Comment
DQR forms and activities	Both their format and the individual forms themselves need controlling.
DQR process	This tends to be somewhat organic and develops uniquely for each project, but some simple statements of process are essential especially in the early stages of each project.
DQR repository	Depending on the technology used this can be independent of the DQR forms ('old-school' spreadsheets) or fully integrated (often using support desk, issue management technology).
Reports	• The format, creation, readership and versioning of data migration project reports and dashboards need to be controlled. • The format, creation, readership of the execution reports need to be controlled.
Mapping definitions	Extract rules, exclusion rules, transformation rules and loading rules need to be controlled both for the target and for archiving.
Migration design	• Extract design, transformation design, load design, fallback design and decommissioning design (including archive design) need to be controlled. • The integration of elements needs to be controlled. • The cutover plan needs to be controlled. • The transitional data store design needs to be controlled.
Migration build	• Depending on the technology, the scripts and executable code needs to be controlled for ETL and fallback for both the target and archive. • The decommissioning build (where appropriate) will also need to be controlled, as will the integration build (where necessary). • The transitional data store build needs to be controlled.
Test build and execute	Test cases, test scripts, test data, test failures (including design and performance issues) need to be controlled.
Legacy decommissioning	IT asset lists, recoverable software licences and decommissioning reports need to be controlled.
Data migration strategy	See Appendix A3 for full contents.
Project plans and planning	Modern project planning software has its own versioning, but the mechanism for briefing out the current plan needs to be agreed.
Risks and issues	Modern risk and issue management software has its own versioning.
DMZ	The DMZ is to an extent defined in the contract, but also in the definitions of the items that pass across it (like the target model). Ensure that they all align and that changes to one are cascaded across the others.

A2 IMPACT ANALYSIS FRAME

In the impact analysis list given in Table A2.1, there are some items that can be clearly linked. In other cases, especially for technology-specific items like mapping specifications or even the format and relationship of data quality rules forms to data quality rules repositories, there is such a variety of possibilities that I have had to indicate the module/submodule (e.g. gap analysis and mapping), not the specific project deliverable.

Table A2.1 *PDMv2* impact analysis frame

Item that changes	Can impact
Legacy data store (LDS) list	• SRPs; • KDSH lists; • Other LDS documentation; • DQR; • Topography documentation; • Mappings in GAM; • Design in migration design and execution.
Topography documentation	Legacy data store lists.
System retirement plans (SRPs)	• DQR; • Scope; • User requirements within GAM, and migration design and execution; • Decommissioning trigger for migration execution and legacy decommissioning; • KDSHs.

(Continued)

Table A2.1 *(Continued)*

Item that changes	Can impact
Key data stakeholder (KDSH) list	• SRPs; • DQR process; • Migration design and execution non-functional requirements; • Migration strategy and governance; • Legacy decommissioning; • LA LDS list; • Gap analysis third-party data.
Conceptual entity model	• Key business data area decomposition; • Data migration strategy; • DQR; • LDS list; • Other documentation that filters on conceptual entities.
Legacy data store (LDS) models	• Profiling; • DQR; • GAM.
Migration model	• Profiling; • DQR; • GAM.
Target model	• Profiling; • DQR; • GAM.
Other data models	• Profiling; • DQR; • GAM.
Project initiation document	• Data migration strategy.
Master data management repository	• GAM; • Migration design and execution.

(Continued)

Table A2.1 *(Continued)*

Item that changes	Can impact
DQR process	• KDSH roles;
	• Migration strategy and governance.
DQR forms and repository	• Profiling;
	• Mapping design;
	• Data quality tool;
	• Post-migration transitional business process and DQR handover;
	• Dashboard;
	• KDSH activities.
Reports	• KDSH lists.
Mapping definitions	• DQR;
	• Migration design and execution.
Migration design	• SRP;
	• Test build and execute;
	• Transitional business processes;
	• Migration build.
Migration build	• Legacy decommissioning build;
	• Migration execution.
Test build and execute	• Mapping;
	• DQR;
	• SRP;
	• Migration design.
Execution reports	• DQR;
	• Execution dashboard;
	• Mapping;
	• SRPs.
Legacy decommissioning plan	• DQR;
	• Transitional business processes.

A3 DATA MIGRATION STRATEGY CHECKLIST

Table A3.1 Data migration strategy checklist

Section/subsection	Comment
Project overview	Should be available from the PID.
Scope	
Programme scope	Should be available from the PID.
Data migration project scope	Check each item below and clearly articulate if it is in your scope or not.
Budget	Standard project office function.
Formal project organisation	Standard project governance function.
Elements of PDM being used and local substitutions including:	It is perfectly normal that a supplier may have their own way of doing things within the DMZ, but are the interfaces clear to PDM elements outside the DMZ?
Definition of DMZ	Essential even if the whole migration is being done in-house.
Landscape analysis	This can be divided between either side of the DMZ.
Gap analysis and mapping	Normally the responsibility of the client, but make sure the target definitions are part of the configuration management set.
Migration design and execution	Normally a mix of responsibilities between client and supplier. Remember that archive design is also part of MDE.
Key data stakeholder management	Nearly always the responsibility of the client.

(Continued)

Table A3.1 *(Continued)*

Section/subsection	Comment
System retirement plan	Essential part of *PDMv2*. Always the responsibility of the client.
Data quality rules	Essential part of *PDMv2*, but can take many forms. Always a joint activity between the client and the delivery partner.
Legacy decommissioning	Essential part of *PDMv2*, but how much of it is part of your project?
Policies	
Generic project methodology (Lean, Waterfall, Agile, Prince)	Usually well understood from the outset of the project.
Architectural (software, data structure)	Varies from client to client.
Quality versus time versus budget (risk aversion)	Always have this discussion up front, but expect it to be tuned by experiences within the project.
Master data management	Often a necessary part of a data migration project, but can you link to a matching project outside to gain maximum synergy?
Regulatory	Everyone has regulators these days. Ensure you know all the ones that might impact your project.
Local	Every company has these.
Conceptual entity diagram	Best practice recommendation, but not compulsory.
Project decomposition	Essential on all but the smallest migration.
Migration form	Normally known at outset, but can change with technology and design impacts.
Proposed migration architecture	Not always available at the outset.
Initial migration plan	There should be at least an understanding of when the migration is targeted for delivery and the *PDMv2* phases can provide the rest of the plan, but there may be a significant LA phase after which the rest of the plan and budget are built.

(Continued)

227

Table A3.1 *(Continued)*

Section/subsection	Comment
Migration software (including a proposed budget)	May not be known at this stage, but an indicative budget and a description of the selection method should be included.
SI selection	May not be known at this stage, in which case a selection process can be part of the plan or may not be appropriate if the project is to be accomplished in-house or the use of PDM in this instance is for an SI.
Generic project office functions	Should be present in any project.
Risk, issue and change control management	Not the same as DQR list. Often it is the bigger programme RAID and CCM list.
Formal communication strategy	Surprisingly often absent from initial data migration project proposals.
Scope management	For both the bigger programme and the data migration project.
Project board establishment	Often the data migration project works without a full project board, but understand how it is represented on the bigger programme board.
Plan management	Does it match horizontally and vertically with the planning needs of *PDMv2* and the rest of the programme?
Budget management	Another item that is often surprisingly overlooked.
Library services	Plan in advance for where the *PDMv2* deliverables are going to be held and their links maintained.
Configuration management	Essential on all but the smallest projects.
Initial key data stakeholder list	This will be an input into KDSM and LA.
Initial legacy data store list	Usually only the biggest enterprise applications are known in advance, but add any others that come to your attention.
Initial DQR list	This often is only known anecdotally within the enterprise.

A4 SPECIMEN DQR FORM

Table A4.1 Specimen DQR form

Identity	
Short name	
Cross reference	
Raised by	
LDS/entity	
Date raised	
DQR ID	
Priority	
Version	
Status	

Data quality assessment	
Description	
Qualitative assessment	*Initial assessment*
Quantitative assessment	*Number of records etc. impacted. State calculation method.*

Method	
Method statement	*Outline of how we are going to fix the problem ('ignore' is also an option). Can be broken down into optional subtasks below.*

(Continued)

Table A4.1 *(Continued)*

	Method		
DQR tasks *Optional*	**Description**	**Who**	**When**
	Metrics		
Metrics	*Description of how the metrics are to be calculated.*		

A5 DATA MAPPING EXAMPLE

The following mapping example aims to populate a target system equipment register as described in Table A5.1 within an ERP application.

You can see the fields that need to be populated (mandatory) from a target system viewpoint. This is, however, only the technical view of 'mandatory'. Although the target system might allow you to create records with some fields unpopulated, the business processes mandate the completion of many other fields. You would also like to provide as rich a dataset as possible, so in the course of your analysis you have found source data for as many fields as possible. Looking at Table A5.1 field by field:

- **Equipment ID** – This is a system-generated unique key, so you do not have to provide any values.

- **Description** – It has been agreed that this field will hold the additional information about the condition of the asset and its precise location. This exists in a matching field (Equipment Item) in the asset inventory LDS table. It is therefore a 1:1 mapping with a simple navigation.

- **Type** – This is trickier. It has been decided that you need to expand the number of types on the new Equipment register from the limited number on the old Equipment Item register. This is so that you can apply the correct maintenance routines against them. The LDS Equipment Item had the allowed values for its Type fields as seen (in part) in Table A5.2. The new system Equipment Types can take more values, at least where pumps are concerned (see Table A5.3). You have a 1:M mapping. That is, one value on the old system can be one of many values on the new. Assuming there is no way of finding the correct new value from other data, then you must appeal to the business domain experts to give you the correct new value. Normally this would be done via a transitional data store. The first step would be to list all the valid old to new combinations in a cross-reference table as shown in Table A5.4. This is not usually a particularly onerous task. The next one, however, asking the business domain experts to link existing Equipment Items to the new Equipment Types, can be huge. The equipment table might contain tens of thousands, even millions, of rows. If you need the enterprise to inspect each record, compare it with what exists in reality and then report back, you might need to allow a substantial amount of time, effort and money in your plan.

Table A5.1 Target system equipment table

Table name	Field name	Field type	Field length	Mandatory	Description	Validation
Equipment	Equipment ID	Integer		Y	Primary key	Must be unique across the equipment table.
	Description	Character	200	N	Free text	None
	Type	Integer		Y	Key of Equipment Type file	Must exist on the equipment type table.
	Status	Character	2	Y	• Operational; • Scrapped; • On standby etc.	Must exist on the Equipment Status file.
	Location ID	Integer		Y	Key of Location file	Must exist on Location file when status set to operational, mothballed or standby.
	Owner	Character	8	N	Key of Owner file (some equipment is owned by third owned parties, but maintained by us)	If present must exist as 'owner' on Owner file with status set to 'current'.
	Input by	Character	8	Y	Key of Employee file	Must exist as 'employee' on Employee file with status set to 'employed'.
	Operator	Character	8	N	Key of Employee file	Must exist as 'employee' on Employee file with status set to 'employed'.
	Warranty date	Date		N	Date warranty expires	Valid date
	Warranty description	Character	200	N	Mandatory if warranty date not null	
	Account code	Integer		Y	Key of the asset account file	Must exist on the Asset Account file with a status of 'active'.

Table A5.2 Legacy Equipment Item Type table

Type	Description
HD	Beam lifter
GN	Generator
MC	Macerator
PM	Pump

Table A5.3 Target Equipment Type table

Type	Description
3999	Beam lifter
4000	Macerator
4001	High lift pump
4002	Rotary pump
4003	Impellor pump
4004	Oil pump
4005	Generator >10,000 kW
4006	Generator <10,000 kW

Table A5.4 Equipment Type cross-reference table

Old type	New type
HD	3999
GN	4005
GN	4006
MC	4000
PM	4001
PM	4002
PM	4003
PM	4004

This is where an open-door policy to LDSs and a virtual team of data stake-holders are essential. With the help of the business domain experts, go back through the LDS catalogue. In this example, although you are getting most of the equipment information from the legacy Equipment Item table, all this equipment was being maintained prior to the new system being implemented. You find that the maintenance routines allow you to infer the Equipment Type from the LDS sources of the maintenance records.

This, of course, assumes that the LDS holding the maintenance records and the Equipment Item LDS have keys in common that allow you to link the two. It also assumes that all records that have a 1:M relationship of legacy Equipment List type to new system Equipment Type exist in both systems. You need to plan and perform a DQR exercise to evaluate this. You might then have to create a second DQR to correct any that are missing from one or other LDS.

To keep the example simple, you find out that the two LDSs are a perfect match (unlikely as that might be in reality!). This is an illustration of the need to have performed an adequate analysis of LDS via the LA process before you get to the mapping. If you had to find additional data stores at the point when you hit these problems you risk compromising the end dates of the project.

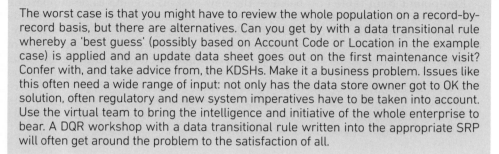

HINT

The worst case is that you might have to review the whole population on a record-by-record basis, but there are alternatives. Can you get by with a data transitional rule whereby a 'best guess' (possibly based on Account Code or Location in the example case) is applied and an update data sheet goes out on the first maintenance visit? Confer with, and take advice from, the KDSHs. Make it a business problem. Issues like this often need a wide range of input: not only has the data store owner got to OK the solution, often regulatory and new system imperatives have to be taken into account. Use the virtual team to bring the intelligence and initiative of the whole enterprise to bear. A DQR workshop with a data transitional rule written into the appropriate SRP will often get around the problem to the satisfaction of all.

The eventual outcome will be a cross-reference table that will be used at data load time to pick up the new Equipment Type from the old Equipment Item ID. This transient data store will have to be created and maintained during the life-time of the migration project. Although in this example it is fairly static, there will be some churn in equipment, as new machines replace old ones. You will need to create a transitional data store that will make sure that as the, soon to be legacy, Equipment Item table is updated with new rows, the Equipment cross-reference table is also updated with matching rows (see Table A5.5).

Table A5.5 Equipment cross-reference table

Equipment item ID	New type	Old equipment item type
SG421	3999	HD
VP563	4003	PM
CX470	4002	PM
JM378	4003	PM
PJ334	3999	HD

The 1:M example, therefore, has both a complex mapping and, possibly, a complex navigation.

- **Status** – The enterprise has decided to rationalise the plethora of old statuses that existed in the Equipment Item table (many now obsolete), so Equipment Status is going to be a M:1 mapping. A simple Old to New Status table is all that is needed. At data load time, as each Equipment Item is selected, the migration software will go to the cross-reference table and pick up the new code, substituting it in place of the old.

- **Location ID** – This presents you with the biggest challenge. The target system Equipment Location field corresponds to the Site field in the legacy Equipment Item table but, because the new system is going to be supporting maintenance as well as asset repository information, the new system needs a finer granularity of information. The new system needs to know where, within the bigger sites, the equipment is located. However, over the course of time some of the smaller sites have been amalgamated into larger units. This information has not always been reflected in the LDS, so you have a situation where, although some legacy Equipment Item records will be split over more Locations than previously, many Equipment Item records will have their Site fields combined into a single Location. You have a M:M relationship. In report terms this might appear as shown in Table A5.6.

Table A5.6 Location cross-reference table

Legacy site		New location	
Description	ID	Description	ID
Hartleson depot	HD	Hartleson depot	3702
Gibb Creek machine shop	GM	GCM Floor 1 Bay 1	3703
Gibb Creek machine shop	GM	GCM Floor 1 Bay 2	3704
Gibb Creek warehouse	GW	GCM general stores	3705
Farnham Bay stores	FS	Farnham Bay	5602
Waring Bro's Fabricators	WB	Farnham Bay	5602

How do you tackle issues like this? There are a number of practical options available:

- o **Single cross-reference table** – As with the Equipment Type example, you could review each Equipment Item and decide where it belongs in the new Equipment Location schema, thus creating an Equipment Item–Equipment Location cross-reference table prior to data load time. The load program would then read the cross-reference table for each item encountered and write the correct Location ID into the new Equipment table as it is created.

- o **Default to M:1 with exceptions** – When you look at the data in detail, you find that 70 per cent of legacy Equipment Items have Site IDs that map 1:1 with new Equipment Location IDs. There are 25 per cent of cases where the legacy Sites are being combined (i.e. are M:1) into a single Location ID and only 5 per cent where a decision has to be made as to which new Location an old Site ID should be changed to (i.e. 1:M). In this case you might decide to run the load program with an Old Site–New Site cross-reference table, and where Equipment Location records are found that could belong to more than one new Location, you default them to a designated Location. A report is created that allows the users to correct the system post implementation. This illustrates the value of observing Golden Rule 3. A solution that is good enough, but less than perfect, is often acceptable. In this case, provided there is enough ancillary data to get the right worker to the right machine for maintenance purposes you can settle for sub-optimal data in the medium term.

In this worked example, because you know which Sites are being split into multiple Locations, you would be more likely to extract those Equipment records that belong to those Sites. However, in the real world, M:M relationships are not always easy to separate in advance of the load, especially where the navigation is complex. This is the stage where a DQR exercise should be carried out to decide the best way forward. A data migration analyst can provide the data analysis of the percentages of records that fall into each category to inform the decision-making process. The data store owner and business domain expert need to be involved to tell you what is permissible and what is possible from an enterprise perspective. The technical data experts and the program experts will confirm what is needed technically, and you will possibly need to consult the audit and regulatory experts on their requirements.

HINT

It is often tempting at this point to go for the 'obvious' technical option. This usually involves dumping a whole lot of work on the user population because their records failed validation. The users are either asked to sift, unaided, through a pile of rejected records or expected to prepare a population of records, again with little support. The difficulty of this data preparation is often compounded by the fact that the new system will have its own set of nomenclature and definitions. These might not have been briefed out. The results of a poorly motivated, poorly trained, poorly briefed, poorly supported workforce carrying out a data review and preparation under tight time pressures are often poor!

---

o **Syncretistic option** – This option is the one that usually prevails either wittingly or unwittingly. Syncretistic means 'the attempted bringing together of differing viewpoints' and here I use it to cover the mixing of a bit of data preparation, a bit of error handling and record rejection at load time, with a bit of defaulting in valid values and a recovery exercise after the event.

Whatever option you choose, make it a conscious choice. The earlier you are aware that a choice needs to be made, the better prepared you are to pick, not an option forced on you by time pressures and circumstances, but an option both the technical and the enterprise sides are proud to live with. This book shows you how to best set up your project so that it meets that ideal.

- **Owner** – This is an optional field in the Equipment table, reserved for those items of equipment that the enterprise does not own directly but uses, manages and maintains (like lease hire cars, for example). You have identified from the gap analysis an LDS that will do the job.

Now you have a tenable navigation, you need to:

- o move the Lessor spreadsheet data to a location that is searchable by your migration tool;
- o check for an entry on the Lessor spreadsheet as each Equipment Item is read in;
- o read a second cross-reference table because the Owner Code is different from the local code being used by the originator of the spreadsheet (but it is 1:1);
- o apply the correct value to the Equipment Owner field.

You will probably also need a transitional rule to operate between the time you take a copy of the spreadsheet and the date the new system goes live to capture changes to the spreadsheet.

- **Input by** – All new records on the Equipment table need to be tracked back to the person who created them, for audit purposes. For the sake of completeness, and for fallback, you will know which of the multiple anticipated runs of the load program created a record. It has been agreed, therefore, that Input By will be a concatenation of 'DM' and the run date.

This means that you will need to create dummy employee records for each run. This is a simple example of concatenation. Often a new field needs to be made of two old fields (M:1) or one old field is split (also known as 'parsed') over more than one new field (1:M). There are also cases where two or more fields are parsed, then concatenated over two or more new fields (M:M). Each field, of course, has its own validation and navigation rules which can be a compound of the examples above. Data mapping can become very complex: it is not often as easy as lifting one set of data from an LDS and placing it into the new system.

ANECDOTE

The real-life experience on which this example is based included whole Equipment Items being split into more than one Equipment Item for maintenance purposes (1:M), and multiple Equipment Items being combined into single Equipment Items (M:1) on the basis of smallest maintainable unit. There were even situations, in some of the more complex engineering processes, where two existing Equipment Items became five new Equipment records (M:M) to reflect maintenance rules better. However, the principles remain the same: enlist the data stakeholder; express the problem in enterprise terms; seek out other LDSs to help; complete a DQR exercise; and update the data mapping rules.

- **Operator, Warranty Date, Warranty Description** – You are leaving these blank. The Operator field is a transient data item (in other words its value changes regularly), in this case possibly more than once a day. It would not be possible to pre-fill it at system load time. The Warranty fields come with the new system and are new to the enterprise. The enterprise has never held this data before, so there is no LDS to get the information from. It has been decided that once the system is up and running, an audit of purchase records will be made and the local managers responsible for Equipment maintenance will be responsible for updating it. This has, of course, been agreed with the data store owner and business domain expert. Had it been decided that the information was needed prior to the system going live, then a transient data store would have had to be built to house the legacy Equipment Item ID and the Warranty Date and Warranty Description. A transitional rule would have been needed to keep the data store up to date.

- **Account code** – This is a straight 1:1 relationship with the legacy Equipment Item Cost Centre Code. However, the DQRs have shown that the data in it is only 97 per cent correct. Some plant with a long working life still has cost centre codes that relate to a previous accounting package. The Equipment Item table was not linked to the accounting system, so being out of step did not matter enough to the business for them to correct it. The new system, however, needs accurate Account Codes because the new link to the maintenance system means that work has to be charged against the correct account. After running a DQR workshop with the data store owner and business domain experts, it was agreed that updating the legacy Equipment Item table was not tenable because of the awkwardness of the LDS that held the Equipment Item table. The favoured alternative was to error out the records that fail to provide a valid Cost Centre Code at data load time and amend these in the soft copy. A piece of software has been written specially to allow the users to do this. The amended records will be resubmitted in a secondary run. Business domain experts are primed and will be standing by to carry out this task.

HINT

In reality, it is extremely unlikely that you would proceed with a data load knowing as many as 3 per cent of the key records would fail to load over something as easy to correct as a single coded value. What I am illustrating here is that because you have already evaluated the data quality via DQRs, there will be no surprises. Where the navigation transformation and validation rules are complex, rejecting records at data load time can be an expedient way of identifying those records that need enhancing. You do not want the project to be in the position that a lot of migration projects find themselves, that is where wholesale validation failures are not identified until the data migration is run for real.

Table A5.7 shows what the (partially) completed data mapping table might look like.

Table A5.7 Partially completed example data mapping table

Target

Source

Table name	Field name	Field type	Field length	Man-datory	Description	Validation	Transfor-mation	Navigation	Table name	Field name
Equip-ment	Equip-ment ID	Integer		Y	Primary key	Must be unique across the Equipment table.			System generated	
	Descrip-tion	Character	200	N	Free text	None			Equipment item	Descrip-tion
	Type	Integer		Y	Key of Equip-ment Type file	Must exist on the Equipment Type table.		Link to user entered data in equipment cross refer-ence using original Equip-ment Item ID.	Equipment item/Equipment cross ref-erence	See Navi-gation
	Status	Character	2	Y	• Operational; • Scrapped; • On standby etc.	Must exist on the Equipment Status file.		Link to Equip-ment Sta-tus cross reference using Equip-ment Item Sta-tus ID to find the new status	Equipment item/Equipment status cross ref-erence	See Navi-gation

(Continued)

Table A5.7 *(Continued)*

Target

					Source			

Table name	Field name	Field type	Field length	Man-datory	Description	Validation	Transfor-mation	Navigation	Table name	Field name
	Location ID	Integer		Y	Key of Location file	Must exist on Location file when Status set to operational, mothballed or standby.		Use Site on original Equipment Item to get a new value from Location cross reference file. Where this returns more than one value, use the first record and write a record to the Equipment Location Control file for later manual correction.	Equipment item/Location cross	See Navigation

(Continued)

Table A5.7 *(Continued)*

Target						Source			
Table name	Field name	Field type	Field length	Man- datory	Description	Validation	Transfor- mation	Navigation	Table name	Field name

Table name	Field name	Field type	Field length	Man-datory	Description	Validation	Transformation	Navigation	Table name	Field name
	Owner	Character	8	N	Key of Owner file (some equipment is owned by third parties but maintained by us)	If present must exist as Owner on owner file with status set to 'current'.		Use Item ID on original Equipment Item to check for value in Lessor table. If a match is found look up the Owner ID in he Lessor/Owner ID cross reference file.	Equipment Item/ Owner cross reference	See Navigation
	Input by	Character	8	Y	Key of employee file	Must exist as 'Employee' on employee file with status set to 'employed'.	Will be a concatenation of 'DM' and the migration cycle.			See Transformation

(Continued)

Table A5.7 *(Continued)*

Target							Source			
Table name	Field name	Field type	Field length	Man-datory	Description	Validation	Transfor-mation	Navigation	Table name	Field name
	Operator	Character	8	N	Key of Employee file	Must exist as 'employee' on Employee file with status set to 'employed'.			Leave blank	
	Warranty date	Date		N	Date warranty expires	Valid date			Leave blank	
	Warranty description	Character	200	N	Mandatory if Warranty Date not null				Leave blank	
	Account code	Integer		Y	Key of the Asset Account file	Must exist on the Asset Account file with a status of 'active'.			Equipment Item	Cost centre code

HINT

It is normal, in fact almost universally applied, that a senior end-user signs off the mapping at this point. On a major programme, where possibly many hundreds of mapping tables with complex validation, navigation and transformation are being sanctioned, this is not an insignificant bottleneck. Each complex operation must be explained and justified etc. However, if you have applied the techniques covered above, the data store owner will have made the journey with you, making the sign-off that much easier. Although it might seem expedient to go for obvious solutions to mapping issues and then place the finished article before the user population, experience shows that it is not. If you compound this by tying the sign-off to some late point on the delivery timeline, you increase the risk of compromising end dates, quality and user–technologist relationships when your working assumptions are challenged.

Impact of technology

This example is based on the 'old-school' approach of creating the mappings by hand, recording them (generally) in a spreadsheet, then handing them over to the programmer to instantiate in code. The steps are reduced with the use of ETL tools. You drag and drop the links between source and target using a graphical user interface, and the tool generates the code. It is still the case that any difficult processing (either selection, exclusion, navigation, parsing or concatenation) will still have to be written by hand, although most simple examples will be accomplished using functions provided in the software.

INDEX